The Living History Sourcebook

THE LIVING HISTORY SOURCEBOOK

Jay Anderson

The American Association for State and Local History
Nashville, Tennessee

To "Bill" Murray, enthusiastic father of Iowa's Living History Farms, my mentor and friend.

And to Jan Anderson, my loving wife, who patiently helped parent this book as it grew to maturity.

Library of Congress Cataloging-in-Publication Data

Anderson, Jay.
   The living history sourcebook.
   Includes index.
   1. Historic sites—United States—Guide-books. 2. Historical museums—United States—Guide-books. 3. Historic sites—Canada—Guide-books. 4. Historical museums—Canada—Guide-books. 5. United States—History, Local—Bibliography. 6. United States—History, Local—Audio-visual aids—Catalogs. 7. Canada—History, Local—Bibliography. 8. Canada—History, Local—Audio-visual aids—Catalogs. 9. United States—History, Local—Societies, etc.—Directories. 10. Canada—History, Local—Societies, etc.—Directories. I. Title.
E159.A53 1985   917.3'04927   85-19945
ISBN 0-910050-75-9

Designed by Gary Gore

Contents

Preface: Jeremiah at the Bridge

ONE hot summer afternoon about ten years go, we were harvesting a field of hay at the Colonial Pennsylvania Plantation, a 1770s living historical farm just outside Philadelphia. The field was oxbowed by a swift, deep stream, and Jeremiah Hayes, one of our farmers, had to cart each load of hay over a very narrow bridge on his way up to the barn. It was a tricky maneuver at best, and late in the day the inevitable finally happened. One wheel of the Scotch cart slipped over the edge of the bridge. Cart, hay, horse, and farmer followed. Jeremiah, holding the horse's inert head above the water, hollered for help. We dropped our sickles, scythes, and rakes, ran to the stream, and jumped into the breast-high water. While a crowd of visitors gathered on the banks to look on, we unfastened the harness, freed the cart, and dragged it up onto dry land. There was a ripple of applause. Meanwhile, Jeremiah tried to coax the horse to stand up, but it seemed to be in a state of shock, its heavy head cradled in Jeremiah's arms. Finally, too exhausted to hold his equine burden any longer, Jeremiah cursed and let go. The horse, being a rather intelligent beast, decided that this was not a day for drowning and shakily stood up, shook himself, and meandered up onto the bank. The crowd of onlookers now numbered about fifty or sixty, and one of them—an older lady with a pronounced New York accent—tapped me on the shoulder and said, "Now, that was *so* interesting! When are you going to do it again?"

I often thought about this experience while working on *The Living History Sourcebook*, for this book has its genesis in another, earlier volume called *Time Machines: The World of Living History* (1984). Writing *Time Machines* was intense, exhaustive. While it was an interesting experience, I certainly didn't want to "do it again." At the suggestion of Betty Doak Elder and her publications staff at the American Association for State and Local History, I began work on this very different book—a guide to some of the best resources that make it possible for us vicariously to enter other periods of time and, with luck, to understand them better.

The Living History Sourcebook is not a complete listing, a comprehensive directory, or an inclusive compendium of living history resources. Rather, it's an annotated *selection* that is meant to serve as an introduction to many of the best resources available today. There are roughly 360 entries divided into ten chapters: museums, events, magazines, books, articles, organizations, suppliers, sketchbooks, games, and films. I have written a brief introduction for each chapter and have grouped each chapter's entries chronologically by historical periods, which are not meant to be exact but are offered as a general outline for the reader. At the end of the book are a glossary and an index.

Writing a book is always an education. The main lesson I learned from *The Living History Sourcebook* is how really extensive, serious, and valuable the living history movement has become in North America. I hope the book enjoyably illustrates this fact. Communicating this message to a varied audience of museum interpreters, reenactors, buckskinners, history buffs, hobbyists, and academic historians has been my primary purpose. *Time Machines* documented the history of the movement; this second volume suggests with concrete examples just how broad and deep the field of historical simulation is. My selection of entries is based on a careful consideration of thousands of examples of museums, events, books, games, films, and so on. It is a subjective yet informed selection, and my criteria for including some examples while omitting others can be found in the introduction to each chapter. If I have missed anything really significant, I hope readers will let me know by writing me in care of the AASLH Press. The living history movement is rapidly growing, especially in Europe, and if an updated edition of this book appears in the future, no doubt it will include new entries from both North America and overseas.

I'd like to thank my wife, Jan Anderson, and my graduate assistant, Sharli Powell, for their patience, understanding, and valuable help in all phases of the book's preparation.

PART I.
INTO THE TIME WARP

1. Museums

DAVE ARMOUR, who works for the Michigan Historical Society and was a childhood friend, talked with me a few years ago about why otherwise normal people get into living history. We were sitting on the porch of the post doctor's house at Fort Mackinac, which overlooks the beautiful strait linking Lake Huron and Lake Superior. It was well after midnight on a warm summer's night. In the moonlight Dave pointed out some of the fort's most historically significant features, frozen in an everlasting past, and then said, "I think a lot of us got into living history because we visited a fort or historic site like this when we were children and were scared. Fear can be an alluring emotion. For some people, like me, deep emotion became associated with history. Ever since, I've wanted to reexperience that heightened sense of reality that I felt as a child."

Historic sites and outdoor museums often have a powerful effect, especially if they use living history—the simulation of life in another time. The first museum seriously to use living history to enliven its historic collection was Skansen, the Swedish national open air museum in Stockholm. Founded in 1891 by

3

Artur Hazelius, Skansen was a daring experiment. Hazelius argued that, without activity, historic buildings could easily become dry shells of the past. He brought in folk musicians to play their fiddles, Lapps to herd reindeer, and peasants to demonstrate traditional crafts. Swedes liked their history "exhibited in living style," and for more than ninety years Skansen has drawn enthusiastic crowds.

During the 1930s, Hazelius's successful idea was transplanted by Henry Ford to Greenfield Village and by John D. Rockefeller, Jr., to Colonial Williamsburg. Ford wanted his museum to "demonstrate, for educational purposes, the development of American arts, sciences, customs, and institutions by reproducing or re-enacting the conditions and circumstances of such development in a manner calculated to convey a realistic picture" (quoted in Geoffrey Upward, *A Home for Our Heritage* [Dearborn: Henry Ford Museum Press, 1979], p. 75). And Rockefeller asserted that "an authentic, three-dimensional environment was essential to understanding the lives and times of early Americans." (quoted in Cary Carson, "Living Museums of Everyman's History," *Harvard Magazine* 83 [July-August 1981], pp. 25–26). In the half century since these two pioneer American living history museums opened, their influence on hundreds of other, smaller institutions in North America has been profound. You can easily make a case for living history as the "American way of history."

Two types of living history museums have emerged: the historic site and the outdoor museum. Historic sites, like Williamsburg, are still in their original locations. Outdoor museums like Greenfield Village, however, consist of buildings relocated to safer, more accessible spots which are often free of modern intrusions as well. All of the more than seventy living history museums described in this chapter are either outdoor museums or historic sites and include many forts, farms, houses, villages, and historic districts of old cities. Despite their differences, each one honors its responsibility as a museum; it collects, preserves, studies, and interprets historically significant artifacts—some of which may actually be accurate reproductions. Especially noticeable at these museums is the emphasis placed on interpretation and education, for living history can do both superbly.

The reasons for selecting living history as a way of simulating the past vary from one museum to another. Some institutions aim to emphasize historical ecology, re-creating natural and man-made landscapes and contexts. Farm buildings, for example, are more realistic if they are surrounded by fields, pastures, crops, and livestock. Other museums need to demonstrate how their buildings were used. Mills saw lumber or grind corn, and craft shops or factories are primarily workplaces. Still other museums find it necessary to stress the social or cultural function of a structure. Forts were once manned by soldiers, churches were used as houses of worship, and taverns were social centers.

Museum staff realized early, that living history not only was an effective means of interpreting context, process, and function but also appealed to visitors and catalyzed their interest. Three "methods" of simulation were developed: animation, demonstration, and participation. A field of oats could be *animated* by simply placing a costumed interpreter with a scythe in it. Going one step further, the same interpreter could actually *demonstrate* for visitors how small grains were once harvested. Or the interpreter could involve visitors in the work itself. All three methods are successful, but the more interaction between interpreter and visitor, the more information can be conveyed. At some living history museums the staff achieves an even greater measure of realism by shifting from the third person ("This is how they once cut oats") to the first person ("We Pilgrims stack our oats this way. How do you do it?"). Nevertheless, each of these methods and points of view can enliven the past.

Of all the criteria I used in deciding which living history museums to include in this book, perhaps the most important was the museum's determination to use historical simulation effectively to provide visitors with a true account of the past. At each of the museums and historic sites described below, you will sense that the staff is concerned not only to enliven the past but also to help you imagine life as it must have seemed at a particular place and time and to communicate the importance of understanding with your head and your heart. In addition I tried to provide a good cross section of historic periods and geographic regions, with museums large and small and old and young, even including a few that are still in the developing stages.

Greenfield Village • P.O. Box 1970, Dearborn, Michigan 48121 • (313) 271–1620

Massive in scope, this outdoor museum is the American counterpart of Sweden's Skansen. Founded in 1929 by Henry Ford, Greenfield Village contains more than one hundred historic buildings representing three centuries of American history. They are clustered in six theme areas: historic homes, community, trades and manufactures, recreation, and complexes memorializing Henry Ford and Thomas Alva Edison. Not all the structures use living history as the primary mode of interpretation, but many do, including Henry Ford's boyhood home, the Firestone Farm, and many mills and factories where historical crafts are demonstrated.

Both Greenfield Village and its indoor museum complement, the Henry Ford Museum, provide a sumptuous array of educational programs, including on-site courses in blacksmithing, glassblowing, woodwork, and the domestic arts. Recently, a series of "great escape weekends" has been initiated. They focus on important decades in twentieth-century American life, and the participants in these "live-ins" are guided back in time by actors playing the roles of historical personages such as Babe Ruth and Charles Lindberg. Imaginative living history programs such as these weekends have established Greenfield Village as an innovator in living history in interpretation.

Ross Farm Museum • New Ross, Lunenburg County, Nova Scotia, Canada BOJ 2MO • (902) 389–2210

Roughly twenty miles north of the picturesque early nineteenth-century fishing port of Lunenburg, in a quiet river valley settled by Scots and Germans, is Ross Farm, one of Nova Scotia's fine local history museums. The farm was cleared from forest in 1816, and for five generations the family of William Ross successfully worked the holding. Ross, like many of his neighbors, was a retired soldier and had been especially recruited to develop the isolated mountains and valleys of central Nova Scotia. The labors of men like him bore results that can still be seen in the many quiet farms and villages of the province.

When I visited Ross Farm in the summer of 1984, the first sound I heard was the clatter of the farm's ox team being driven up to the nearby agricultural exposition at New Ross (population 516), where they subsequently competed with *fifty* other teams of oxen from other farms in the area. A robust respect for the past is evident throughout the region.

The museum consists of the original 1817 Ross house, "new" 1893 barn, the family's small store and workshop, and two operating cottage industries: a cooper shop and stave mill. The latter enterprise immediately undercuts the myth that Ross and their neighbors were simple pioneers eking out a living in the wilderness. In fact, they were tough-minded creative entrepreneurs planting seeds of both an agricultural and an industrial revolution in a new, rich land. Ross Farm, through its collection and programs, interprets this complex theme of rural development in the nineteenth and early twentieth centuries.

Village Historique Acadien • CP 820, Caraquet, New Brunswick, Canada EOB 1KO • (506) 727–3467

Situated on the northeast coast of New Brunswick, the Village Historique Acadien is a superb open air museum on the Skansen model. From the Acadian tricolor at the entrance to the French-speaking interpreters, the village proclaims its mission as *the* museum of Acadian culture.

For an American, it is a stimulating foreign place abounding in the unexpected: farmers are skilled in marshland irrigation agriculture; fishermen still hand process cod; housewives bake crusty Canadian loaves in outdoor ovens; and French-speaking children scamper about in wooden clogs. The orientation exhibit features a moving sound-and-light show in the French style, and the museum's restaurant offers excellent local dishes.

The village quickly reveals its major theme: the function of traditional regional culture in a modern postindustrial nation. It is a contemporary, highly political message that the village's primarily French-Canadian audience deemed relevant. The issue is addressed by only a few American museums; Living History Farms is one good example.

Harvesting wheat on a pioneer Iowa farm. —*Iowa Living History Farms; photograph by Mimi Dunlap*

Kings Landing Historical Settlement • P.O. Box 522, Fredericton, New Brunswick, Canada E3B 5A6 • (506) 363–3081

After the American Revolution, ten thousand British Loyalists fled the United States and settled along the St. John River valley in central New Brunswick, Canada. During the next century these political refugees developed a unique regional culture that remains, in substance and style, interestingly British colonial. Kings Landing celebrates that culture in a beautifully situated folk park along the St. John River, just above Fredericton, the provincial capital.

The landscape is simply breathtaking; picture postcard views open up wherever you walk. Many of the buildings, such as the water-powered sawmill and Quebec-style barns, are massive. Animators using generally third-person interpretation are drawn from the local area and communicate their deep attachment to their land and heritage.

Kings Landing contrasts interestingly with Old Sturbridge Village, its closest counterpart in scope and period of interpretation. Both are immensely relaxing places to visit. My favorite activities at Kings Landing were a harvest service at St. Mark's Anglican Chapel-of-Ease, a pint of bitter at the Kings Head Inn, and an enjoyable summer's evening spent listening to dramatic readings of local writers. All *very* English.

Upper Canada Village • Box 740, Morrisburg, Ontario, Canada KOC 1X0 • (613) 543–2911

Established in the late 1950s on the north shore of the St. Lawrence River, Upper Canada Village re-creates the regional folklife that flourished along the river valley from 1784 to 1867. During this period, Loyalists from the United States, followed by immigrants from the British Isles, settled the land upriver from Quebec, hence the descriptive name, Upper Canada.

The museum consists of historically representative buildings relocated when the St. Lawrence Seaway was constructed and many older farms and villages were flooded. Many of the village's more than thirty-five buildings are rare: a wool blanket mill, water-powered sawmill, canal lock, and cheese factory. Also represented are farms, stores, churches, and the shops usually associated with early nineteenth-century life.

Although the village never really existed in history, it looks and feels historically accurate—in large measure because of its setting. The river sweeps along on the south side, while to the north and west are a dozen broad fields and a large mill pond. The ambiance is intensely rural.

Two annual events well worth attending are the Queen's Birthday in late May and the recreated Fall Fair and Ploughing Match. The latter is an accurate re-creation of a typical 1850s small agricultural exposition.

Sleepy Hollow Restorations • 150 White Plains Road, Tarrytown, New York 10591 • (914) 631–8200

Strung out along the Hudson about twenty miles north of New York City are the three historic sites that comprise Sleepy Hollow Restorations: Philipsburg Manor, Sunnyside, and Van Cortland Manor. Together they illustrate three hundred years of Dutch-American history, beginning in the early 1600s. The two "manors" were once owned by wealthy Dutch-American families. As you walk around their buildings, gardens, orchards, and fields, the influence of Holland is clear. The families who settled this beautiful valley in the seventeenth century were *the* progressive farmers of their times. Even more

Hauling hay with oxen and sled. —*Iowa Living History Farms; photograph by Mimi Dunlap*

Reaping oats on the 1900 Farm. —*Iowa Living History Farms; photograph by Mimi Dunlap*

nostalgic is Sunnyside, the whimsical home of Washington Irving, whose literary creation Rip van Winkle illustrated the imaginative potential of "time travel" in 1848.

All three restorations make appropriate use of living history interpretation. Throughout the year, Dutch colonial calendar customs are celebrated. The holiday season beginning with St. Nicholas Day (December 6) and ending with Twelfth Night (January 6) is particularly appealing. Philipsburg Manor has both a small farm and a mill where historical agriculture of the 1720–1750 period is accurately interpreted. Especially interesting here are the corn- and wheat-milling and cheese-making demonstrations.

Farmers' Museum and Village Crossroads • New York State Historical Association, Cooperstown, New York 13326 • (607) 547–2533

Cooperstown evokes nostalgia. This little town seems frozen in the nineteenth century, comfortably isolated from the modern world by the Catskills to the south and the Adirondacks on the north. In this home of baseball's Hall of Fame, the Jeffersonian belief in a nation respectful of its yeoman farmers is treasured. For almost a half century, Cooperstown has been a Mecca for history buffs. The Farmers' Museum and Village Crossroads interprets the regional folklife of the central New York area in the nineteenth century. The Farmers' Museum is located in a magnificent stone dairy barn and contains excellent orientation and thematic exhibits. The Village Crossroads is a classic open air museum consisting of about a dozen representative buildings clustered to form a pre–Civil War village. Buildings include a country store, schoolhouse, tavern, church, lawyer's and doctor's offices, apothecary, blacksmith shop, newspaper office, church, and farm. The last named is one of the first living historical farms. The museum is open year round and sponsors many special events. My favorite is the mid-June Firemen's Muster, which includes a parade of antique hand- and horse-pulled fire-fighting equipment, a cornet band concert, hose cart and ladder races, a bucket brigade in which children can participate, and traditional foods.

Quiet Valley Living Historical Farm • R.D. 2, Box 2495, Stroudsburg, Pennsylvania 18360 • (717) 992–6161

Quiet Valley is an apt name for this Pennsylvania German farm. It is located on a sixty-acre site in a beautiful, isolated valley just south of the Pocono Mountains. The farm was settled in 1765 and remained in the hands of one family, which farmed it successfully for four generations. Two periods of the farm's history are interpreted: the late 1700s and the 1890s. Staff members using the first person and adopting the roles of family members take visitors back to the 1770s and 1780s and then gradually lead them through the nineteenth century. This chronological approach is successful, and visitors feel that they are watching a farm and its family grow from colonial infancy to Victorian maturity. Quiet Valley has more than ten original structures: a farm house; two barns; "houses" for smoking, washing, ice, dried fruits, and milk; an outdoor bake oven; a sheep pen; a chicken house; and sheds for storage and maple sugaring. Animals are everywhere, and the staff grows abundant garden and field crops. The farm is open for groups from May 1 to June 20 and receives visitors until Labor Day. Quiet Valley also holds its very popular Harvest Festival on the Columbus Day weekend.

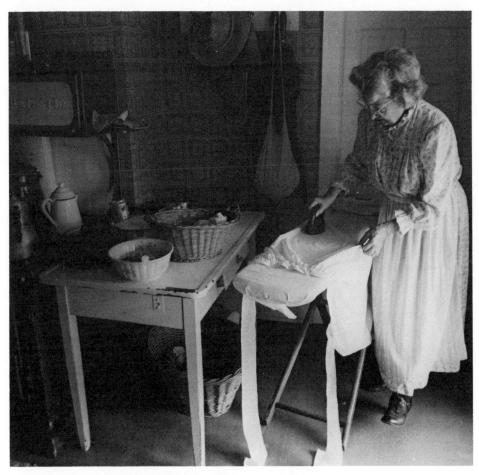

Afternoon ironing in the kitchen of the 1900 Farm. —*Iowa Living History Farms; photograph by Mimi Dunlap*

Blue Ridge Institute • Ferrum College, Ferrum, Virginia 24088 • (703) 365–2121

The Blue Ridge Institute was organized in the early 1970s as a division of Ferrum College, which has a long history of serving the rural people of western Virginia. Among the institute's varied programs is a farm museum located in a scenic hollow just across from the college.

Two farmsteads make up the museum. The first is a German settlers' log house, kitchen, bank barn, and outbuildings dating to 1800. Set amid small fields, an orchard, and gardens, this early farm recalls both German and Pennsylvania Dutch traditions. The second farm dates from the 1900 period and consists of a remodeled single-pen log cabin with a crimped tin roof, smokehouse, and root cellar. All the farm buildings are authentic to their particular periods and were relocated from the Blue Ridge Mountains nearby. Together the farms illustrate both cultural tenacity and innovation in the region during the last century.

The museum is open daily in summer and provides the serious visitor with quiet, thoughtful interpretation. For people interested in a considerably noisier experience, the institute sponsors a "Market Days" antiques show in early June, an exceptionally authentic folklife festival in late October, and a draft horse and mule show in July.

Museum of Appalachia • Box 259, Norris, Tennessee 37828 • (615) 494–7680

John Rice Irwin, owner-operator of the Museum of Appalachia, began serious collecting of southern mountain artifacts in the early 1960s. More than 150,000 items later, he presides over a fifty-acre "folks museum" characterized by a lived-in atmosphere. Irwin has noted that he has "above all else,

Sunday's chicken dinner in its first stage. —*Iowa Living History Farms; photograph by Mimi Dunlap.*

Hands-on history at the farm. —*Iowa Living History Farms, photograph by Mimi Dunlap*

striven for authenticity" and has tried to make his dwellings "appear as if the family has just strolled to the spring to fetch the daily supply of water."

All of the museum's thirty log structures were moved in from the central Appalachian region, primarily eastern Tennessee and western Virginia and North Carolina. Most date from the 1790–1840 period, when settlement took place, and each is fully documented.

Rather than simulate the folklife of the region's pioneer past, Irwin uses the museum as a setting for preserving artifacts of folk culture. The primary mode of interpretation is demonstration, practiced by local folk for whom the museum is a cultural center. One of the best times to visit is in late May, when the museum sponsors a "homecoming" for musicians, folk artists, and practitioners of various crafts.

Jarrell Plantation • Route 1, Juliette, Georgia 31046 • (912) 986–5172
For more than a century the Jarrell family worked a small plantation in the red hills of Jones County about sixty miles southeast of Atlanta on the road to Savannah. Sidney Lanier's "Thar's more in the Man than thar is in the Land" applies to both the Jarrells and their farm. From the 1840s on, the family lived here, enduring Sherman's march to the sea, half a dozen economic depressions, soil erosion, and the boll weevil. They survived, and their isolated, weathered, self-sufficient farm is now operated as a historic site by the state Department of Natural Resources. The farm has been preserved as it was in the 1940s, an extraordinary above-ground artifact. Visitors can see the original 1840s dwelling, a mill complex (cotton, lumber, grist, and cane), a syrup "factory," shops (blacksmith, carpenter, wheelwright, cooper), grain storage "houses," a barn, a chicken house, a smokehouse, a scuppernong grape arbor and beehives, a garden, and various sheds. Interpretation is often

in the first person and is emotionally arresting. Jarrell Plantation attracts its largest crowds on the Fourth of July and Labor Day. A fascinating time to visit is November, when the sugarcane crop is harvested and the staff members begin milling and cooking down the syrup.

Living History Farms • 2600 111th Street, Des Moines, Iowa 50322 • (515) 278–5286

From a six-hundred-acre site just west of Des Moines, Iowa, Living History Farms interprets the story of farmers and farming in the Midwest in five particular periods: 1700, the 1840s, the 1870s, 1900, and the near future. Each period except the first, which re-creates an Ioway Indian lodge and farm, has several operating living history components. The 1840s site, for example, has both a pioneer farm and a small general store. The 1870s area contains a town and a large progressive farm. The 1900 farm is one of the best living historical farms in the nation, and the futuristic complex demonstrates conservation farming and energy-efficient technology. Interpreters use the third person and help visitors adjust to the rapid time traveling that a visit requires.

Special events occur every other weekend and range from plowing and corn-picking matches to generic seasonal festivals, such as the "Old-Fashioned Fourth of July," Fall Harvest Days, and the homemade pie social.

A visit to the farms is a trip deep into a region that just happens to be the center of America's heartland. It is a poignant experience. Especially moving is the rural church that marks the site of Pope John Paul II's pilgrimage to rural America in October 1979.

Spring plowing near the Crossroads Village. —*Old World Wisconsin, State Historical Society of Wisconsin*

Threshing wheat with a fanning mill and horse-powered treadmill. — *Black Creek Pioneer Village*

Heritage Hill • 2640 South Webster Avenue, Green Bay, Wisconsin 54301 • (414) 497–4368

Located on a hillside overlooking the Fox River, Heritage Hill is a forty-acre historical enclave within Green Bay, Wisconsin. Looking down over the museum from the visitor's center is akin to visually traveling through northern Wisconsin's past. Buildings are thematically grouped to preserve and interpret four periods: a pioneer heritage which mixes Indian and French culture, Scandinavian and Moravian colonization, military life in the early 1800s, and finally the robust mid-Victorian period, with its small towns and Belgian farms. Each theme area centers on significant buildings relocated from the surrounding countryside and the old neighborhoods of Green Bay. The museum is essentially a folklife park in the classic European local history tradition.

What makes Heritage Hill special? Since its dedication in 1976, the staff has been devoted to living history interpretation. Most of the museum's two dozen structures, from the 1776 Tank Cottage to Fort Howard's 1826 hospital, where Dr. William Beaumont practiced his pioneering intestinal surgery, feature first-person interpretation.

Heritage Hill hosts a number of authentic events, including an excellent Civil War encampment in late June, complete with a band concert and military ball.

Old-World Wisconsin • Route 2, Box 18, Eagle, Wisconsin 53119 • (414) 594–2116

Located in a state forest just west of Milwaukee, Old-World Wisconsin interprets the immigrant experience in Wisconsin from 1845 to 1915 by means of a series of living history farms and an 1870 village.

Many of the ethnic enclaves hail from northern Europe, especially the Scandinavian countries. It's possible to trace the history of Norwegian Americans as reflected through their farmsteads, for example, since the museum has brought in examples of Norwegian buildings and artifacts from key historical periods. The same is true of several other ethnic groups: the German, Swedish, Danish, Finnish, and—most recently—New England Yankee. The museum's interpreters use the third person and are generally engaged in traditional farming or crafts activities.

The architecture really sets the museum apart. A tremendous effort was made to find stellar examples of the European vernacular. You could spend a full week just comparing different traditions in the architectural and decorative arts.

A good time to visit the museum is June, for the Scandinavian Midsummer Celebration, or on winter weekends when the cross-country skiing trails open. In the best European tradition, the museum also has an excellent restaurant built into a magnificent 1897 octagonal barn.

Black Creek Pioneer Village • 5 Shoreham Drive, North York, Ontario, Canada M3N 1S4 • (416) 661–6610

Since 1960 Black Creek has been interpreting the social history of south central Ontario in the period before confederation (1867). Operated by the Metropolitan Toronto and Regional Conservation Authority, the museum is a re-created village consisting of more than thirty buildings relocated on roughly fourteen acres. Interestingly, Black Creek has a noticeable Pennsylvania German atmosphere. Many of its buildings were originally constructed by refugees from Pennsylvania who migrated to Ontario after the Revolutionary War. These structures include Daniel Strong's farm, Edgeley Mennonite

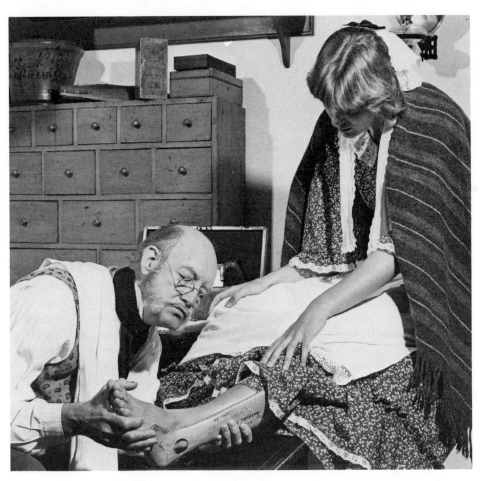

Interpreting mid-Victorian health care. —*Black Creek Pioneer Village*

Meeting House, Henry Snider's cider mill, and the magnificent 1806 John Dalziel barn. The village also includes a variety of other representative structures, including a halfway house, blacksmith, cooperage, carriage works, emporium, post office, and quarters for a weaver, a gunsmith, and a broom maker. Open year round (except February), Black Creek manages to retain its rural atmosphere, in contrast to the encroaching urbanization of modern Toronto.

Old Cienega Village Museum • Route 2, Box 214, Santa Fe, New Mexico 87501 • (505) 471–2261

Scattered across three hundred and fifty acres of rolling hills and rich marshland on El Rancho de las Golondrinas (The Ranch of the Swallows), now almost three hundred years old, is Old Cienega, an atmospheric living museum interpreting the regional folklife of colonial New Mexico. The museum takes its name from La Cienega, a nearby village which once served as a stop on the highway from Santa Fe (fifteen miles north) to Albuquerque.

Old Cienega was opened in 1971 and includes two historical complexes. The first is a late 1600s placita (adobe house built around a plaza) complete with chapel, kitchen, outdoor bake ovens, well, weaving rooms, and fortified tower as well as corrals and pens for livestock. The atmosphere is quintessentially medieval, reminiscent of a Spanish feudal manor. The second complex dates from the mid-1700s and includes the home of the Baca family (which owned the ranch for more than two hundred years), a butchering area, barns, various shops, several mills, a school, a winery, and many fields. Burros, goats, sheep, chickens, and other farm animals help animate the entire ranch, creating an impression of a self-sufficient, successful enterprise.

On the first weekend in May and October, traditional festivals heralding

A winter outing in Ontario.—*Black Creek Pioneer Village*

On the eve of Christmas. —*Black Creek Pioneer Village*

spring and harvest are celebrated. Mass is said in honor of San Ysidro, patron saint of farmers, and there is a procession followed by folk music, dances, and plays. For staff and visitor alike, these events are both authentic and deeply moving.

Ontario Agricultural Museum • P.O. Box 38, Milton, Ontario, Canada L9T 2Y3 • (416) 878–8151

Located within an hour's drive of Toronto, the Ontario Agricultural Museum interprets the province's changing rural lifestyles in an eighty-acre complex. The more than thirty buildings include rare 1830 and 1850 period farmsteads and a wide assortment of 1930s structures, including a McDuffe implement dealership, a Ford garage and repair shop, and a steel-truss barn.

Another unusual feature of the collection is the variety of central Ontario rural "industries": an apple butter and cider plant, a wooden pump manufacturer, carriage works, a shingle mill, and a slaughterhouse. Most of these structures are operated in a historically accurate manner and are integrated into educational programs for both school groups and adult visitors.

The museum is open from May to October and has two autumn events that are particularly intriguing. In mid-September an 1884 fall fair is re-created, complete with livestock and food judging. During the first week of October, the Canadian Thanksgiving, Harvest Home, is celebrated in late Victorian fashion. Included in this event are special butchering demonstrations.

For visitors familiar with John Kenneth Galbraith's *The Scotch,* an autobiographical memoir of life in southern Ontario, the Ontario Agricultural Museum will be particularly poignant.

Preparing for the wheat harvest in colonial New Mexico. —*Old Cienega Village Museum*

White House Ranch • 3202 Chambers Way, Colorado Springs, Colorado 80829 • (303) 578–6640

With the Colorado Rockies providing a towering backdrop to the west, White House Ranch presents one of the living history movement's most effective programs. The ranch is part of the thirteen-hundred-acre Garden of the Gods National Landmark on the edge of Colorado Springs. Three periods of central Colorado's social history are interpreted on the site: the ages of homesteading (1860s), ranching (1890s) and "estate living" (1910s).

The "walk through Colorado's past" begins with Walter C. Galloway and his 1868 homestead. An interpreter adopts the role of Galloway, a pioneer who was described by a contemporary in 1885 as "a plain, plodding day-laborer" who successfully "cultivated the regulation patch of garden demanded by Uncle Sam." Contrasting dramatically with his primitive cabin and holding is the Rock Ledge Ranch, where the Robert Chamber's family prospered in 1895. Here the product of twenty years' hard work is seen: a substantial stone farmhouse, greenhouses irrigated year round from a reservoir, a frame barn for the ranch's horses, cattle, sheep, goats, chickens, and burros, a blacksmith and carpentry shop, and extensive gardens. The last stop is the "White House" itself, an estate built by General William Palmer, a Union Civil War hero who made his fortune running narrow-gauge railroads up to Colorado's nearby mining camps. The fourteen-room mansion was completed in 1907 and is eclectic in style, combining Spanish, Dutch, and Edwardian English motifs. First-person interpretation is also used effectively at both the ranch and estate.

Open from June through October for walk-on visitors, the ranch also hosts a variety of seasonal events and programs in autumn and spring, including a "Pike's Peak or Bust" reenactment in April.

Grove Farm and Homestead • P.O. Box 1631, Lihue, Kauai, Hawaii 96766 • (808) 245–3202

On the island of Kauai, roughly one hundred miles west of Honolulu, is Grove Farm Homestead, a historical museum of Hawaii plantation life. Founded in 1864 by George Wilcox, the eighty-acre homestead is one of the earliest sugar plantations in Hawaii. The original buildings and furnishings, the farm's orchards, exceptional trees, kitchen gardens, and cattle pasture, and the traditional work routine and processes have all been preserved. History here is not simulated; rather it has been stabilized and allowed to continue so that the homestead is a functional unit in situ, or what the French would call an "eco museum." The museum is worth studying as a model by individuals who want to preserve and interpret a more recent historic site.

Fewer than ten thousand people visit the farm each year, and half of them are island residents. For Hawaiians, this plantation functions as their own folklife museum, a tangible reminder of their own culture's recent history, a history which continues to shape their lives in the modern world. The farm's interpretive program, an unhurried tour, allows visitors to understand the plantation as a functioning economic, social, and cultural unit.

Plimoth Plantation • P.O. Box 1620, Plymouth, Massachusetts 02061 • (617) 746–1622

A re-creation of the Pilgrims' 1627 village, Plimoth Plantation is one of the most exciting living history museums in North America.

The enclosed village is harshly realistic; it really *looks* and *feels* like a Jacobean peasant community. The same attention to historical detail carries over to the simulated folklife. Interpreters remain in the role of Pilgrims and

Storing dried seed corn. —*Old Cienega Village Museum*

Eighty-eight year old Catalina Barela weaves a *jerga*, or New Mexican rug. —*Old Cienega Village Museum*

convey spontaneity, suggesting what T. S. Eliot called "felt life." Walking into the village is akin to stepping into a historical drama. It's exhilarating.

My favorite times to visit the plantation are early spring, late fall, or bad-weather days when the crowds are thin. For a truly absorbing ramble, other visitors should be as few as possible. On a slow day, you have the chance to talk at length with individual interpreters or to poke in the village's odd nooks and crannies. Special events such as weddings and Harvest Home are crowded but worthwhile. A visit takes at least a day, especially if you want to tour the *Mayflower* and spend time in the museum's excellent store.

Historic St. Mary's City • P.O. Box 39, St. Mary's City, Maryland 20686 • (301) 944–0776

Situated on a peninsula jutting out into the salty expanse of Chesapeake Bay, Historic St. Mary's City is one of the newest and most ambitious living history museums in North America. The original city, founded in 1634, was Maryland's colonial capital for the next sixty years. The city flourished, blessed by religious toleration and the benign rule of Cecil Calvert, second Lord Baltimore. The restoration, scarcely in its tenth year, successfully captures the earthy excitement of the original settlement.

A number of projects stand out. The *Maryland Dove* is a full-scale replica of an early seventeenth-century ship large enough to cross the north Atlantic but small enough to maneuver through Maryland's coastal bays and rivers. Her architect was William Baker, who designed the *Mayflower II*, and she regularly takes to sea. The *Dove's* cargo is often tobacco from the Godiah Spray Tobacco Plantation, an operating and very realistic living history farm of the 1640s. Carved out of forest and set beside St. Andrew's Creek, the plantation includes both dwelling and tenant houses, tobacco barns, cow and

Grinding corn on a stone metate or hand mill. —*Old Cienega Village Museum*

hog pens, pasture, orchard, gardens, and fields for corn and the "Devil's weed." About a mile away are the 1676 State House and Farthing's Ordinary, two imposing public buildings. The State House was re-created in 1934 but has only recently been interpreted using living history simulation. Farthing's Ordinary, on the other hand, was designed as a functioning inn and serves period meals to both staff and visitors. The view of the bay is spectacular from both buildings. First-person interpretation is used at all four complexes. Lord Baltimore's World, a private venture, located just behind the State House, provides an even heavier dose of living history on eight summer weekends. More than one hundred actors present the story of early Maryland using live interpretation, skits, improvisations, and formal dramas set amid simulated taverns, theaters, homes, and urban shops. The experience is worthwhile if you totally suspend disbelief. Finally, a number of archaeological digs are under way on the site of the original city. Nearby at Chancellor's Point Natural History Center, Errett Callahan, the foremost experimental archaeologist, began constructing an Algonquian longhouse in 1984.

Sainte-Marie among the Hurons • c/o Huronia Historical Parks, P.O. Box 160, Midland, Ontario, Canada L4R 4K8 • (705) 526–7838

Isolated on a remote peninsula in Georgian Bay, about an hour and a half north of Toronto by car, is a painstakingly accurate reconstruction of the first European settlement in the interior of North America, the Jesuit mission to the Hurons, Sainte-Marie. Within a palisade are twenty-two dwellings, workshops, barns, longhouses, churches, and a cookhouse and hospital. Here in 1639–1649 lived sixty Frenchmen, one-fifth of the European population of New France in the mid-seventeenth century. The everyday life of this significant frontier settlement is simulated daily throughout the summer from the

Victoria Day weekend in May through Labor Day. The level of interpretation is exceptionally high, and as you walk about the smoky Huron longhouses and dank French structures, the place seems to have a true historical feel.

A visit to this living museum may be coupled with one to the nearby Historic Naval and Military Establishment at Penetanguishene, a center of British military might for forty years following the War of 1812.

Sainte Marie de Gannentaha • Onondaga County Department of Parks and Recreation, P.O. Box 146, Liverpool, New York 13088 • (315) 457–2990

Constructed in 1933 as a public works project in Syracuse, Sainte Marie de Gannentaha commemorates the French Jesuit mission to the Iroquois in 1656–1658. For two years, forty colonists lived among the Onondaga Nation and developed a small self-sufficient European outpost. In addition to farming, they practiced blacksmithing, carpentry, tailoring, and related domestic arts. Iroquois politics eventually forced them to withdraw to Montreal.

The present project is similar to many other city- or county-sponsored living history programs. Efforts are being made to restore and expand the old "French Fort" located in a park on the north bank of Lake Onondaga. Volunteers have been recruited from voyageur units interested in interpreting the early period of North American French history. A small professional staff has developed programs with assistance from experimental archaeologists at Syracuse University and from the nearby Onondaga Council of Chiefs. Sainte Marie de Gannentaha's potential as one of the few sites focusing on the mid-1600s is rapidly being realized.

Vaqueros, or cowboys, braid rope. —*Old Cienega Village Museum*

Pilgrim militia members drill under the scrutiny of Miles Standish. —*Plimoth Plantation, Inc.*

Pennsbury Manor • 400 Pennsbury Memorial Road, Morrisville, Pennsylvania 19067 • (215) 946–0400

The official residence of William Penn when he was governor of Pennsylvania in the late seventeenth century, Pennsbury Manor was re-created in the 1930s by the state of Pennsylvania. The forty-acre site sits along the Delaware River about twenty-five miles north of Philadelphia. The historic buildings include the manor house plus outbuildings for baking, brewing, smoking meats, and storing ice. In addition, there is a plantation office, a joiner's shop, and a barge shelter (transportation to and from Philadelphia was by barge), a large barn, a sheepfold, and smaller structures for livestock (horses, cows, pigs, and assorted poultry). Pennsbury Manor was designed by the well-known colonial revival architect Brognard Okie and describes life in the early colonial period as historians in the 1930s thought it was lived.

William Penn lived at the manor only twice, in 1683–1684 and in 1700–1701. The staff has developed an excellent first-person program, "Meet the People," which simulates and contrasts these two visits. A good time to experience this program is in the winter, when there is plenty of time to talk at length with the interpreters. The museum also sponsors an authentic Market Fair on a mid-September weekend. Juried reenactors join the staff in presenting a really accurate English-American rural celebration with fascinating Quaker overtones.

The Museum of San Agustin Antiguo • Historic St. Augustine Preservation Board, St. Augustine, Florida 32084 • (904) 824–3355

The Museum of San Agustin Antiguo is a living eighteenth-century Spanish colonial barrio in the very heart of modern "downtown" St. Augustine, a tiny city of twelve thousand which was founded on the north-

Erecting a post hole, mortise, and tenon house.—*Plimoth Plantation, Inc.*

east Florida coast in 1565. The museum consists of five traditional houses, a pottery, a smithy, and a weaver's and cabinet maker's shop. Three of the houses are constructed of tabby (homemade oyster-shell concrete) and coquina, a shell rock quarried from the nearby beach near the well-known Castillo de San Marcos. Another is frame, and the last is pure coquina coated with a pink stucco. The overall ambiance of the neighborhood is "vernacular" in the extreme and fascinating.

Enthusiastic staff members, a number of whom live in the barrio, use living history to demonstrate colonial Spanish-American foodways and local crafts. Especially interesting is the potter who produces San Marcos earthenware, an Indian pottery characteristic of northern Florida.

The Saint George Street Players, a troop of actors, perform in translation the short rustic comedies of Lupe de Rueda, the sixteenth-century Spanish playwright who first employed natural dialogue. The players work from a traveling show wagon which, like the barrio itself, is a veritable time machine.

Fortress of Louisbourg • Fortress of Louisbourg National Historic Park, Box 160, Louisbourg, Nova Scotia, Canada BOA 1M0 • (902) 733-2630

Awesome in scale, the Fortress of Louisbourg lies isolated at the end of Nova Scotia's beautiful Cape Breton Island. It's well worth the trip, especially if you are planning a Canadian maritime vacation.

Focusing on the year 1744, interpretation at Louisbourg varies from third-person animation to excellent static exhibits that tell the story of the site's restoration. The number and variety of the interpretive staff is daunting—the fortress was, after all, a small city, made up of soldiers, sailors, fishermen, merchants, and craftsmen of all sorts. You could spend a day just looking at all the different types of clothing.

Although the museum provides adequate orientation by means of a "time tunnel," Louisbourg has four excellent books and numerous brochures that, if read beforehand, would enrich a visit. Inside the fortress, canteens provide historically accurate eighteenth-century French food.

The living history buff should plan to spend at least a couple of days at Louisbourg. The Feast of St. Louis, celebrated on August 25, is the highlight of the year and a great time to visit. Candelight tours during July and August, however, are also extraordinary ways to experience a "moment in time."

Fort Necessity • Fort Necessity National Battlefield, R.D. 2, Box 528, Farmington, Pennsylvania 15437 • (412) 329–5512
The battle that took place at Fort Necessity on July 3, 1754, was an important first in two ways. It was the opening engagement of the French and Indian War, and it marked the only time that George Washington ever surrendered to an enemy force. His force of four hundred Virginia and South Carolina troops was besieged by a French and Indian army almost twice as large, and Washington wisely capitulated and was allowed to return home. In 1933 the site of Fort Necessity, in southwestern Pennsylvania close to both the West Virginia and Maryland borders, was designated a national park. The fort's stockade, storehouse, and entrenchments were reconstructed. The park also includes Mount Washington Tavern, a large stone and brick inn built in 1827 on the National Road—the turnpike which connected western Pennsylvania, Virginia, and Ohio with the eastern seaboard in the first half of the

Spring gardening at the Godiah Spray Tobacco Plantation. — *Historic St. Mary's City; photograph by John Ennis*

Moments before the day's work. —*Historic St. Mary's City; photograph by John Ennis*

nineteenth century. National Park Service staff and volunteers present first-person living history programs at the tavern in mid-May on "Old Pike Days" and on the two mid-December weekends. A major French and Indian War event commemorates the Battle of Fort Necessity on the weekend closest to July 3. Since battle reenactments are not permitted in national parks, the weekend activities consist of an authentic encampment and period drills and displays.

Fort Niagara • Old Fort Niagara Association, Inc., Box 169, Youngstown, New York 14174 • (715) 745–7611

One of the oldest remaining structures in the Great Lakes area, Fort Niagara was constructed in 1726 at the mouth of the Niagara River on Lake Ontario. Occupied successively by the French, British, and Americans, it controlled access to the Great Lakes and the westward waterways into North America's heartland. Its strategic significance diminished only after the completion of the Erie Canal in 1825.

In 1934 the fort's restoration was completed. By far the most impressive structure is the "French Castle," a fort within a fort constructed in 1726 and containing barracks, storerooms, a bakery, a powder magazine, officer's apart-ments, and a sacristy and chapel. The fort's massive bastions have also been restored, and the view from them over Lake Ontario and the Niagara River to Canada is worth the visit.

The staff at the fort conducts daily musket and cannon firings, military drills, and eighteenth-century cooking demonstrations. With the assistance of serious reenactors, the fort also offers a variety of special events, including a celebration of the King's Birthday in June, a French and Indian encamp-

Hoeing tobacco, Maryland's major cash crop in the seventeenth century. —*Historic St. Mary's City; photograph by John Ennis*

ment in July, and theme weekends focusing on eighteenth-century crafts and army life throughout the year. Fort Niagara is regarded as a leader in the movement to bring together museum professionals and living history buffs.

Fort Michilimackinac • Mackinaw City, Michigan 49701 • (616) 436–5563

Within sight of the seemingly endless Mackinac Bridge, which links lower and upper Michigan, Fort Michilimackinac re-creates its colorful history from 1715 to 1781. Restoration began in 1960 under the auspices of the Mackinac Island State Park Commission. Extensive archaeological and historical research preceded construction, and the fort today houses informative static exhibits as well as ongoing archaeological excavations. Both interpret the research effort.

Set in a park at the water's edge, the fort contains eight major buildings, including a French Catholic church, a priest's house, a blacksmith shop, barracks, the commanding officer's house, a storage building, a merchant's house, and a guardhouse. A large parade ground gives one-half of the fort an open feeling, while the buildings cluster in the other half, reminding me of a small eighteenth-century Quebec village. A massive palisade wall complete with fortified gates encloses the entire fort, limiting the view of modern intrusions.

Interpretation varies from excellent first-person improvisation at the merchant's store and guardhouse to a sound-and-light show in the Church of Sainte Anne. There are also a number of indoor museum exhibits, life-sized dioramas, and, in summer, an interpreted archaeological excavation. Nearby, you can board the *Welcome,* a reconstruction of the supply sloop built at the fort in 1775.

Fort Ligonier • Fort Ligonier Memorial Foundation, Inc., South Market Street, Ligonier, Pennsylvania 15658 • (412) 238–9701

The staging site for the British and Provincial Army which captured Fort Duquesnes from the French in 1758, Fort Ligonier is of major historical significance in the French and Indian War. The restoration, located in the small town of Ligonier, about forty miles east of Pittsburgh, is a good example of a modest site which has revitalized itself by adopting living history interpretation and enlisting the support of reenactors.

Western Pennsylvania is the heart of French and Indian War reenactment activity. The Eighteenth-Century Society has its headquarters in nearby Bushy Run. Sites like Fort Ligonier and Fort Necessity have opened their gates to serious reenactment units and have developed special events, both closed and open to the public, which allow buffs to become acquainted with authentic historic sites. The opportunity to bivouac in an eighteenth-century space is one most reenactors cherish.

Fort Ligonier contains an officer's mess, barracks, quartermaster's supply room, armory, commissary, hospital, huts, and several stockaded gun platforms and redoubts. It is a good context for the fort's major annual event, Fort Ligonier Days Encampment, held every October to commemorate the severe attack by French and Indian forces in 1758, which failed and essentially ended French influence in western Pennsylvania.

Grand Portage National Monument • Box 666, Grand Marais, Minnesota 55604 • (218) 387–2788

Grand Portage commands one of the most beautiful vistas in North America. Located on the north shore of Lake Superior a few miles from the

Riving a clapboard from a piece of white oak with a froe. —*Historic St. Mary's City; photograph by John Ennis*

An indentured servant grinds corn using a mortar and pestle. —*Historic St. Mary's City; photograph by John Ennis*

Canadian border, this reconstruction of the original post as it was in 1778–1803 looks eastward toward Isle Royale. Not a single modern intrusion mars the view. Two hundred years of "progress" seem to have disappeared. The only sound is the lapping of icy water on the shore.

The National Park Service has built four structures: the massive great hall, its kitchen, a canoe warehouse, and a trader's cabin. The post is partially surrounded by a stockade, and the entire site impresses the visitor as a well-kept park. While the tidiness and lack of interpretive garbage are certainly not historically accurate, Grand Portage nevertheless effectively suggests its earlier, more prosperous time.

Interpretation is provided by Park Service staff members, who wear period clothing and use the third person, and by Chippewa Indians from the nearby Grand Portage Reservation, who build birchbark canoes and demonstrate traditional crafts. A poignant, informative film, *Northwest Passage— The Story of Grand Portage,* sets the site in its historical and geographic context.

Each August, Grand Portage hosts a major event, Rendezvous Days, which attracts voyageur reenactors from throughout North America.

Old Fort William • Vickers Heights Post Office, Thunder Bay, Ontario, Canada POT 2Z0 • (807) 577–8461

In 1816, Old Fort William on the north shore of Lake Superior was the Grand Central Station of the Great North Woods. As headquarters of the North West Company, the fort was the center of a vast trading empire stretching from Montreal to the Pacific.

The company was the historical prototype of today's international conglomerates. Its fort was a microcosm of Canada: a miniature city in the wilderness, populated by French voyageurs, Ojibwa Indians, and Anglo-Scottish merchants.

Comparable to Louisbourg in scope, the fort contains more than forty buildings within its towering palisades and teems with entrepreneurial activity. There are carpenters, blacksmiths, armorers, tailors, and coopers at work. In a huge canoe shed, thirty-six-foot Montreal freight canoes are being built of birchbark. The kitchens smell of bread, the taverns of wine. Shops are stocked with trade goods from Europe, and sheds are piled high with bundles of fur. Animation is provided by almost 150 interpreters who use a variety of living history techniques, including very effective role playing.

One day at the fort is not enough: the site and the subject it interprets are too grand. It is best visited as part of a cool summer vacation in western Ontario.

George Washington Birthplace National Monument • Washington's Birthplace, Virginia 22575 • (804) 224–0196

Popes Creek Plantation, the birthplace and boyhood home of George Washington, was substantially re-created in 1968 as a typical Tidewater farm of the 1730s era. The National Park Service staff performs such day-to-day tasks as plowing and cultivating field crops, gardening, cooking on a fireplace, wool and flax spinning, blacksmithing, coopering, and woodworking. Great efforts have been made to use the livestock and plants of the period. Historical accuracy has long been important in the plantation's program.

Located on the west shore of the Potomac River about ninety miles south of Washington, D.C., the plantation suggests the preferred atmosphere of the

Godiah Spray and his household pause for their midday meal. —*Historic St. Mary's City; photograph by John Ennis*

Stitching a sampler at Sainte-Marie among the Hurons. —*Huronia Historical Parks, Ontario Ministry of Tourism and Recreation*

genteel planter and contrasts nicely with the yeoman earthiness of Turkey Run nearby. The staff has pioneered "hands-on" educational programs for groups of all ages. The basic interpretive tour is first rate and gives the serious visitor a sound introduction to the everyday plantation life of the early 1700s.

The National Colonial Farm • 3400 Bryan Point Road, Accokeek, Maryland 20607 • (301) 283–2113

Established in 1958 by the Accokeek Foundation with the support of the National Park Service, the National Colonial Farm differs in purpose from most other living historical farms. First, it protects the Maryland shore directly across from Mount Vernon from modern intrusions, perpetuating a mid-eighteenth-century landscape of the kind Washington himself would have seen from his front lawn. Second, it maintains a repository of historical plants and livestock for study and use by other farm museums. One of its most notable projects is an American chestnut grove where blight-resistant trees are being developed. Third, the farm demonstrates to visitors, especially school groups, middle-class life and agriculture on an eighteenth-century tobacco plantation. It therefore contrasts directly with Turkey Run, its nearby poor cousin.

The farm's setting in the secluded center of Piscataway Park across the Potomac from three other historic parks (Mount Vernon, Fort Hunt, and Fort Washington) is pastoral. It is an ideal place to escape the hurly-burly of Washington, D.C., approximately a half-hour's drive to the north.

Colonial Williamsburg • P.O. Box C, Williamsburg, Virginia 23187 • (804) 229–1000

A pioneer in the field of living history, Colonial Williamsburg has been simulating life in the late eighteenth century for more than fifty years. Millions of Americans are familiar with the "old" colonial capital of Virginia, as dignified, courteous, and properly attired as a Southern gentleman.

There has been a change. The "new" Williamsburg is populated with women, blacks, workers, and other ordinary folk. The interpretive program is determined to communicate the city's social history.

Many of the museum's 550 costumed staff employ first-person interpretation in innovative and effective ways. Actors roam the streets, servants show visitors through the Governor's Palace; and in 1984, the Publick Hospital of 1773, the first insane asylum in the United States, reopened.

In addition, the museum offers some of the finest crafts demonstrations in the nation as well as lantern tours, concerts, plays, military tattoos, and a variety of seminars. You could spend months in Williamsburg and not experience all its programs. Off season, especially winter, is a good time to visit. The pace is slower and the crowds thinner.

Colonial Pennsylvania Plantation • Ridley Creek State Park, Media, Pennsylvania 19063 • (215) 566–1725

In 1974, a group of living history buffs, experimental archaeologists, and museum interpreters, united by a mutual interest in living history, founded the Colonial Pennsylvania Plantation, a 1770's Quaker family farm. Located fifteen miles west of Philadelphia in a hilly, densely forested state park, the plantation had once been a prosperous farm, established in about 1710 by a

A French Jesuit missionary shares a text. — *Sainte-Marie among the Hurons, Huronia Historical Parks, Ontario Ministry of Tourism and Recreation*

In the bleak midwinter. —*Sainte-Marie among the Hurons, Huronia Historical Parks, Ontario Ministry of Tourism and Recreation*

Quaker family which worked it for over a century. Most of the original buildings still stood, along with a few stone walls, mature shade trees, and the outlines of a colonial field system. The plantation was opened to the public almost immediately as a "museum in the making," an outdoor historical laboratory where the primary interpretive theme was historical research. Visitors readily grasped the concept of a 120-acre land version of *Kon-Tiki*, and the plantation became an innovative, popular Bicentennial project.

Today the plantation is alive and well, functioning primarily as a "folks museum" for many reenactors in western Pennsylvania who appreciate an informal home base. It hosts a variety of special events, ranging from Revolutionary and Civil War encampments to a harvest feast, Quaker style. The staff also operates a variety of educational programs for adults and children.

One of the most beautiful living historical farms in the East and totally isolated from modern intrusions, the plantation in every season speaks to the visitor of its peaceful Quaker origins.

Claude Moore Colonial Farm • Turkey Run, 6310 Old Georgetown Pike, McLean, Virginia 22101 • (703) 442–7557

Just a musket shot away from Central Intelligence Agency headquarters in McLean, Virginia, is Claude Moore Colonial Farm, a poor man's farm of the sort found in the northern Virginia Tidewater on the eve of the American Revolution. The farmstead is actually twelve cleared acres in the heart of a dense forest. The setting of this National Park Service living history project is isolated, and the whole place has a precarious, eerie feel about it.

This colonial farm was begun in 1973 during the initial boom in living history projects before the American Bicentennial. What set it apart then was the Park Service's goal of re-creating a small dirt farm where an obviously poor farmer and his family eked out a meager existence on land worn out from fifty years of tobacco cropping. The project reflects the new social history movement and its concern with minorities, in this case, the often neglected small farmer.

A rough log cabin, outbuilding, kitchen garden, pigpen, two weedy cornfields, and a pasture circled with a stake-and-rider snake fence make up the physical farm. But the *living* colonial farm is the sum of the relationships between the poor family, its livestock (quarterhorses, Devon cattle, razorback hogs, and dunghill fowl), and the worn-out land. The effect of the material and social characteristics of Claude Moore Colonial Farm on the visitor can be powerful and informative.

The staff uses first-person interpretation and conducts a variety of educational programs, including a weekend live-in for teachers.

U.S. Frigate *Constellation* • The Ship's Company—1800, 9411 Boulder Road, Frederick, Maryland 21701 • (301) 663–1829

Launched in 1797, the *Constellation* is the oldest existing American warship. She fought the French in the Caribbean during the 1799 undeclared "Quasi War," blockaded Tripoli in the 1802 struggle against the Barbary pirates, served in the Mediterranean during the Civil War, and in 1871 became a training ship at the Naval Academy. In 1914, the frigate returned home to Baltimore, and in the early 1960s she was restored and became both a National Historic Landmark and a tourist attraction in the revitalized inner harbor once protected by Fort McHenry.

The *Constellation* is interpreted on the first Saturday of every month,

Everyday life in the 1640s. —*Sainte-Marie among the Hurons, Huronia Historical Parks, Ontario Ministry of Tourism and Recreation*

Evaluating a young ox at the Market Fair. — *Pennsbury Manor, Pennsylvania Historical and Museum Commission*

spring through fall, by the "Ship's Company—1800," a devoted group of twenty volunteers with a strong reenactment background. They muster a cannon crew and twelve marines, enough to portray a cross section of deck ratings, boys, and sea soldiers. Their goal is the accurate depiction of life on board the *Constellation* in about 1800.

The Ship's Company's interpretation is important as a model for the other restored ships. Vessels are "bounded" entities, and like forts, farms, and villages, they have great potential as living museums. The capacity of ships for research experiments (*Kon-Tiki, Brendan,* and *Hokule'a* are notable examples) has been demonstrated. The *Constellation* project indicates the educational value of shipboard interpretation.

Fort Mackinac • Mackinac Island State Park Commission, Mackinac Island, Michigan 49757 • (906) 847–3328

Fort Mackinac crowns a high bluff overlooking Mackinaw City, the harbor, and the straits connecting Lakes Huron and Michigan. The view from its ramparts is both breathtaking and romantic. The island has been a popular resort since the 1830s, in part because of its natural beauty, kept relatively unspoiled by a ban on all motor vehicles. One of the loudest sounds heard on the island is the clip-clop of horses' hooves. It is a wonderful place to vacation, the more so if you are a living history buff.

Mackinac Island was discovered by the Jesuits in 1670. The British made it a center for both their fur trade and their military activity in 1781. It lay directly on the route from Montreal and Grand Portage and dominated three Great Lakes: Huron, Michigan, and Superior. An American force occupied the fort in 1783, then lost it in the early days of the War of 1812. After the war it once again was garrisoned by the American army, which made it the center of the American fur empire after 1817. The government made the island a national park in 1875, but not until the 1950s did serious restoration and interpretation of the fort begin.

Interpretation of the huge complex uses both static displays in period rooms and some excellent living history demonstrations. My favorite is a carefully scripted and well-acted dramatization of a common soldier's court-martial which actually took place in 1797.

A visit to Forts Mackinac and Michilimackinac takes several days and is well worth the time.

Historic Fort Wayne • 107 South Clinton Street, Fort Wayne, Indiana 46802 • (219) 424–3476

Constructed in 1815–1816, the original Fort Wayne was one of the largest, most complex all-wooden forts in North America. The solid oak barracks, officer's quarters, blockhouses, hospital, privies, and even magazine of the reconstruction are equally impressive. Located in a riverside park in downtown Fort Wayne, the fort has, since 1974, become one of the continent's best interpreted historic sites.

The staff uses the first person and portrays historic persons connected with the fort and the northeastern Indiana area in 1816. Training is creative and rigorous and a large percentage of the more than 130 interpreters are volunteers many of whom have a reenacting background. The fort is open from mid-April through October, and the daily program re-creates the everyday life of soldiers, civilians, and Indians during the tense years following the War of 1812. The staff also re-creates a bucolic July 4, 1816, on the basis of an

A Quaker farm laborer feeds William Penn's best team. —*Pennsbury Manor, Pennsylvania Historical and Museum Commission*

Respite for three voyageurs in Boucher's House, a tavern at Fort William. —*Old Fort William, Ontario Ministry of Tourism and Recreation*

eyewitness account. Historical accuracy characterizes the fort's everyday and special events.

Close cooperation with serious reenactor groups is crucial to the success of the War of 1812 Weekend, held every September to commemorate the Indian siege of 1812. First-person interpretation is required of all invited units. Less formal is the Trappers' and Traders' Rendezvous, generally held the last weekend in October when Indiana's foliage is as colorful as the late eighteenth- and early nineteenth-century buffs who come to enjoy one more rendezvous before winter sets in.

Fort Snelling • Minnesota Historical Society, St. Paul, Minnesota 55111 • (612) 726–9430

At the point where the Mississippi River meets the Minnesota, on a towering bluff commanding the river routes north and west, stands Fort Snelling, the Minnesota Historical Society's premier living history museum. Here men and women of the Fifth Regiment of Infantry re-create everyday life at the fort in the 1820s. Once the gateway to the great Northwest, Fort Snelling now leads visitors into Minnesota's past.

Fort Snelling rivals Louisbourg and Old Fort William in the variety and accuracy of its interpretations. Officers strut on the gravel parade ground, soldiers gripe about the loneliness and hardship of garrisoning a frontier. The echo of the blacksmith's hammer ricochets off the barrack's walls and mingles with the crackle of musket fire and a cannon's bellow. In the hospital, the post surgeon practices medicine, while nearby, in the sutler's store, a soldier bargains for credit. There is the slosh of the washerwoman's everlasting laundry and the smell of fresh-baked bread. Soldiers' songs mix with the

Williamburg's mayor and other distinguished citizens enjoy the gaming at the Colonial Fair. — *Colonial Williamsburg Foundation*

cackle of gossip. Few other sites are as sensually complete. The Fort Snelling experience is living history at its best.

Restored at considerable expense during the 1970s, the fort contains a variety of authentic components: magazine, school, guardhouse, barracks, officer's quarters, batteries, towers, shops, and stores. Most are manned by a well-trained staff effectively using first-person interpretation. In addition to excellent daily programs, the fort presents a series of theme weekends highlighting the domestic arts (dressmaking, quilting, soap and candle making, foodways), and there are intriguing evening events, including a wedding, dinner party, court-martial, and lantern tour of the off-duty garrison in 1827.

Historic Naval and Military Establishments at Penetanguishene • c/o Huronia Historical Parks, P.O. Box 160, Midland, Ontario, Canada L4R 4K8 • (705) 526–7838

Following the War of 1812, the British government built a series of forts and military posts to protect Canada against any future invasion from the south. The Naval and Military Establishments at Penetanguishene served as a naval dockyard and supply base and later as an army garrison. For over forty years, the Establishments secured the Georgian Bay and Lake Huron. Today the Ontario government has reconstructed the original residences, offices, workshops, officers' quarters, and the naval dockyard and storehouse. The site is open from the Victoria Day weekend in May through Labor Day. My favorite time to visit is late July, when the site celebrates Liberty Days. The H.M. Schooner *Bee* (a full-scale replica) returns to port, and its sailors celebrate with music, dancing, drills, and festivities.

Interpreters enjoy a sporting match at the Colonial Fair. —*Colonial Williamsburg Foundation*

Fort Henry • Box 213, Kingston, Ontario, Canada K7L 4V8 • (613) 542–7388

Dominating Wolfe Island at the point where Lake Ontario funnels into the St. Lawrence River, Fort Henry was built after the War of 1812 to defend Upper Canada from possible American invasions. During the 1830s, a rebellion swept what is now Quebec and Ontario, and a small American force actually invaded Canada downriver near Ogdensburg, New York. The invaders were defeated, and many of the prisoners of war ended up in the dungeons of the fort. Today the only Americans who invade Fort Henry are tourists.

In 1938, the Fort Henry Guard was formed to re-create military life and ceremony at the fort. One of the finest "reenactor" units, it interprets 1867, the year of Canada's confederation. This "thin red line" performs a variety of drills, including a ceremonial retreat, a tattoo, a feu de joie, and a royal salute. The guard also interprets the daily life of the mid-Victorian British line regiments and Royal Artillery which once garrisoned the fort. Made up entirely of university and secondary school students, the guard is "activated" every summer from mid-May through mid-October.

The fort was opened in 1948 and contains a major military museum in addition to a number of restored period rooms and facilities. An ideal visit also takes in Upper Canada Village, about eighty-five miles downriver at Morrisburg, Ontario.

Fort Wellington National Historic Park • P.O. Box 479, Prescott, Ontario, Canada KOE IT0 • (613) 925–2896

Fort Wellington is located on the St. Lawrence River between Fort Henry and Upper Canada Village. Set on a forty-acre site across the river from Ogdensburg, New York, the fort consists of a blockhouse, latrine, officers' quarters, a *caponnière*, and extensive defensive works. These structures were built in 1837–1838 when Canadian rebels with American help threatened Upper Canada. Although the fort itself was never attacked, its garrison helped defeat a force of two hundred invaders which landed about a half mile away in November 1838. The site of this "Battle of the Windmill" is a part of the Fort Wellington park.

Administered by Parks Canada since 1923, the fort interprets the year 1845, when a company of the Royal Canadian Rifle Regiment garrisoned it. In summer, the small permanent staff is augmented by twenty students who form a period guard unit and by a number of women and children who portray the soldiers' families. This well-trained staff re-creates the daily routine of Fort Wellington at a time when Canadians looked across the St. Lawrence with understandable fear and suspicion. Only after the threat of Irish-American "Fenian" invasions waned in 1870 did the fort cease to function as a frontline defense.

On the third weekend in July, Fort Wellington plays host to five hundred members of the Brigade of the American Revolution for a Loyalists Days military pageant.

Fort Ross Historic Park • c/o California Council for Living History, 1630 La Plaza Way, Sacramento, California 95611 • (916) 485–3172

One of California's most recent living history projects, Fort Ross is also one of the state's most exotic and tenuous. Each summer, interpreters re-create life in the Russian American Fur Company's hunting and trading post in 1836. The fort is located about seventy-five miles north of San Francisco on

Social history hits the street in Colonial Virginia. —*Colonial Williamsburg Foundation*

Colonial Black folklife re-created in Virginia's capitol. —*Colonial Williamsburg Foundation*

the spectacular but treacherous Highway 1, the scene of frequent rock slides which sometimes close the road. The fort was also difficult to reach in the 1830s, one reason why the Russians eventually cut their losses in 1841 and sold it.

Two or three times each summer, sixty reenactors portraying Russian colonists, militia, Hudson's Bay Company traders, and visiting Mexican officials re-create a day in the life of the old fort. A skewered lamb slowly turns on an outdoor fire, the Slavojanka men's choir practices its liturgical hymns in the Orthodox chapel, seal and otter skins are traded in the fur barn, and commander Alexander Gavrilovich Rotchev and his wife, Elena Gagarina, ready their fine wines, crystal, and rose garden for the visitors from Monterey. Inside the stockade, the atmosphere is an exotic mixture of Russia and Old California. Outside, Kashaya Pomo Indians mixing with Canadians give the scene the more familiar look of a fur trade rendezvous.

The program, sponsored by the council and the Department of Parks and Recreation with help from the New Helvetia Brigade of Mountain Men, is authentic, exciting, and well worth the visit. It's crucial to write ahead to confirm information regarding the schedule of events.

Bent's Old Fort National Historic Site • 35110 Highway 194 East, La Junta, Colorado 81050 • (303) 384–2596

Many living history aficionados feel that the best living history program in the National Park Service is at Bent's Old Fort. Located in southeastern Colorado near La Junta, the original fort was built of adobe by a hundred Mexican laborers between 1830 and 1833. The financiers were the Bent brothers, who saw the economic potential of a large trading post along the

An officer and his lady enjoy a moment of peace in 1816 Indiana. —*Historic Fort Wayne*

Arkansas River near the Santa Fe Trail. It didn't hurt either that the main hunting grounds of the Cheyenne, Arapaho, Commanche, and Kiowa were nearby. The post did an extraordinary business in the 1840s, especially in buffalo robes and Indian trade goods. Its heyday was 1846, during the Mexican War, the year interpreted at the reconstructed fort today.

Since 1976 the staff has been refining a complex living history program that includes first-person interpretation of eight stock fort figures: a trader, a trapper, a dragoon, a blacksmith, a carpenter, a Mexican laborer, and, perhaps most unusual, an Arapaho Indian—played sensitively by an Arapaho. Most of the interpreters are seasonal, and a successful effort has been made to hire experienced living history professionals or reenactors, including members of the American Mountain Men.

The fort looks just as authentic as its staff. The most exciting time to visit is the weekend after Labor Day, when the fort hosts an authentic fur trade rendezvous with more than three hundred participants.

Sutter's Fort Living History Program • c/o **Interpretive Services, Department of Parks and Recreation, P.O. Box 2390, Sacramento, California 95811 • (916) 322–8554**

California specializes in revitalizing older restored historic sites by arranging well-planned, authentic, and believable special events. Russian colonial life in 1836 is re-created at Fort Ross; Fort Tejon is the setting for Civil War skirmishes; and Sutter's Fort, in downtown Sacramento, captures the drama of 1846, the tumultuous year when California became a U.S. territory.

John Sutter operated his fort from 1830 to 1850. It served as both a refuge for travel-weary pioneers and a major emporium for trappers, settlers, moun-

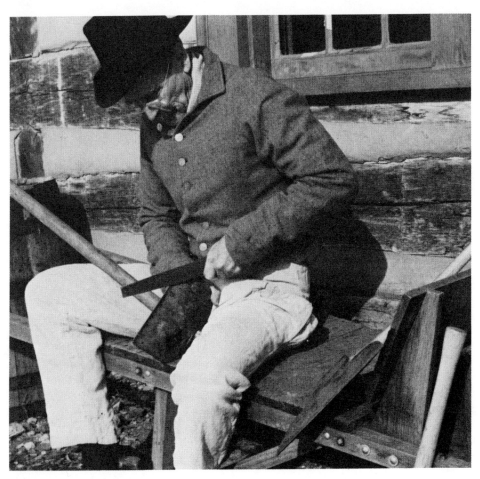

Preparing for spring on the Indiana frontier. —*Historic Fort Wayne*

tain men, Indians, and traders of all nationalities. After gold was discovered at Sutter's nearby sawmill in 1848, the fort was Mecca for the Forty-niners. Eventually Sacramento grew up around it, and in 1958 a city mindful of its history rehabilitated the site.

The living history program, which interprets a series of events in the year 1846, is in its fifth year. Using Sutter's diary and other eyewitness accounts, a corps of seventy experienced volunteers re-creates the fort's daily life on five weekends in March, June, August, October, and November. As the "year" progresses, the focus shifts from Mexican California to the Bear Flag Revolt, war in the South, rumors of invasion, and the prospect of a lean winter. Throughout, the militia is drilling, guns are being repaired, craftsmen are turning out their wares, women are cooking, and children are busying themselves with school and chores. In short, life goes on.

This successful program is best seen on Saturday or Sunday mornings before the crowds develop. Normally, visitors number two thousand a day. In March 1983, when Queen Elizabeth and Prince Philip attended, it was considerably higher!

Four Mile Historic Park • 715 South Forest Street, Denver, Colorado 80222 • (303) 399–1859

Constructed in 1859, the Four Mile House is the oldest building in Denver. For its first ten years, the house served as a wayside inn on the Cherokee trail, a major artery through the Rockies. After 1870, Levi Booth and his descendants turned the inn and property into a large and profitable farm, raising wheat, corn, oats, potatoes, and stock cattle. The family developed a successful irrigation system using water from nearby Cherry

Creek and prospered for the next seventy-five years. In 1975, the Denver Parks and Recreation Department acquired the historic house and twelve acres of land and set up a nonprofit organization to administer it.

Almost from the outset, the staff used living history interpretation to tell the story of the inn and the farm. Traditional tools and methods are being employed in the reconstruction of outbuildings (barn, granary, carriage house, tool shed, hog pen, chicken house, sheep shelter, and so forth), and farming and household chores are demonstrated in historically accurate detail. A tour which traces the history of the farm and area introduces visitors and students to many of the representative groups that passed through Four Mile House: trappers, miners, farmers, and native Americans. Although the focus of the interpretive program is 1859–1864, a much longer period of regional history is introduced.

The farm is supported by a network of volunteers who enable the staff to sponsor eight to ten special events each year, keyed into the agricultural and civic calendar. Particularly boisterous is the 1859 Fourth of July.

Hopewell Village National Historic Site • RD 1, Box 345, Elverson, Pennsylvania 19520 • (215) 582–8773

In the heart of the Pennsylvania German country roughly midway between Philadelphia and Lancaster, Hopewell Village re-creates daily life on an "iron plantation" in the 1820–1840 period. During that time, two hundred men and their families lived in the village, cutting cordwood for charcoal; repairing the huge furnaces; casting stoves, plow parts, holloware, and other iron articles; and tending their livestock, gardens, orchards, and fields—the primary source of food. Hopewell was a rural manufacturing community

Close order drill on Fort Snelling's parade ground. — *Fort Snelling, Minnesota Historical Society*

Paperwork on the Minnesota frontier in the 1820s. —*Fort Snelling, Minnesota Historical Society*

typical of those found where charcoal could be produced in quantity, in the forested areas just west of the major eastern cities.

Restoration of Hopewell Village began in 1938 soon after its acquisition by the National Park Service. The village runs a fine living history program every summer, with demonstrations of both factory and domestic work. Included are flask molding and carpentry, textile work, blacksmithing, gardening, and foodways.

The village is now on the edge of French Creek State Park. An ideal visit would take in both the restoration and the environmental interpretive programs at the park. My favorite time to visit is Establishment Day, the first Sunday in August, when a charcoal pit is constructed of five to seven cords of wood and is lit for a week of supervised burning.

Old Economy • 14th and Church Streets, Ambridge, Pennsylvania 15003 • (412) 266–4500

Old Economy Village, the successful nineteenth-century communitarian venture of the Harmony Society, is situated on the Ohio River about twenty miles downriver from Pittsburgh. Now surrounded by Ambridge, a small historic river town, the center of the industrious Harmonists is a quiet early Victorian enclave which successfully recaptures the tone and texture of life in the 1830s and 1840s, the period of the society's furthest advance. Old Economy was once an impressive manufacturing center, producing shoes, hats, textiles, wines, whiskey, and flour. A planned community of twenty acres, the original village included homes, a church, feast halls, mills, textile factories, and gardens, twelve of which have been carefully restored.

Administered by the Pennsylvania Historical and Museum Commission,

Old Economy has long been an innovator in living history interpretation. In 1970 the village became one of the first museums to offer a live-in participatory program for students. It has served as a model for countless other serious outdoor museums. The staff also helped pioneer first-person role playing, re-creating original members of the Harmony Society. This mode of interpretation continues to be used in conjunction with third-person tours and craft and domestic arts demonstrations. A very high percentage of the village's interpreters are volunteers recruited locally and well trained.

Old Economy offers a variety of adult seminars, workshops, and special events. The most popular of these are the Kunstfest (craft festival) in June, the Erntefest (food festival) in September, and Christmas, which was for the German Harmonist—as for visitors today—a time of traditional celebration and joy.

Old Sturbridge Village • Route 20, Sturbridge, Massachusetts 01566 • (413) 347–3362

Situated in the hills of central Massachusetts, Old Sturbridge Village re-creates the regional folklife of inland New England on the eve of the Industrial Revolution and the nineteenth century—a time when the atmosphere was no longer colonial. The United States was fiercely independent and was beginning to look inward as it shaped its own culture. In addition to a complete traditional village, the museum also operates one of the finest living historical farms. Both are intensely rural and are wrapped in an aura of realistic nostalgia.

The interpreters at Sturbridge look as if they had stepped out of a painting by an itinerant folk artist. Interpretation is generally in the third

Tea time in the captain's house at the Naval and Military Establishment at Penetanguishene, Ontario. —*Naval and Military Establishment at Penetanguishene Huronia Historic Parks, Ontario Ministry of Tourism and Recreation*

A student practices charting the shoreline of Georgian Bay. —*Huronia Historic Parks, Ontario Ministry of Tourism and Recreation*

person, but special events such as the town meeting often use role playing. This is a great place to escape from the late twentieth century and return to a cultural landscape that melds forest and field, meadow and green. A winter weekend is perfect.

Hale Farm and Village • 2686 Oak Hill Road, P.O. Box 256, Bath, Ohio 44210 • (216) 861–4573

Carved out of the hardwood forests of Cuyahoga Valley National Recreation Area midway between Cleveland and Akron, the Hale Farm and Village depicts rural life in Ohio's Western Reserve in about 1825–1850. Completion of the Erie Canal in the late 1820s opened the northwestern Ohio frontier to commerce, and the area around Cleveland flourished. The museum therefore represents not the pioneer era but rather a period of hard-won prosperity, when the region was inextricably bound to the industrialized eastern seaboard states.

The living museum is divided into two sections: the Jonathan Hale farm, begun in 1826 by a prosperous Connecticut family, and a reconstructed village consisting of representative buildings relocated from their original sites in the Western Reserve area. The village includes a blacksmith, woodworker's shop, pottery, sawmill, meetinghouse, glassworks, law office, school, and two Greek revival houses.

Both the operating Hale farm and the village lie on the floor of a lovely valley, isolated from all modern intrusions save the Oak Hill road which bisects them. The setting reminds the visitor of prints by Currier and Ives.

Interpretation primarily involves third-person tours and demonstrations, with a wide variety of special events scheduled in May through October.

These include Morgan Horse Days in July and an October harvest home observance.

Conner Prairie Pioneer Settlement • 13400 Allisonville Road, Noblesville, Indiana 46060 • (317) 773–3633

Situated on the northern outskirts of Indianapolis, Indiana, Conner Prairie Pioneer Settlement re-creates life in an 1836 first-generation frontier village. Its inhabitants are a heady mixture of immigrants from New England, the Hudson River Valley, Kentucky, and the eastern Midwest. The community is a small town in the rough. Interpreters use the first person, a technique that was pioneered by Conner Prairie in the early 1970s.

The museum contains more than thirty very different examples of original vernacular architecture on 240 acres. The atmosphere is realistic and contrasts nicely with the earlier, more eastern Old Sturbridge Village.

My favorite annual events are the reenacted camp meeting and the 1836 election rallies. Both communicate the vigor of early American frontier religion and politics. Conner Prairie's own black powder militia provides the fireworks at the museum on the Fourth of July.

Lincoln Boyhood National Memorial • Lincoln City, Indiana 47552 • (812) 937–4757

For the student of Abraham Lincoln who is also a living history buff, several sites in Indiana and Illinois are well worth visiting. The first is the Lincoln Living Historical Farm (part of the Lincoln Boyhood National Memorial) operated by the National Park Service. Here in the heavily wooded hills of southern Indiana, Lincoln lived from 1816 to 1830, the

Preparing sea cakes in the captain's kitchen. —*Naval and Military Establishment at Penetanguishene, Huronia Historic Parks, Ontario Ministry of Tourism and Recreation*

A budding young shipwright tries his hands at caulking a bateau. —*Naval and Military Establishment at Penetanguishene, Huronia Historic Parks, Ontario Ministry of Tourism and Recreation*

formative years of his boyhood and youth. The farm re-creates the years 1827–1830, when Lincoln was rapidly coming of age and was preparing, with his father, Thomas, to take the family to Illinois.

The re-created farm consists of five log buildings—cabin, barn, chicken house, smokehouse, and carpenter shed—on one hundred acres. The staff grows corn, cotton, flax, and tobacco and tends an extensive kitchen garden and orchard. Cows, pigs, sheep, and chickens are kept for food, draft horses for work.

Interpretation is in the third person. From April to October the staff demonstrates the daily routine of the Lincoln family. Regular activities include cooking, spinning, soap making, chicken plucking, flax breaking, quilting, milling, and field work. In addition, the staff presents six different weekend "how-to" sessions, including "How to Rive and Split," "Making Gluts, Mauls, and Handles," and "Lincoln's Horsepower." There are two tours, one through the kitchen garden and the other an evocative candlelight walk.

Lincoln's New Salem • New Salem State Park, Rural Route 1, Box 244A, Petersburg, Illinois 62675 • (217) 632–7953

From 1830 to 1836 Abe Lincoln lived in the small village of New Salem, about twenty miles northwest of Springfield. Here Lincoln said he developed from an "aimless piece of driftwood" into a lawyer. Along the way, he tried being a storekeeper, surveyor, postmaster, soldier (militia captain during the Black Hawk war), flatboat pilot, and politician. Two years after Lincoln left, New Salem rapidly declined; deserted by its population, it virtually disappeared. In the 1930s the state undertook serious reconstruction. Eventually twenty-three buildings were reconstructed on their original sites. They include the Rutledge Tavern, the Lincoln-Berry store, Miller's blacksmith shop, a carding mill, the village school and church, the sawmill, the gristmill, and more than a dozen cabins and homes. A large volunteer corps of interpreters in 1830s dress demonstrate period work and tell the village story. Isolated in a dense forest, the village looks much as it must have when Lincoln walked its muddy streets. A great time to visit is mid-October when there is a candlelight tour.

Lincoln's Log Cabin Historic Site • Rural Route 1, Box 175, Lerna, Illinois 62440 • (217) 345–6489

Abraham Lincoln's father and stepmother lived on this Goosenest Prairie farm in east central Illinois from 1840 to their deaths in 1851 and 1869. Thereafter the farm remained in the Lincoln family until 1892, when the cabin was sent to the 1893 Chicago Columbian Exposition. In 1929, the state of Illinois purchased the building and returned it to its original site. By 1975 serious re-creation of the entire farmstead was under way. The results are impressive.

The site includes the original "cabin," really a large double-room, southern-style "saddlebag" house, which in 1845 (the year re-created at the museum) accommodated eighteen members of the extended Lincoln family. There are also a barn, corncrib, smokehouse, root cellar, two fenced pastures, an orchard, and a kitchen garden. Sheep and barnyard fowl roam about, and the atmosphere is earthy.

Lincoln's Log Cabin uses first-person interpretation, and the staff has developed more than twenty historic characters which are played in various

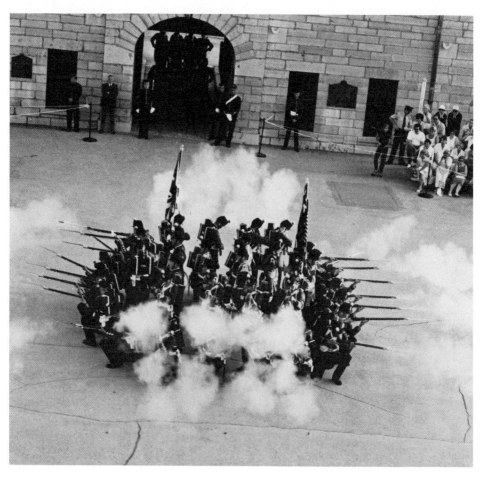

The British Square, part of Fort Henry's ceremonial Retreat, performed by the Fort Henry Guard. —*St. Lawrence Parks Commission*

Drums of the Fort Henry Guard. —*Fort Henry, St. Lawrence Parks Commission*

combinations throughout the year. Many trained volunteers have been recruited and realistically evoke the folklife of the 1840s as well as communicate essential information about the Lincolns, including Abe, who from time to time visited the old family farm from his new home in Springfield.

The staff also sponsors an excellent Mexican War–period militia muster in September, a harvest frolic in October, and an 1845 Glorious Fourth.

Old Bethpage • Round Swamp Road, Old Bethpage, New York 11804 • (516) 420–5280

Located about forty miles east of New York City in the heart of Long Island, Old Bethpage re-creates the regional folklife of a farm community in the decade before the Civil War. The community consists of forty-five historic buildings, including two general stores, a smithy, an inn, a Methodist church, several farms, eight residences, a carpentry shop, and many other smaller buildings. All structures were relocated on the museum's two-hundred-acre site during the last twenty years and collectively represent a near-complete architectural record of the Long Island vernacular tradition of building. Care has been taken to re-create the 1850s historical landscape as well. To modern eyes, the village looks strange, rough, and historically very accurate.

Operated by Nassau County, Old Bethpage is a fine outdoor museum. Interpretation is excellent, whether at the Powell site (a fully operating living history farm) in the shops of the blacksmith, tailor, or carpenter; or at the Noon Inn. Interpreters are obviously well trained.

Old Bethpage is open year round and features a different, historically appropriate event each month. These events include the Long Island Fair, St.

Nicholas Day, Washington's Birth Day, and an innovative Civil War Union training camp (which enlists the support of several hundred experienced reenactors). The museum also offers a variety of creative educational programs, including many nineteenth-century folk and popular arts, for school and special interest groups.

The Homeplace 1850 • Land Between the Lakes, TVA, Golden Pond, Kentucky 42231 • (502) 522–8500

Operated by the Tennessee Valley Authority in its extensive recreation area Land Between the Lakes, the Homeplace is a representative family farm typical of western Kentucky and Tennessee just before the Civil War. It is one of the few living history museums portraying the folklife of the upper South. The farm has sixteen structures, mostly log, and includes a superb dogtrot house and a tobacco barn. Its setting is isolated from all modern intrusions, and the atmosphere is realistic. The Homeplace has the texture of an early daguerreotype.

Activities vary with the season. My favorites are the summer's eve play party and the husking bee in late autumn. Besides farming and going about daily activities common in the 1850s, the staff takes time to celebrate a wedding and the visit of neighbors for a gospel sing. Interpretation is basically in the third person, and the staff is a delightful mixture of older local residents and student interns. The orientation slide show in a nearby earth-covered visitors' center is excellent.

Land Between the Lakes abounds in campsites. A family weekend vacation with a day at the Homeplace is an ideal way to renew an acquaintance with history and nature.

Blast furnace, casting house, and other related structures at Hopewell Village, a restored ironmaking village from the nineteenth century. — *Hopewell Village. Photograph provided by the National Park Service*

Blast furnace at Hopewell Village. In the early nineteenth century, iron was made here using iron ore, limestone, and charcoal. —*Hopewell Village. Photograph provided by the National Park Service*

Shakertown at Pleasant Hill • Route 4, Harrodsburg, Kentucky 40330 • (606) 734–9111

One of my most pleasant memories is of walking along the country lanes on the outskirts of Shakertown one Sunday morning and *not* hearing or seeing one twentieth-century sound or sight. No televisions blared, no auto engines revved, and no billboards interrupted the view of rolling hills, stone walls, Georgian brick buildings, and Kentucky bluegrass. A weekend at Shakertown can be a pastoral idyll.

Restoration of Shakertown began in 1961. In addition to restoring nearly thirty original pre–Civil War buildings, the founders purchased more than twenty-five hundred acres of surrounding farmland and opened a hostelry featuring guests' rooms fitted out with reproduction Shaker furniture and an inn offering authentic nineteenth-century Kentucky dishes. Shakertown quickly became a favorite stop for history buffs and epicures.

Living history interpretation is primarily demonstration. You can see a spinner, weaver, cooper, broom maker, and cabinet maker at work. In addition, some period agriculture is practiced, especially gardening and food processing. Theme weekends of particular interest to adults focus on Shaker dance, music, and religion. With Cincinnati, Louisville, and Lexington only an hour's drive away, these events are fully subscribed, so advanced reservations are necessary.

Westville • South Mulberry Street, Lumpkin, Georgia 31815 • (912) 838–6310

Westville is about halfway between Plains, Georgia, and the Chattahoochee River, the state's natural border with Alabama. This is the Deep

South. Founded in 1968, the museum re-creates a small 1850 Georgia town and is open year round. Within its fifty-eight acres, almost forty original pre-1850 buildings have been relocated. These include the Chattahoochee County courthouse; an academy; a cotton gin mill and screw press; a pottery pug mill, kiln, and shop; a camp meeting arbor; a whiskey still; a sugarcane mill; a mule barn; various shops (cabinet maker, blacksmith); offices; a Presbyterian church; an inn; and a variety of homes once inhabited by rich and poor, black and white. Very few outdoor museums manage to achieve the historical atmosphere and regional feel that Westville captures. As you walk its dusty streets with the sharp smell of pine filling the warm air, the real old South comes alive. There is not a hint of *Gone with the Wind*. The museum re-creates an authentic 1850s rural fair in the late fall.

Meadow Farm Museum • General Sheppard Crump Memorial Park, County of Henrico, Division of Recreation and Parks, P.O. Box 27032, Richmond, Virginia 23273 • (804) 788–0391

Meadow Farm opened in 1983 and is already a favorite of reenactors. The staff hosts a Civil War reenactment every September and a colonial muster in October. Both events are appropriate, since the farm was owned and operated by the Sheppards from 1713 to 1980, a family whose papers tell of experiences in both wars. Located on 150 acres of parkland, there are a restored farmhouse, a smokehouse, a doctor's office, and unrestored outbuildings. Meadow Farm also has an apple orchard, kitchen garden, and livestock collection (two wild boars, chickens, geese, and ducks). The site interprets the period 1850–1865, when Dr. John Sheppard, a graduate of the University of Pennsylvania Medical College, practiced medicine and operated the farm with his

Dinner in the dining room of the Salem Towne House. —*Old Sturbridge Village; photograph by Robert S. Arnold*

Carrying buckets of maple tree sap to the sugar camp. —*Old Sturbridge Village; photograph by Robert S. Arnold*

wife and ten children. First-person interpretation is used in most of the farm's programs. Staff members, assisted by experienced reenactors from the Richmond area and beyond, have already achieved a high standard of authenticity in their presentations. Besides the two military events, a good event to visit is the Yuletide Fest, when the "Sheppard family" celebrates with members of Longstreet's Corps, Army of Virginia, C.S.A., who bivouac there over Christmas.

Sherbrooke Village • P.O. Box 285, Sherbrooke, Nova Scotia, Canada BOJ 3CO • (902) 522-2400

Gold was discovered near the small shire town of Sherbrooke in the summer of 1861. For the next twenty years, Sherbrooke was the industrial, commercial, and business center of southwestern Nova Scotia, with a population of twelve hundred, consisting predominately of Scottish Presbyterians. The town included several churches, a jail and courthouse, a school, a bank, a post office, many stores and shops, boardinghouses, and several "grand" residences. The opening of western Canada and the industrialization of New England drained away Sherbrooke's prosperity in the twentieth century, stranding it in the past.

In 1969, both the provincial government of Nova Scotia and the citizens of the town saw Sherbrooke's potential as a living museum. Since then, the town has gradually been restored to its 1860–1880 status, and although the timber trade, shipbuilding, and goldmines no longer support it, tourism does. Walking along Sherbrooke's streets, always within sight of St. Mary's River and the encircling wooded hills, you often feel as if you had entered a time warp. Many of the historic shops and businesses are open and operate with realistic interpretation provided by villagers and a small professional staff. Services are actually held in the Anglican and Presbyterian churches, tea is served at the village inn, and minor trials take place in the courthouse. Sherbrooke has not yet attained the sophisticated interpretation of Upper Canada Village or Kings Landing, but the potential is there. It's well worth a visit, especially if you are already on the road to Louisbourg, about two hours' drive to the east on Cape Breton Island.

Old Cowtown Museum • 1871 Slim Park Drive, Wichita, Kansas 67203 • (316) 264–0671

Founded as a county-city museum in 1960, Old Cowtown re-creates the social history of Wichita during its formative years, 1865–1880. An outdoor museum, it is located on twenty acres of parkland along the Arkansas River in downtown Wichita. About forty historic buildings have been relocated to simulate the original town center. Included are log houses, a Presbyterian church and manse, a one-room school, undertakers, a clothing and dry goods store, a post office, a hotel, and a saloon. Since 1981 the staff has worked hard to improve the historical accuracy of the structures and to develop comprehensive living history programs. On alternate weekends during the summer, the interpretive staff—augmented by reenactors—simulates everyday life in the 1870s using first-person interpretation and historical vignettes. The museum's highly dramatic interpretation is also well researched. Old Cowtown is a good example of an older institution which has provided a realistic and interesting account of post–Civil War life in place of the commercial "Gunsmoke" stereotype.

Unloading the kiln. —
*Old Sturbridge Village;
photograph by Robert S.
Arnold*

Washing sheep in the
farm creek before summer
shearing. —*Old Sturbridge
Village; photograph by
Robert S. Arnold*

Oliver H. Kelley Farm • 15788 Kelley Farm Road, Elk River, Minnesota 55330 • (612) 441–6896

The son of a Boston tailor, Oliver Kelley emigrated to the Minnesota Territory in 1849, bought some land on the Mississippi River about thirty miles from St. Paul, and literally taught himself to farm. He was never very successful, but the organization he helped establish in 1867, the Order of the Patrons of Husbandry, or Grange, profoundly influenced farmers and farming in late nineteenth-century America.

"Father" Kelley's 189-acre farm was purchased by the Grange in 1935 and was donated to the Minnesota Historical Society. Since 1980, the farm has been open May through October, interpreting the progressive agriculture Kelley advocated. This national landmark is becoming one of the most ambitious historical farming programs on the continent. Great pains are taken to "farm by the book" and to recapture Kelley's enthusiasm and experimental spirit.

Since 1982, the staff has re-created each September an accurate nineteenth-century agricultural fair complete with a plowing match between horses and Durham oxen, trials of a flopover horse hayrake, demonstrations of "new" threshing machines, a band concert, uplifting speeches by local notables, and even a lady's sidesaddle riding contest.

The museum also features an earth-covered, energy-efficient interpretive center that effectively places Kelley and the Grange in their historical context.

Georgia Agrirama • P.O. Box Q, Tifton, Georgia 31793 • (912) 386–3344

The Georgia Agrirama depicts rural society in the southern "pine belt" region during the 1890s. The open air museum contains a subsistence herding farm, a progressive farm, and a small railroad town. Activities include cane grinding, sheep shearing, log rolling, and "frolics." The frolics feature traditional dancing, games, feasting, and storytelling.

Interpreters use the third person and encourage visitor participation, especially during the Agrirama's county fair and Christmas celebrations. The Agrirama's staff has carried out an extensive research program with the goal of establishing a solid historical base for its simulation of the material culture and traditional folklife of the region.

The museum's location is fortuitous—just off a north-south interstate highway. It is a good place to stop on the way to Florida, especially during the winter. A summer visit is worthwhile, if only to experience the good heat of the Deep South. It helps you to appreciate Faulkner.

Mystic Seaport Museum • Mystic, Connecticut 06355 • (203) 536–2631

Mystic Seaport had its genesis with the founding of the Marine Historical Association in 1929. The museum, located in the shipyard of George Greenman and Company in the heart of Mystic harbor, grew rapidly after World War II. It now contains, on its own seventeen acres of waterfront property, more than forty historic buildings, three large sailing ships, and more than one hundred small craft. Buildings include a meetinghouse and chapel, tavern, ship chandlery, cooperage, shipsmith shop, sail loft, rope walk, shipwright's shop and shipyard office, general store, school, and numerous homes. The sailing ships on exhibit include the *L. A. Dunton,* a two-

Civilization comes to the Indiana prairie. —*Conner Prairie Pioneer Settlement*

Bringing in the hay in nineteenth-century Minnesota. —*Oliver H. Kelley Farm, Minnesota Historical Society*

masted schooner; *Joseph Conrad,* a Danish merchant marine training ship; and the *Charles W. Morgan*—the last wooden whaler in existence and the pride of the museum's collection.

Although Mystic's collection and exhibits span nearly all of the nineteenth century, there is an emphasis on the 1870s and 1880s, especially when the interpretive staff presents living history programs. Since 1979 the museum has utilized role players who dress in period costume and use first-person interpretation to give visitors a feeling for the speech, manners, and attitudes of townsfolk and seamen in the year 1876. Primary interpretive themes include the influence of the sea on everyday life, the social structure of a maritime community, and the impact of technological change.

Open year round, Mystic Seaport offers an extensive variety of educational programs (live-ins, classes in blacksmithing, sailing, and so forth); boat races; and special events such as Photo Day in September, when the museum is filled with interpreters in period clothing, Independence Day 1876, and my favorite—Chowder Celebration on the Columbus Day weekend.

Washburn Norlands • R.F.D. 2, Box 3395, Livermore Falls, Maine 04254 • (207) 897–2236

Norlands was the home of the politically important Washburn family. The museum staff interprets Maine folklife during the 1870s, a period of peace and prosperity in inland New England.

The subject of an extensive article in the June 1983 *History News,* Norlands features a unique adult live-in program. The program was begun in 1977 and is held on ten weekends each year. Fifteen adults adopt the personae of two families and a collection of villagers—including schoolteachers, a

In rural 1850 Georgia, a mule was a farmer's best friend. —*Westville*

preacher, a blacksmith, a pauper, a widow, and so on. Billie Gammon, the program's director, notes that people today want to "experience another period in time." They see Norlands as a "'Fantasy Island,' a respite from the pressures of the 1980s." She cautions that the adult live-in is no vacation or nostalgic trip to Grandma's. Rather, it is a voyage to a good but hard land in a fascinating period of history. In addition to the adult live-ins, the museum has programs for children and student internships. Norlands also welcomes summer visitors. Sitting atop a gorgeous mountain in Maine, Norlands is also a *very* beautiful aristocratic farm well worth a detour.

Pioneer Farm • 11418 Sprinkle Cut-Off Road, Austin, Texas 78754 • (512) 837–1215

On the northeastern outskirts of Austin, the Austin Natural Science Association has established a seventy-acre living history farm along Walnut Creek in the "blacklands" country. Originally settled in 1852, the farm was homesteaded by Frederick and Harriet Jourdan, who gradually added to the original holding. By the Civil War, they had two thousand acres of cotton under cultivation. Their grandchildren gave the original farmstead to the city as an educational center.

The farm is modest: the Jourdan's original dogtrot cabin, a later "homestead" house, a barn, a kitchen garden, and livestock structures. The site's educational programs are special. For the staff, the farm's chief function is to provide a context for didactic "stimulation," not "simulation." The emphasis is not on re-creating central Texas folklife in the 1880s but rather on using the land and historic buildings as a center for a very wide variety of programs. These include workshops on hog butchering, sausage making, beekeeping, open fireplace cooking, and gardening; thematic events focusing on calendar customs, music, and folk crafts; and tours for groups of varying ages and interests.

Jensen-Alvarado Ranch Historic Park • c/o Riverside County Parks Department, P.O. Box 3507, Riverside, California 92519 • (714) 787-2551
Located in Riverside, one of the many large cities which make up greater Los Angeles, the Jensen-Alvarado Ranch is still in its infancy but is rich with potential. A thirty-acre historic enclave in the midst of a highly developed urban area, the ranch is one of the few California projects in which living history interpretation is used year round, not just for special events.

The ranch was pioneered by Cornelius Jensen, a Danish immigrant, in 1868. He had been stranded in California in 1848, married Mercedes Alvarado, and settled in the rich Santa Ana River valley, within sight of the Santa Ana and San Bernadino mountains. Jensen purchased three hundred acres from another settler, built a large house in the Danish vernacular style of architecture with which he had grown up, and began to graze sheep and cattle. Later, he and his wife had twelve children. They grew apricots and oranges as well as grapes for wine and raisins. Eventually the family built a winery and a small dairy. The ranch prospered, and Jensen, who had become a respected member of the growing Riverside community, served as a county supervisor for more than twenty years.

The ranch house was acquired by the county parks department and is now slowly being restored to its 1880s condition. Following the model of the Colonial Pennsylvania Plantation, during the next ten years the project will interpret historical research and restoration for visitors interested in how a complete living history site is developed.

Mattie Cannon quilts an Eight-Pointed Star in Georgia, 1850. — *Westville*

Mystic Seaport's role players reenact an 1870's Decoration Day. —*Mystic Seaport; photograph by Kenneth E. Mahler*

Fosterfields Living Historic Farm • Route 24, Kahdena Road, Morris Township, New Jersey 07960 • (201) 285–6166

Fosterfields is one of the most beautiful living museums in North America. Its two hundred-acre farmstead, fields, orchards, and gardens were developed by Charles Foster, a gentleman farmer, and his daughter, Caroline, in the 1880s and 1890s. Located a few miles from historic Morristown and the railway to New York City, their farm was to the Fosters both an idyllic haven and a prosperous enterprise. The Fosters shipped milk, fruit, and produce to the city for more than half a century. They were able to maintain the farm's commercial success by practicing soil conservation, continually improving their plant and animal stock, and using modern technology and processes. Both Fosters also appreciated agriculture as an appealing way of life, and they invested their energies and resources in maintaining their buildings and grounds.

The Morris County Park Commission began developing the museum in the late 1970s. The Fosters' home, The Willows, is an exceptional example of Hudson River Gothic. Built in 1854 by Paul Revere's grandson, it was placed on the National Register of Historic Places and was restored. The farm's four barns, machinery shed, springhouse, cribs and granaries, and extensive fields, orchards, and pastures were stabilized and were gradually returned to operation. The staff reintroduced historical agricultural processes representative of the 1880–1900 period as well as demonstrations of various domestic arts. The Park Commission constructed a multifunctional visitors' center and museum where the larger history of northern New Jersey's commercial agriculture and rural history could be introduced.

Fosterfields is twenty-five miles west of New York City and hosts a variety of seasonal activities and events for the serious visitor and student. It is open year round.

Slate Run Living Historical Farm • P.O. Box 29169, Columbus, Ohio 43229 • (614) 891–0700

On the outskirts of Columbus in a seventeen-hundred-acre woodland park, Slate Run Farm re-creates life in central Ohio in the two decades before the twentieth century. The small professional staff, augmented by a corps of volunteers, does a first-rate job of interpreting the complex operation of a family-owned, horse-powered, preelectric mixed crop and livestock farm.

The farm was acquired by Metro Parks (Metropolitan Park District of Columbus and Franklin County) in 1964 and is operated year round. It consists of an 1856 Gothic revival farmhouse, an 1881 barn, a summer kitchen, a smokehouse, and a granary. The major buildings are original to the site. Livestock include Percheron draft horses, Guernsey cattle, Merino sheep, Poland China hogs, and a veritable host of chickens, ducks, geese, turkeys, and guineas—a selection that is historically completely accurate. The crops grown are corn, wheat, oats, and hay. The farm also has a large kitchen garden, an orchard, and a grape arbor. It is an impressive, well-researched site, isolated from modern intrusions, and with the settled, prosperous look of a thirty-year-old, second-generation 1900 farm.

The staff offers several dozen authentic seasonal activities, which include putting up kraut and horseradish in September, cooking down apple butter in October, and hosting a small Chautauqua in midsummer. Many of these events have a German-American tone; all are well researched, educational, and fun.

Dixie Lee Saloon
girls. —*Old Cowtown
Museum*

Planting "King Philip"
corn. —*Oliver H.
Kelley Farm, Minnesota
Historical Society*

Stuhr Museum • 3133 West Highway 34, Grand Island, Nebraska 68801 (308) 384–1380

Established in 1961 on a two-hundred-acre site along the Platte River just outside Grand Island, Stuhr is one of the largest open air museums on the Great Plains. Its focus is on the period 1850–1900, a time of ferment and change for the region's native Americans and homesteading Euorpean immigrants. Stuhr tells their story by means of three large indoor museums and a re-created railway town. The latter is impressive and consists of more than sixty original buildings moved in from central Nebraska. The town includes a wide variety of late Victorian structures: offices, shops, houses (including Henry Ford's birthplace), a farm, a school, a superb Danish Lutheran church, a railroad depot, an engine house, a maintenance shop, and an operating 1908 Baldwin locomotive complete with gondolas, cattle and flat cars, passenger coaches, a baggage and mail car, and other stock from the Nebraska Midland Railroad. Many of Stuhr's visitors come just to ride the train. Many of the town's buildings and shops are brought to life by trained interpreters, however, and you could easily spend a day here. The outdoor component of Stuhr is open May through September.

Ukrainian Cultural Heritage Village • Historic Sites Service—Alberta Culture, 8820 112th Street, Edmonton, Alberta, Canada T6G 2P8 • (403) 421–7065

Scattered over three hundred acres of Alberta prairie about thirty miles east of Edmonton, a new outdoor ethnic museum is being developed by the historic sites service of the provincial government. Consisting of more than thirty structures, the Ukrainian Cultural Heritage Village will tell the story of the settlement of east central Alberta by Ukrainian pioneers from 1890 through the 1930s. The village is scheduled for completion in 1987 and will have three components: representative farmsteads (houses, barns, granaries, sheds, and so forth); a rural community (churches, school, grocery, hall); and a rural town (hardware store, lumber company, market square, police post, woodworking and blacksmith shops, livery, railway station, and grain elevator). More than half of the village's buildings have already been relocated and restored and are being interpreted by staff members trained to use both the first and the third person.

Open from the last weekend in May to Labor Day, seven days a week, the village is already drawing more than fifty thousand visitors annually. Many come for Ukrainian Day, August 12, when a major folklife festival is held. The museum draws heavily on volunteer support from the Ukrainian community, some members of which have formed a historic acting troupe to perform folk plays and historical vignettes. Volunteers regularly demonstrate folk crafts and arts and perform traditional sacred music in the museum's three Orthodox churches. One of the best reasons to visit the village soon, however, is to see it gradually spread out over the prairie, much as the Ukrainian settlements did a century ago.

Pioneer Farmstead • Great Smoky Mountains National Park, Gatlinburg, Tennessee 37738 • (615) 436–5615

Pioneer Farmstead is a re-created Smoky Mountain farm consisting of twelve original buildings on an accessible fifteen-acre site. The primary interpretive purpose of the farm is to give visitors to the national park an idea of life in the central Appalachians between 1900 and 1920. The farm is an

Cultivating corn. —*Oliver H. Kelley Farm, Minnesota Historical Society*

ideal place to begin exploring the extraordinary mountains, hollows, gaps, and coves of the park itself, which straddles the Tennessee–North Carolina line and includes almost one thousand square miles of unspoiled forest and highland wilderness.

The farm includes separate substantial log "houses": one for the farm family and the others for its chicken, meat, milk, apples, and gear. There is also a barn, a woodshed, a blacksmith shop, a sorghum mill, two corncribs, a large kitchen garden, a bee gum stand, and an outhouse. The clear, fast-running Oconaluftee River races by on the east, and majestic forested mountains tower overhead on all sides. The Pioneer Farmstead, nestled peacefully in its remote cove, evokes a way of life gone forever from the mountains.

From May through October, interpreters, recruited locally, demonstrate traditional farming, household chores, crafts, and folk arts. On any given summer day, the patient visitor is likely to see such activities as shake splitting, moonshine making, spinning, cooking, and the firing of a muzzle-loading rifle. Although third-person interpretation is used, the past never seems far away.

Raking mixed timothy-clover hay with a flop-over hayrake. —*Oliver H. Kelley Farm, Minnesota Historical Society*

2. Events

WHEN I was a kid growing up in a small town in western Pennsylvania, every Saturday was special. Saturdays weren't part of the week; they existed in a timeless world, and you could use them—we always did—as a bridge to the past. On Saturdays we were cowboys and Indians, knights in shining cardboard and aluminum foil armor, Johnny Rebs and Billy Yanks, or very clean-shaven G.I. Joes. History for us was not only involving, exciting fun; it was the great liberator.

Of course, it still is. And one of the best gauges of living history's popularity in North America today is the number of events that are held every year. There are quite literally thousands of first-rate living history events: battle reenactments, militia musters, encampments, rendezvous, patriotic celebrations, agricultural fairs, traditional rural calendar customs, military tattoos, and civilian frolics.

Most living history events are sponsored by outdoor museums, historic sites, historical societies, or reenacting groups. Discovering where and when events will take place is not difficult. Many museums publish annual or seasonal calendars. All the living history museums listed in this book, for example, will send out detailed descriptions of their special activities, often with press releases and copies of newspaper clippings. Historical societies are particularly proud of their battle reenactments, rendezvous, military musters or camps, and assorted "historic weekends, days, and festivals" and will rain publicity upon you in the form of tourist's kits, brochures, and guides.

The most comprehensive descriptions of serious events, however, are to be found in living history magazines and journals. Publications like *Living History Magazine, F & I War,* and *Camp Chase Gazette* (to name three excellent examples) regularly list, describe, and *review* events. They also carry advertisements by sponsors and, perhaps more revealing, letters from participants extolling the virtues of one reenacted battle or criticizing another as an inaccurate "farb fest" totally lacking in authenticity. Newsletters and bulletins of organizations such as the North West Territory Alliance or the Association for Living Historical Farms and Agricultural Museums are also packed with information. In fact, the often ephemeral newsletters bind together thousands of living history units and individual buffs. Like an almost invisible "bush telegraph," the newsletters let reenactors know what will be happening and when.

Many living history events are also finding their way into the

Festivals Sourcebook (Detroit: Gale Research Company, 1984), a compendium which can be found in most larger libraries. Since the *Sourcebook* includes a wide variety of festivals, fairs, and other celebrations, the reader must search through it carefully to find the really authentic historical simulations.

Although great fun is one of the hallmarks of living history events, many are planned to fulfill functions other than that of pure entertainment. Most have a serious interpretive or research purpose. Museums use events to focus attention on historically significant occasions: community holidays like Harvest Home or Thanksgiving, patriotic celebrations such as the birthday of George Washington or King George III, or annual social reunions at militia musters or agricultural fairs. Living history reenactors use battle reenactments, cantonments, or rendezvous to experience realistic facsimiles of past events, thereby learning by imitative experimentation. Events can be excellent mediums for buying and selling, enlisting recruits, for evaluating the reproductions of sutlers, for cementing old friendships, and for making friends for living history.

Putting the following list of recommended events together was difficult because I had to choose from so many excellent examples. I eventually tended to limit my entries to "classics"—older events which have stood the test of time. Most here have a good authentic "period feel" and were seriously planned to be far more than entertainment. I also tried to include a mix of large and small events, examples from throughout North America, and even one or two unknowns.

Pennsic War • Society for Creative Anachronism, Slippery Rock, Pennsylvania • For information, write Darkblade Press, c/o Dan and Judy Kirk, 722 West Willard Street, Kalamazoo, Michigan 49001 • August

Since 1971, the Society for Creative Anachronism has held its annual "war" in western Pennsylvania. More than four thousand members from all parts of the continent and overseas attend. Visitors from the modern world are welcome if they dress and behave medievally. The site is pastoral and includes a lake, grassy hill and woods. Members create a veritable city of colorful pavilions, rustic booths, and small shops. The August event lasts a week, Tuesday through Sunday, and apart from mock warring, of which there is a great deal, members hurl themselves into country dancing, costuming workshops, bartering, chugging and wet chemise contests, archery, swimming, Viking soothsaying, Shakespeare readings, madrigal singing, belly dancing, processions, courts, gaming, and gamboling. A daily newspaper, the *Pennsic Progress*, keeps everyone informed: "A call to all jugglers! Meet at Pennsic Progress camp at 4:00 P.M. today." "Traveling magician seeking new friendships—will perform at your camp at night." "Harry the Doppelganger of the Willow Point Road is hosting a crutch-making contest due to a recent need," and so forth. For members of the society, the Pennsic War is Mecca. Nonmembers should probably try a regional event or two before attempting the pilgrimage to Pennsylvania.

Harvest Home • Plimoth Plantation, P.O. Box 1620, Plymouth, Massachusetts 02360 • Columbus Day Weekend

The forerunner of the American Thanksgiving holiday was the Pilgrims' Harvest Home feast. First celebrated in 1621, the feast lasted almost a week and took place after the corn was ripe, probably in October. Harvest Home was an informal joyous affair, certainly the high point of the Pilgrims' year.

Plimoth Plantation re-creates the 1627 feast, when Isaack de Rasieres, secretary of the Dutch Colony of New Netherlands, visited the Pilgrims with his men. Interpreters reenact the main events of de Rasieres's visit and the subsequent feast. Speeches and gifts are exchanged; a huge, traditional two-course feast of goose, duck, venison, pumpkins, pork, rabbit, corncake, custard, "sallet," and fruit tarts is prepared; and there are military displays, swordsmanship contests, and games of pillow bashing, running the quintain, and tug-o-war. Visitors can not only join in many of the activities but also listen to the discussions between Governor Bradford and the Dutch concerning trade, military matters, and life in the New World. Like Plimoth Plantation's other annual events (the militia muster, the Wampanoag summer feast, and the English country wedding), Harvest Home is meticulously researched and authentically interpreted.

French and Indian War Seminar • Bushy Run Battlefield State Park, Jeannette, Pennsylvania 15644 • Mid-June

In August 1763, Colonel Henry Bouquet with a British force of five hundred defeated an allied Indian army just east of Fort Pitt at Bushy Run. The conflict effectively ended French and Indian control of western Pennsylvania and laid the foundation for British settlement of the Midwest. The battlefield is

Every second Wednesday in July, Plimoth Plantation re-creates a traditional English country wedding. —*Plimoth Plantation, Inc.*

Isack De Rasieres, secretary of the Dutch Colony of New Netherlands, shares the Pilgrims' harvest feast in 1627. — *Plimoth Plantation, Inc.*

now a state historic park and the site for many events belonging to the period of the French and Indian War. These include military encampments, a first-rate reenactment of the battle, and the French and Indian War Seminar. This last event brings together historians and serious reenactors for a weekend of lectures, discussions, and demonstrations, all focusing on the challenges of interpreting the period of the French and Indian War. Established in 1982, the seminar has rapidly become an event which bridges the worlds of academic and living history. The seminar is open to all serious French and Indian War units and generally attracts to its encampment half a dozen of the best groups.

Kethtippecannunk Eighteenth-Century Fashion Fair • Tippecanoe Battlefield, P.O. Box 225, Battle Ground, Indiana 47920 • Mid-July

The Midwest has long been fertile ground for folk festivals. A recent guide lists almost a thousand such events. It's not surprising, therefore, to see festivals being developed around historical themes and using living history as a primary mode of presentation. A good example is the Kethtippecannunk Fair. There was in fact an important Northwest Territory town by this name; Kethtippecannunk is Shawnee for Tippecanoe. Located on the Wabash River just north of present day Lafayette, Tippecanoe had more than a hundred houses and taverns and was considered a center of French and Indian culture. (Before their defeat in 1811, Tecumseh and his brother, the Prophet, planned to make the town site the capital for their Indian confederation.) The weekend fair is organized by the museum staff at the Tippecanoe Battlefield Museum and by area reenactors who specialize in period arts and crafts: weavers, spinners, tailors, leather workers, cordwainers, cobblers, potters, cabinet makers, puppeteers, musicians, and assorted food vendors. Authenticity is enforced, and special workshops on eighteenth-century frontier folklife are presented.

Governor's Invitational Firelock Match • Fort Frederick State Park, P.O. Box 177, Big Pool, Maryland 21711 • Last weekend of September

Fort Frederick was built by the colony of Maryland in 1756 to protect its western frontier settlements from the French and Indians. The fort was converted into a prison for captured British and German soldiers during the Revoluntionary War and saw brief action in 1861 when Confederates raided it on Christmas Day. The Civilian Conservation Corps in the 1930s restored Fort Frederick to its 1758 appearance. The fort's staff sponsors a number of excellent living history programs each year. All are "spectator" events, and the general public is invited to visit, but only invited groups may participate. In this way, authenticity is kept at a very high level. Three of the fort's events are considered classics. An eighteenth-century rendezvous, first started in 1974, is held on the last weekend in May. On Military Field Days, invited military units from the French and Indian War, American Revolution, and Civil War set up camps and engage in tactical demonstrations. The Field Days take place on the last weekend in June and feature 350 men in uniform. Finally, in late September, the fort hosts an eighteenth-century firelock match. This popular event was started in 1965 and features friendly competition between "reactivated" eighteenth-century units. Matches include drills with muskets, rifles, pistols, and tomahawks.

Feast of the Hunter's Moon • Tippecanoe County Historical Association, 909 South Street, Lafayette, Indiana 47901 • Late September or early October

The Feast of the Hunter's Moon began in 1968 as the historical society's fall outing at re-created Fort Ouiatenon, a 1717 French fur trading post on the

Arrival of the voyageurs at Grand Portage's Rendezvous Days. —*Grand Portage; photograph provided by the National Park Service*

Rest and relaxation at Rendezvous Days. — *Grand Portage; photograph provided by the National Park Service*

Wabash River. The event grew rapidly and is now one of the premier Midwest living history events. In recent years, it has drawn several thousand serious reenactors and well over fifty thousand visitors. Buffs bivouac in three separate camps—Indian, voyageur, and military. French and Indian War, Northwest Territory, and voyageur and early fur trade units are represented. For reenactors, evenings teem with historical activity—dancing, piping and fiddling, good food and tobacco, and some serious swapping of tales and trade goods. During the day, the feast is a carnival. In addition to demonstrations of eighteenth-century crafts, canoe races, fashion shows, and parades, there are literally hundreds of booths and blanket traders selling period food, crafts, clothing, and accoutrements. The site, on the outskirts of West Lafayette, is isolated from modern intrusions and has a good historical feel about it, especially at night. During the day, Ouiatenon is crowded but great fun for both visitor and buff.

Fort de Chartres Annual Rendezvous • Fort de Chartres State Historic Site, Prairie du Rocher, Illinois 62277 • June

Fort de Chartres lies about forty miles south of St. Louis on the east bank of the Mississippi River and has been holding a summer rendezvous since 1970. The event draws many competitors for its rifle, pistol, smooth base, and military team shoots. The fort also hosts smaller spring and fall events in April and November. The success of all three of the fort's events is due in large measure to the experience and the creative enthusiasm of the site's interpretive staff. Staff members are able to create a real eighteenth-century atmosphere, especially during the "course competitions," when small teams are led through the forest by a "coeur de bois de Fort de Chartres" in a simulated hunt. While the three rendezvous are enjoyable and informative for visitors, they are particularly challenging time trips for participants. The buff who wishes to take part in competitions should write ahead for information.

Fort Crevecoeur Rendezvous • Fort Crevecoeur, Inc., Box 23, Creve Coeur, Illinois 61611 • Fourth weekend in September

Fort Crevecoeur was the first French settlement in what is now Illinois. Built hastily in 1680 by the explorer Robert La Salle and his thirty men, the fort was soon abandoned after a mutiny. Nevertheless, Gallic influence continued, and for well over half a century, trade flourished between the Peoria Indians and the French. In 1980, the fort was rebuilt in a ninety-acre park just south of Peoria. The Fort Crevecoeur rendezvous, begun in 1976, is now held in the park. It's an ideal natural setting. The event is completely authentic, and all participants must preregister and be approved. Over the years the rendezvous has gained a reputation in the Midwest as a first-rate event for the buff interested in the French and Indian frontier era (1680–1830). Visitors are welcomed, and there is a good mixture of historically accurate foods to eat, activities to join in, and reenactors to meet. In short, this is a smaller, less hectic event.

Eastern Rendezvous • National Muzzle Loading Rifle Association, P.O. Box 67, Friendship, Indiana 47021 • September

Since 1976, this NMLRA rendezvous has attracted some of the most serious and enthusiastic buckskinners in the eastern United States and Canada. The rendezvous is held at a different site each September. In 1983, it took place in the rugged mountains of northeastern Pennsylvania in the heart of

Bartering trade goods at Rendezvous Days. —*Grand Portage; photograph provided by the National Park Service*

Chippewa nimi-iding or pow-wow, the Native American component at Rendezvous Days. —*Grand Portage; photograph provided by the National Park Service*

what had once been Iroquois territory; in 1984 muzzle loaders traveled to the banks of Schroon Lake in upstate New York, a few miles from historic Fort Ticonderoga. Historical authenticity is required. Although the cutoff date is 1840, recent rendezvous have encouraged earlier time periods. Usually there are both modern and primitive camps, and membership in the association is required of at least one person in each camp. The rendezvous lasts at least a week, and many families make this their annual vacation from the chaos of late twentieth-century life. Complete information on the "Eastern" can be found in the spring and summer issues of magazines such as *F & I War*.

Rendezvous Days • Grand Portage National Monument, Box 666, Grand Marais, Minnesota 55604 • Second weekend in August
Sponsored by the Grand Portage Band of the Minnesota Chippewa Tribe in cooperation with the National Park Service, Rendezvous Days is unique. The event successfully re-creates the great rendezvous that took place in Grand Portage every summer from 1778 to 1803, when hundreds of voyageurs, trappers, traders, and guides would join with the nearby Ojibwa (Chippewa) people for a week of trading, feasting, dancing, and canoe races. Two cultures—native American and new American—blended on these occasions. The same is true today. The voyageur part of the rendezvous includes activities such as fire making, pack races, leg wrestling, axe throwing, and tug-o-war. Nearby, members of the Chippewa Tribe from the Grand Portage Indian Reservation sponsor a nimi-iding (powwow). They are often joined by dancers from other tribes, with or without dance outfits, and many drum groups. Older and newer dances are performed, including some in which spectators are invited to participate. In short, Rendezvous Days combines a

living history program which simulates life in an earlier time with a native American powwow, an actual historic event that lives on in the lives of the Ojibwa people.

Fur Trade Weekend, 1827 • Fort Snelling History Center, St. Paul, Minnesota 55111 • Last weekend in July

Unlike many fur trade rendezvous which might be described as "historical smorgasbords," Fort Snelling's weekend is highly specific. The year portrayed is 1827, the event is the last gathering of the Columbia Fur Company at Fort Snelling, and the participants involved, using the first person, portray actual traders and soldiers who were present at the time. This rendezvous was begun in 1979 and is one of the finest living history events in North America. Cohosted by the Minnesota Historical Society and a volunteer reenactment group, La Compagnie des Hivernants de la Rivierre Sainte Pierre, the rendezvous is carefully researched. Preregistered participants who "pass inspection" by documenting their clothing and equipment are sent an excellent packet of interpretive materials to familiarize them with the educational goals of the event and the rendezvous's history. A camp is established outside the fort, and a number of skits are scheduled to bring together traders and soldiers. The weekend is an excellent opportunity for visitors to see a really authentic historical re-creation and for professional and volunteer interpreters to share ideas, skills, and experiences.

Reenactors and interpreters gather at Fort Snelling's Fur Trade Weekend. — *Fort Snelling, Minnesota Historical Society*

Re-creating the last gathering of the Columbia Fur Company in 1827. — *Fur Trade Weekend, Fort Snelling, Minnesota Historical Society*

School of the Soldier and Annual Meeting • Brigade of the American Revolution, New Windsor Cantonment State Historic Site, Box 207, Vails Gate, New York 12584 • Late April

During 1782 and 1783, ten thousand men, women, and children of Washington's Continental Army waited in the New Windsor cantonment for news of peace. Here, fifteen miles north of West Point on the banks of the Hudson River, the state of New York preserves the historic sites and allows the Brigade of the American Revolution to hold a series of historically accurate events for its member units. Perhaps the best-known event is held in late April: the School of the Soldier. The model for many other similar events, the school allows brigade members to sharpen their living history skills. Lectures are given, seminars are held, and most important, traditional lore is passed on by word of mouth and by example. Units encamp, practice tactics and maneuvers, enjoy firelock shooting competitions and camp life, and discuss various aspects of late eighteenth-century folklife: social and political patterns, clothing, surgery and medicine, military strategy and tactics, weapons and engineering, and trends in living history interpretation. This description makes the school sound serious, and it is, but it's also great fun and one of the finest events in the reenacting field.

The King's Birthday • Old Fort Niagara, P.O. Box 169, Youngstown, New York 14174 • Early June

Like Fort Frederick in central Maryland, Fort Niagara hosts a series of exceptionally fine living history events every year. They include a Civil War encampment in May, a French and Indian War siege in mid-July, the War of 1812 Revisited in late July, and Soldiers of the Revolution in late August. Each event is by invitation only and stresses both authenticity and interpretation. The French and Indian War program, which reenacts the British and Iroquois siege of the French-held fort in 1759, is a huge three-day spectacle in which visitors are taken on a tour of the siege works and fort in the midst of a simulated battle. Perhaps the most unusual of the fort's living history events, however, is the annual celebration of King George III's birthday on the weekend closest to June 4. Naturally only British, Loyalist, German, and native allies are invited. For the loyal forces which garrisoned Fort Niagara during the American Revolution, the King's Birthday was the only real holiday. This reenactment is therefore truly celebratory for the more than three hundred participants. Particularly impressive is the Grand Review and Royal Salute.

1812 Weekend • Historic Fort Wayne, 107 South Clinton, Fort Wayne, Indiana 46802 • Early September

The War of 1812, in comparison with America's other major conflicts, has been neglected by the living history movement. Few historic sites and reenactor units seriously interpret this second war with Britain. One notable exception is Historic Fort Wayne. In addition to its fine daily interpretation of the period, the fort sponsors an 1812 Weekend, when the Indian siege of the fort in September 1812 is re-created. Held the weekend after Labor Day, the event draws period units from the United States and Canada on an invitation-only basis. All participants use first-person interpretation and carry out tactical demonstrations typical of siege warfare during the period. The fort's daily routine is also simulated. In addition the staff at Historic Fort Wayne hosts a fine Trappers and Traders Rendezvous the last weekend in October, a

The taste of history at the Fur Trade Weekend. —*Fort Snelling, Minnesota Historical Society*

really exceptional 1816 Glorious Fourth of July, and a number of encampments cosponsored with the Brigade of the American Revolution and the North West Territory Alliance in spring and fall. Nevertheless, the 1812 Weekend is the really special event.

Annual Rendezvous • Bent's Old Fort, 35110 Highway 194 East, La Junta, Colorado 81050–9523 • Weekend after Labor Day, Thursday to Sunday

Bent's Old Fort is one of the finest living history sites on the continent. Its annual rendezvous is, similarly, a classic event for participant and visitor alike. The rendezvous is also a first-rate example of effective cooperation between professional interpreters and serious reenactors and buffs. Held the long weekend after Labor Day, the rendezvous draws about three hundred buffs. A strictly primitive camp is established in a bend of the Arkansas River, within sight of the adobe fort. Traders set up inside the fort itself just as they did in the 1830s and 1840s. The atmosphere is strongly Southwestern—no kilts, war bonnets, or Civil War dress or equipment. Traditional shoots, period games, and a "Fandango" with a Hispanic band are featured. The staff also sponsors several contests—chili making, most authentic camp, and so on—and invites well-known historians to talk informally about the fur trade period, 1800–1850.

Western Rendezvous • National Muzzle Loading Rifle Association, P.O. Box 67, Friendship, Indiana 47021 • Summer

Jointly sponsored by the National Muzzle Loading Rifle Association and the National Association of Primitive Riflemen, the "Western" is one of the

Serious play at the King's Birthday Celebration. —*Old Fort Niagara*

A log cabin float, pulled by a team of Devon oxen, leads a Whig parade in support of William Henry Harrison at Old Sturbridge Village's 1840 presidential election—*Old Sturbridge Village; photograph by Robert S. Arnold*

largest and most authentic of the national rendezvous. It's held in a different location each summer, usually deep in the Rocky Mountains. The exact site, along with basic information, is published in black powder magazines such as *The Buckskin Report* which focus on the "primitive" side of muzzle loading. The Western often attracts several thousand serious buffs for a week to ten days. As with most of the really historically accurate events, the Western is closed to the general public on all but one day, when outsiders can come in, chat with participants, snap photographs, and gain an insight into why modern families choose to relive the days of the mountain man.

Thanksgiving • Old Sturbridge Village, Sturbridge, Massachusetts 01566 • Thanksgiving Week

The annual calendar of Old Sturbridge Village is packed with special events characteristic of small New England towns in the 1830s. Each is thoroughly researched and creatively presented. It's difficult to single one out as better than the rest. The serious student of living history should write Sturbridge for information in advance of any visit. Some of my favorite events are the 1840 town meeting and presidential election in early November; Thanksgiving week, which features a turkey shoot with muzzle-loaded firearms, the preparation of traditional regional dishes in many of the village's homes, religious services in the meetinghouse, and dinner in the Bullard Tavern; a George Washington's Birthday celebration in February; Militia Training Day in May, and, of course, Independence Day, July 4. The Village and Freeman Farm follow the old agricultural calendar, so there are many seasonal activities, such as hog butchering in December, maple sugaring in late February and early March, sheep shearing in June, and various harvests in late summer and fall.

Election Day 1860 • Harpers Ferry National Park, Harpers Ferry, West Virginia 25425 • October

"Election Day 1860" is an exceptional living history program. Developed by the National Park Service in the early 1980s, the event re-creates the proceedings on election day 1860, a time of tension, drama, and imminent danger. With the help of experienced living history interpreters from both the National Park Service and invited reenactment units, the Harpers Ferry staff fills the streets of this restored nineteenth-century factory town with a good cross section of the voting populace in 1860. There are political speeches and debates, a grand civic barbecue and torchlight procession, militia drills, actual voting in the re-created polling place (dry goods store), arm wrestling and heated arguments in the tavern, and even a period recruiting tent set up by the U.S. Army. The day "ends" with the reading of the election results. (The elector for Stephen Douglas won the original election but has been known to lose in the reenactment!) The program is well researched and organized and uses first-person interpretation.

Camp Winfield Scott • Old Bethpage Village Restoration, Round Swamp Road, Old Bethpage, New York 18804 • First weekend in August

Since 1979, Long Island's re-created 1850s village of Bethpage has sponsored an authentic 1861 Union army camp of instruction. Cohosted with the reenactors of Company H, 119th New York Volunteers, the camp is open to Union reenactors units and their families. Included are intensive instruction in the manual of arms, bayonet training, marching, an accurate re-creation of an 1861 sutler, a period concert and dance, and activities for ladies such as sewing groups and parlor music and recreations. What makes Camp

Reading the Declaration of Independence during Fourth of July festivities at Old Sturbridge Village. —*Old Sturbridge Village; photograph by Robert S. Arnold*

Contra dancing during Old Sturbridge Village's Fourth of July celebration. —*Old Sturbridge Village; photograph by Robert S. Arnold*

Winfield Scott unusual is the authentic village context and the support of the museum staff, many of whom are skilled in doing civilian impressions. The museum invites serious reenactors to apply and uses a screening process to ensure that everyone involved has a first-rate historical experience.

Confederate Camp of Instruction • Fort Fisher, P.O. Box 68, Kure Beach, North Carolina 28449 • Early March

Fort Fisher, the largest earthwork fortification in the South, guarded the approach to Wilmington, North Carolina, from 1861 to 1865. The fort protected the supply line for "blockade runners" until January 1865 when, after a massive Union bombardment and assault, it was captured. Now a state historic site, Fort Fisher is the scene of a rigorous Confederate Camp of Instruction. Cohosted by reenactors of the Third North Carolina Light Artillery Battery B and the state Division of Archives and History, the event asks its invited participants to do impressions using the first person and to camp over the weekend in accordance with period customs. All instructions follow actual period drills: 1863 Confederate Army Regulations, Hardee's Light Infantry Tactics, McClellan's Bayonet Exercise, and Patten's Artillery Drill. Ladies are furnished with separate sleeping quarters. The camp is an excellent example of a closed event, meant to simulate life in another time and to train reenactors in the craft of living history. Fort Fisher is a great experience but not for beginners.

A toy paper balloon, launched on the Common at Old Sturbridge Village's Fourth of July. —*Old Sturbridge Village; photograph by Robert S. Arnold*

Civil War Garrison Days • Old Fort Mifflin, c/o Fairmont Park Commission, Memorial Hall, West Park, Philadelphia, Pennsylvania 19131 • Early October

One of the most historically significant forts in the United States, Fort Mifflin now sits on the north shore of the Delaware River, overlooking the naval base in Philadelphia's inner harbor. The fort was originally constructed in 1772 on a mud and silt island and was virtually leveled by a British fleet in November 1777—but not before its defenders had given Washington time to establish camp at Valley Forge. President John Adams had the structure rebuilt in 1798, and it was manned during the War of 1812. It was garrisoned in the Civil War and in World Wars I and II and was used for storage during the Korean conflict. In short, the fort has a long history. Of the many living history events which it sponsors, one of the most interesting is its Civil War Garrison Days weekend. In this event, begun in 1981, military and civilian reenactors re-create the daily routine as it occurred from 1861 to 1865. A guard is mounted, and the fort's company is drilled. Artillery training and firing are demonstrated, and the participants even play a period baseball game. Visitors tour the hospital-dispensary and the dark, damp bombproofs in which Confederate prisoners were kept.

Battles of Lexington, Athens, and Pilot Knob • Division of Parks and Historic Preservation, Missouri Department of Natural Resources, P.O. Box 176, Jefferson City, Missouri 65102 • August or September

Every summer the Missouri Department of Natural Resources, in cooperation with the Missouri Civil War Reenactors Association hosts a Civil War reenactment. Following a three-year cycle, the events take place at Lexington

(1985), Pilot Knob (1986), Athens (1987), and so on in rotation. Only serious authentic reenactors are invited to participate. In view of the excellent reviews the events have garnered, it's wise to write well ahead for an application. The three sites are located in different parts of the state (far west, southeast, and north) and are ideal choices—uncrowded, open, and free from modern distractions. State officials, local community groups, and the reenactors' association work smoothly together to provide all amenities—hay, straw, wood, raw foodstuffs, gunpowder, percussion caps, and first-rate leadership and scenarios.

Civil War Muster and Mercantile Exposition • Village of East Davenport Association, 2200 East Eleventh Street, Davenport, Iowa 52803 • Third weekend in September

This popular Iowa event has been drawing large numbers of participants and visitors every year since 1973. It takes place in a thirty-acre park adjoining the historic "village" of East Davenport and overlooking the Mississippi River. The site is historically significant. During the Civil War, Camp McClellan, the primary training facility for Iowa soldiers, was located here.

The weekend includes two battle reenactments, usually from the Western theater (for example, the Assault on Vicksburg and the Battle of Corinth); a military ball in the officer's club at the nearby Rock Island Arsenal; formal retreats; drill, period dress, and live-round competitions; and numerous activities for ladies and families. Because of the event's location in the "Quad Cities" (Davenport, Rock Island, Moline, and Bettendorf) and the excellent reputation of its cosponsor, reenactors of the Sixteenth Iowa Veteran Volunteers, the muster draws upward of five hundred reenactors and ten thousand spectators. It's a good family affair.

The Richmond Grays muster with other militia units at Election Day 1860. —*Harper's Ferry; photograph by Patti Ferguson*

Union soldiers enjoy the national pastime at Fort Snelling's Civil War Weekend. —*Fort Snelling, Minnesota Historical Society*

Battle of Perryville • Perryville Battlefield State Park, Perryville, Kentucky 40468 • First weekend in October

The original Battle of Perryville, fought on October 8, 1862, was a standoff. Kentucky was in the midst of a drought, and the armies suffered terribly from thirst. The engagement itself was marked by confusion and high casualties on both sides. The reenactment of Perryville, hosted by the State Parks Department and the First Kentucky Orphan Brigade, with help from the Seventh Kentucky U.S., captures the realistic desperation of the original fight. The "bluegrass" countryside where the reenactment takes place has changed little in a century. Few modern intrusions mar the scene. Authenticity is stressed, and the battle scenario is carefully followed. Invited units portray the actual forces present in 1862.

Battle of Olustee • Olustee Battlefield National Monument, c/o Raymond Giron, P.O. Box 316, McIntosh, Florida 32664 • Third weekend in February

Olustee lies at the edge of northern Florida's great Osceola National Forest. The only major Civil War engagement in Florida was fought here on February 20, 1864. A small Union force was soundly defeated. Nobody "loses" at the Olustee reenactment, a first-rate event cosponsored by the state of Florida and an alliance of reenacting groups, the Blue/Gray Army, Inc. The first reenactment took place in 1977 in realistic pine flatwoods of the actual battlefield. Since then the event has grown; in 1984 it drew one thousand serious participants and five thousand visitors. Tremendous emphasis is placed on re-creating truly authentic Civil War camps. The Union camp in 1984, for example, was laid out in accordance with the *Revised U.S. Army*

Minnesota veterans enjoy some well-earned refreshment at Fort Snelling's Civil War Weekend. — *Fort Snelling, Minnesota Historical Society*

Regulations (1861) "Plan of Encampment" and was brought to life by a rich assortment of soldiers, sutlers, surgeons, daguerreotypists, officers, cavalrymen, and camp followers. Walking around it, I thought, "If only Mathew Brady were here."

Battle of New Market • New Market Battlefield Park, P.O. Box 1864, New Market, Virginia 22844 • Sunday preceding May 15

New Market is a "granddaddy" of Civil War reenactments. Begun in 1967, the event has drawn large numbers of reenactors and spectators annually. The simulated battle takes place on the exact terrain of the original May 15, 1864, engagement. In 1984, twelve hundred participants from nineteen states and several Canadian provinces took part. The weather was sunny and cool, undoubtedly an attraction for the more than fifteen thousand onlookers. The reenactment is sponsored by the Virginia Military Institute's New Market Battlefield Park, which heightens its historical authenticity each year. In earlier reenactments of the battle, any realistic unit could take part, but participation recently has been limited to only those reactivated units whose precursors actually fought at New Market.

Battle of Saylor's Creek • c/o Chuck Hillsman, Route 1, Box 185, Jetersville, Virginia 23083 • Early April

Saylor's Creek is one of the oldest and most realistic Civil War battle reenactments. It is for authentics only, and participation is by invitation. It is held on the first weekend in April unless Easter falls on that Sunday. The event generally draws eight hundred participants. Saylor's Creek is often described as a participant's event rather than one which caters to spectators, since most of the action takes place in remote areas of the original battlefield, near Rice, Virginia, on Lee's route to Appomattox. When reenactors gather during the winter to evaluate the summer's campaigns, Saylor's Creek is invariably rated as one of the best living history events.

Battle of Dallas • Gaston County Museum of Art and History, P.O. Box 429, Dallas, North Carolina 28034 • Late April

No Battle of Dallas ever occurred in the Civil War. This reenactment is a "what if" event. It depicts what might have happened in April 1865 if a Confederate force had been present to defend the Gaston County Courthouse when Union cavalry entered Dallas. The first "what if" battle took place in 1981 and proved so popular among reenactors and spectators that the sponsors decided to hold the event annually. Apart from a historically realistic battle in and around the old courthouse, the event includes Union and Confederate camps, a parade, a re-created field hospital, period church services on Sunday, and surrender ceremonies. Cohosted by the Eleventh North Carolina Infantry Company reenactors ("Charlotte Grays"), the battle attracts excellent Union reenacting units, who are victorious.

Grenada Wargames • Grenada, Mississippi • c/o Gary Pierce, 606 West Church, Apartment 2, Greenwood, Mississippi 38930 • Irregular

Sponsors vary their reasons for organizing living history events. Some emphasize interpretation, others thoughtful re-creation. Events held primarily as a form of experimental research are often closed to spectators, are deliberately held in remote, isolated sites, and are limited to a very small number of serious simulators. The war games that irregularly take place in Grenada, Mississippi, are a good example of a research-oriented event.

Union camp at Saylor's Creek, Virginia. —*Photograph by Richard Cheatham*

Confederate Camp of Instruction at Fort Boykin, Virginia. — *Photograph by Richard Cheatham*

Limited to one hundred Federal troops and one hundred Confederates, the war games are fought around two original earthen forts using specific, standardized, realistic rules. Trained judges, or referees, accompany the small units, which are restricted to experienced, serious reenactors. The primary purpose of the exercise is to gain insight into the Civil War as it was fought at the small-unit level. The "after-action" reports of the commanders and judges are peppered with questions, answers, and thoughtful observations on the nature of man at war. Some participants are also interested in war gaming on a larger scale and play Simulations Publications' Terrible Swift Sword and a miniatures battle as well. The activity at Grenada and other serious war games make possible a better understanding of living history's potential as a research tool.

Frontier Military Independence Day Celebration • Fort Larned National Historic Site, Route 3, Larned, Kansas 67550 • July 4

From 1860 to 1878, Fort Larned was a central link in a chain of forts guarding both the Santa Fe Trail and the Santa Fe Railway. During the Indian War of 1868–1869, it was a key military post and later an agency of the Indian Bureau. The fort includes original barracks, post hospitals, shops, commissary, quartermaster's storehouse, officers' quarters, and a quadrangular parade ground. Fort Larned's National Park Service staff annually hosts a number of excellent living history events. The Independence Day celebration re-creates July 4, 1868, and includes demonstrations of military cooking, fort life, cavalry drills, and small arms and twelve-pounder mountain howitzer firing. With the help of experienced reenacting units, which are invited to attend, the staff also presents a historical fashion show (1861–1878), patriotic speeches, and a formal evening military retreat ceremony.

Parade of the Fifth Cavalry, Wyoming, and the First Colorado at Fort Larned, Kansas. —*Photograph by John Beck*

Nineteenth-Century Agricultural Fair • Oliver H. Kelley Farm, 15788 Kelley Farm Road, Elk River, Minnesota 55330 • Late September

Oliver Kelley was one of the founders of the Order of the Patrons of Husbandry, or Grange. His farm on the Mississippi River, about thirty miles from St. Paul, is operated by the Minnesota Historical Society and interprets the progressive agriculture that Kelley advocated. It's appropriate, therefore, for one of the museum's primary living history events to be an agricultural fair. The post–Civil War activities presented include a plowing match between draft horses and Durham oxen, a horse-pulled flopover hayrake trial, demonstrations of "new" threshing machines, a brass band concert, uplifting speeches on the nobility of farmers, and a lady's sidesaddle riding contest. The fair has a realistic atmosphere and celebrates in an enjoyable way one of the methods the Grangers and other reformers used to "improve" agriculture.

Great War Re-creation • Shrimpstown, Pennsylvania • c/o Brian Pohanka, 425 Queen Street, Alexandria, Virginia 22314 • Columbus Day weekend

Since 1979 the Great War Association has annually reenacted the trench warfare of World War I on an isolated "battlefield" near Shrimpstown, Pennsylvania, during Columbus Day weekend in October. German, French, British, and American contingents take part for an entire weekend. Trenches are lightly manned, and patrols are sent far into no-man's-land. Visitors are allowed to tour the lines on Saturday morning; thereafter, the event is "closed" and attempts to simulate the pure hell that was the Western Front. There are rolling artillery barrages, gas attacks, night patrols, wiring parties, flares, grenades, adrenaline boosts, anxiety attacks, battle fatigue, and depression. The event is highly realistic and has been well reviewed in *Living History*

A proud moment at The Henry Ford Museum's 1920's Great Escape Weekend. — *Photograph courtesy of The Henry Ford Museum, Dearborn, Michigan*

Magazine (vol. 1, no. 3, Spring 1984). As the centennial of World War I approaches, this event will become more significant in the living history world.

Great Escape Weekends • Henry Ford Museum and Greenfield Village, P.O. Box 1970, Dearborn, Michigan 48121

Greenfield Village and its indoor complement, the Henry Ford Museum, present an array of annual events of interest to the living history buff. The most unusual include a tent Chautauqua, a fire engine muster, and four Great Escape Weekends. While the Chautauqua and muster take place in the open air of Greenfield Village, the weekends are presented inside the vast Henry Ford Museum from January through April, cold months in Dearborn. The weekends are creatively hot, however, and involve visitors in the life of four decades: the 1890s, 1920s, 1930s, and 1940s. A variety of activities are included: period music and dancing (ragtime, swing, waltz, Charleston, jitterbug, rhumba, and so forth); variety shows and historic films; period meals; special "guests" (Annie Oakley, "Diamond Jim" Brady, Babe Ruth, Emily Post, Amelia Earhart, Mae West, Rosie the Riveter, Little Orphan Annie); workshops (making valentines, bicycling); demonstrations of the latest steam engines and electric and gasoline-powered automobiles; and historical plays such as *Shenandoah*. These events use a variety of living history techniques—first-person interpretation, demonstration, and historical workshops.

PART II.
POINTING THE WAY

3. Books

ONE cold, wet March morning, I was sitting with some interpreters in the barn of a living historical farm. It was obvious that we were going to have plenty of time to talk—few visitors take in a farm museum on a raw day in late winter. The conversation came around to the phases a person goes through on the way to becoming an interpreter. Someone said that if you were a male, you first played with toy soldiers, then dressed up in makeshift uniforms and fought mock battles, next became a fanatical reader of old history books, and later passed through the rite of passage that is college. Finally, when you couldn't get a decent job, you became an interpreter, usually at the minimum wage—and of course you were hooked on history for life, or at least until a million tourists' questions ("Do you live here?" "Is that really food you're eating?" "You know, I know you're wrong. People never did that") burned you out. When burnout happened, books brought you back. We all agreed.

The books in this chapter are some of my favorites. They all deal with living history or historical simulation in one way or another. Some are about time travel and the experience of moving from one period of time to another vicariously. I've also included several examinations of the historical experience of time itself. Other books are about museums and run the gamut through philosophies, bibliographies, works on interpretation, and even some excellent "coffee table" books. A third category deals with the use of simulation for research. Many of these accounts are by archaeologists and tell of voyages on experimental ships like *Kon-Tiki* and the *Brendan*. Still another category focuses on simulation games and the theory and practice of war games and role playing. Finally, I've included a selection of how-to books, including some comprehensive introductions to buckskinning and black powder shooting. All the books I've described are serious studies and were well reviewed. Most are available from large libraries or by special order from the publishers. A number have also been reissued in paperback.

For lack of space, I have not covered historical novels—there are just too many. This genre is of obvious importance to the living history movement, however, and many magazines and journals regularly (and critically) review historical fiction. Also omitted are academic histories and secondary sources dealing with various themes and periods in the past. I've left out primary sources of all types, too.

In looking over my list of books about living history, I noticed some real gaps in the literature. There is no anthology of readings nor any in-depth study of methodology. No one has really examined the sociological function of the movement and its place in our popular culture. And there's no guide to the hundreds of unpublished research studies written by staff members at living history museums nor even an annotated list of master's theses and doctoral dissertations which touch on living history. There is obviously much work to be done.

Time Machines by Jay Anderson. Nashville: American Association for State and Local History, 1984.

This is the first book to examine the entire living history movement. Anderson defines living history as "an attempt to simulate life in another time" and suggests that there have been three primary motivations for simulating history: interpretation, research, and serious play. After a preface briefly describing the history of the time travel concept, he traces in three sections the social history of living museums, experimental archaeology, and reenacting. The sections develop chronologically and present case studies of significant outdoor museums, experimental projects, and buffs' organizations. A conclusion argues that living history is a valid complement to academic accounts of the past. Living history, for many groups, is actually folk history, an imaginative way of re-creating the texture and meaning of the relevant past. *Time Machines* is heavily illustrated with photographs and contains a section on living history sources.

The Time Machine and the War of the Worlds by H. G. Wells. New York: Oxford University Press, 1977 (originally published, 1895).

The fictional treatment of deliberate time travel originated with H. G. Wells. Between the years 1888 and 1894, in a series of short magazine articles, Wells worked on the idea of a time machine that could take a person to a particular point of time, past or future. In *The Time Machine,* the real hero is a device that transports an English scientist, the "Time Traveller," eight hundred thousand years into the future. A popular and influential book when it was first published in 1895, *The Time Machine* remains a classic. Wells understood how attractive the idea of man's mastery of time would be. Time hasn't lessened this attraction, as the living history movement has clearly demonstrated.

On Time: An Investigation into Scientific Knowledge and Human Experience by Michael Shallis. New York: Schocken Books, 1983.

Shallis was a film director until 1970, when he began to study physics. In 1978 he received his doctorate in astrophysics from Oxford, where he now teaches. His book is an investigation into the scientific knowledge and human experience of time. The book's success derives from Shallis's ability to interpret current theories of time for the educated layman, often by helping the reader to visualize the subject through the use of metaphors. This learning experience is not easy, for our "commonsense" concept of time as objective, linear, and simple is an ethnocentric one, rooted in our culture and sense of history. Nevertheless, the transcending of our dated ideas and experience of time can be exhilarating, akin to looking back to earth from outer space.

The first introduction of many American readers to the concept of time travel. — *Photograph by Sharli Powell*

Revolution in Time: Clocks and the Making of the Modern World by David Landes. Cambridge, Mass.: Belknap Press of Harvard University Press, 1984.

Living historians have a deep curiosity about the texture of life in the past. They want to know how the past actually looked, felt, sounded, smelled, and even tasted. Throughout most of man's history, these senses were powerful limiting factors, shaping and coloring everyday life. Modern man, however, is beset by a sixth sense—an awareness of time. The "particular interval each person calls a life" is constantly being measured. It is frequently time, not the world, that is too much with us, hence our need to escape vicariously from time, from modern life, into the "timeless" past. This motivation is living history's *raison d'être*. David Landes, a professor of history and economics at Harvard, has achieved in *Revolution in Time: Clocks and the Making of the Modern World* the first "history" of time and its impact on man, especially European man. In three sections, he examines in depth the reasons why clocks were invented, how they were dramatically improved, and what their impact has been on the modern world. This is a provocative and intellectually satisfying book.

Time and Again by Jack Finney. New York: Simon and Schuster, 1970.

Considered one of the five best mysteries ever written, *Time and Again* brings H. G. Wells's *Time Machines* up to date. Finney's hero, Si Morley, travels back to the New York City of 1882 on a secret government project. Not only does Finney explain the feasibility of this time travel, he also brings alive the historical culture of New York by the brilliant device of having Si depict it in words *and* pictures. In fact, Finney calls his book an "illustrated novel." The result is a near-total suspension of the reader's normal disbelief in time travel. Finney captures the good feelings that come with a successful simulation of life in another time.

Voyagers in Time, edited by Robert Silverberg. New York: Hawthorn Books, 1967.

Robert Silverberg is an award-winning author who's specialty is science fiction. For more than thirty years he has been challenging thoughtful readers with his novels and short stories dealing with the theme of time travel. His *Up the Line,* written in 1969, is a classic example of the genre established by H. G. Wells's *The Time Machine.* Silverberg's *Voyagers in Time* is a collection of twelve short stories by science fiction professionals, all of whom are adept at exploring the far frontiers of time travel. Silverberg in his introduction identifies the connection between time traveling and living history: "The story that takes a voyager backward in time has a more solid foundation—the accumulated archaeological and paleontological knowledge of science. In such stories, the past is made strangely vivid in a way rarely achieved otherwise. . . . Science fiction—even the best of it—does not give us literal blueprints. It deals, rather, in images, in ideas, in rearrangements of modern concepts. Its intention is to provoke thought, to dazzle the senses, and to divert the mind wearied with this moment of now" (p. xi).

Sources on Folk Museums and Living Historical Farms by Ormond Loomis. Bibliographic and Special Series, No. 16. Bloomington, Ind.: Folklore Forum, 1977.

Folklorist Ormond Loomis compiled this bibliography of 895 publications on open air museums and living history farms in 1975. It includes references, mostly articles, on the folk museum, its methods and techniques, and specific examples. Many of the important publications are annotated. Loomis also provided an index of authors and museums. Although this sixty-page study is dated, it nevertheless remains a useful and valuable resource.

Bibliography of Books, Pamphlets, and Films Listed in the Living Historical Farms Bulletin, compiled by Sharon Eubanks. Washington, D.C.: Smithsonian Institution, Association for Living Historical Farms and Agricultural Museums, 1976.

This useful seventy-three-page bibliography covers the period December 1970–May 1976, years which saw the rapid growth of the living historical farms movement. Eubanks includes 833 entries organized into the following categories: arts and crafts, crops and livestock, earth and water, gardens and orchards, hearth and home, money and records, odds and ends, and people and places. There is an index. This valuable resource should be updated.

What Time Is This Place? by Kevin Lynch. Cambridge, Mass.: MIT Press, 1972.

In this major theoretical study, Lynch argues that we humans have a particular sense of time, a biological rhythm that may follow a different beat from that dictated by external, official objective timepieces. We need to foster a relationship with the temporal dimension of the places we inhabit while we are living on earth. One way to help people do this is to "support private or semipublic efforts to develop out-door museums: environments in which the entire context of some particular period is preserved and reproduced as accurately as possible, as an educational device. . . . the visitor [could be invited] to play a part himself and thus acquire a direct feeling for the quality of life in the period represented" (p. 236). Lynch suggests that living museums should not be "limited to the Revolution or the Wild West (although these would be very revealing if accurately done) but . . . [should] include many more of the critical eras and subcultures of our relevant past, notable and notorious" (pp. 236–37). In 1972 *What Time Is This Place* was mandatory reading for living historians. It still is.

Interpretation of Historic Sites, **2nd ed. rev. by William T. Alderson and Shirley Payne Low. Nashville: American Association for State and Local History, 1976.**

Alderson and Low's book is a landmark introduction to historic site interpretation. After defining "interpretation" as an attempt to create understanding, they explain exactly how to develop and conduct interpretive programs. They include sections on setting objectives, planning, varying modes of interpretation, special programming for educational groups, selection and training of interpreters, security, and evaluation. In two fascinating appendixes, they illustrate their proposals by presenting a step-by-step account of the interpretation of a hypothetical but very realistic site. At the time the first edition of *Interpretation of Historic Sites* was written, Alderson was director of the American Association for State and Local History; he is now the director of the Margaret Woodbury Strong Museum. Mrs. Low was formerly a supervisor of hostess training for Colonial Williamsburg. Their advice, based on years of experience, was and remains worth heeding.

What time is this place?—*Old World Wisconsin, State Historical Society of Wisconsin*

Interpreting Our Heritage by Freeman Tilden. Rev. ed. Chapel Hill: University of North Carolina Press, 1967.

Freeman Tilden wrote his classic introduction to interpretation in 1957. It is still fresh and insightful. His thoughts about the potential of live interpretation were prophetic. Tilden challenged interpreters to "people" their historic sites: "Architecture and furnishings are much; we admire and draw conclusions from them, but we must find the art to keep them from seeming to have been frozen at the moment of time when nobody was home" (p. 69). He advocated demonstrations, participation, and animation. Tilden was impressed by the sight of visitors to the Farmers' Museum at Cooperstown watching the old-time processes of breaking flax, weaving, and candle making. He liked it even more when visitors could participate physically in a historic activity, even if it was just a leisurely carriage ride at Williamsburg. And he particularly was moved by animation, or the realistic simulation of life in the past. Tilden's challenge was taken up by a generation of interpreters. It still deserves attention.

Meet the Real Pilgrims: Everyday Life on Plimouth Plantation in 1627 by Robert Loeb, Jr. Garden City: Doubleday, 1979.

Working closely with the staff of Plimoth Plantation, Robert Loeb has written an excellent young people's introduction to the everyday life of Plimoth Plantation in 1627. The book takes the form of a tour, led by Loeb, in which the reader meets a selection of Pilgrims, all very earthy and all speaking a colloquial Elizabethan English. The device is effective. Events that heretofore were legends become human, involving real people with work that needs to be done, with stories they want to tell, and with a village they want you to see before you return to your modern world. A series of inviting photographs helps the reader visualize this world. Loeb followed this volume with a similar one, *New England Village*, which was named a "notable children's trade book" by the National Council for the Social Studies.

***Fortress of Louisbourg* by John Fortier. With color photographs by Owen Fitzgerald. Toronto: Oxford University Press, 1979.**

Co-winner of the American Association for State and Local History's Award of Merit, *Fortress of Louisbourg* looks like a coffee table book, but it far transcends that genre. Fitzgerald's fifty-eight photographs capture the color and texture of life in the fortress during the mid-1740s. But it is John Fortier's text that sets the book apart. The former director discusses in an engrossing style the site's history, restoration, and interpretation. Fortier's text, essentially an essay, is one of the most persuasive arguments for living history to date.

***Louisbourg Portraits* by Christopher Moore. Toronto: Macmillan of Canada, 1982.**

Christopher Moore was staff historian at the Fortress of Louisbourg from 1972 to 1975. As he watched the carpenters, masons, and other artificers recreating the fort's physical past, Moore began work on an unusual social history which would breath new life into five people who once garrisoned the town. The result was *Louisbourg Portraits*, a superb book that in 1982 won the governor general's literary award, one of the Canada Council's highest honors. Moore's book certainly stands by itself, but it makes ideal reading for a visitor who has seen the restored fortress. Although my sourcebook generally omits historical novels and nonfiction accounts of the past, I include Moore's book because it dovetails with the site's excellent living history programs.

In the book's preface Moore offers a challenge: "Andy Warhol has said that in the future everyone will be famous for fifteen minutes. It seems a comment on modern technology, but buried there is an assumption that every human life would be worthy of our attention, if we had the means to notice. If in the future, why not for the past, at least on those rare occasions where we do have the means to notice. In Louisbourg, one small community long since overwhelmed by the violence of its times, we have the chance" (p. ix). Both Louisbourg and Moore's book give us the chance to fraternize with our brothers and sisters from another time.

Hier l'Acadie: Scènes de Village Historique Acadien. Texte de Clarence Lebreton, photos de George Jacob. Montreal: Diffusions, 1981.

Clarence Lebreton, historian-researcher at New Brunswick's Village Acadien, and Georges Jacob capture the Gallic spirit of Acadian culture in this warm and friendly book. They provide an insider's view of Acadian community life on the banks of the Gulf of St. Lawrence. Jacob's 131 color photographs—which are discussed by Lebreton—take you into the village's homes, gardens, workshops, and fields and introduce many of the community's folk. The village residents are seen at work and at play, and you can sense their cultural pride and their *joie de vivre*. *Hier l'Acadie* complements a visit to the living museum and contrasts powerfully with *Kings Landing,* a similar pictorial essay.

Kings Landing: Country Life in Early Canada. Photographs by Wayne Barrett, introduction by George MacBath. Toronto: Oxford University Press, 1979.

George MacBath was overall director of the development of Kings Landing, one of Canada's finest living museums. Wayne Barrett is a photographer who specializes in capturing the visual themes that express a regional culture. Together they portray in words and color photographs the folklife of New Brunswick so poignantly re-created at the outdoor museum on the banks of the St. John River near Fredericton, the provincial capital. The book's ninety photographs and thoughtful text somehow capture the texture of everyday life in this Loyalist community. Like the outdoor museum itself, MacBath and Barrett present us with a very human account of country life in the early nineteenth century.

Experimental Archaeology by John Coles. New York: Academic Press, 1980.

John Coles is the foremost historian of the field of experimental archaeology and a reader in European prehistory at the University of Cambridge. His *Archaeology by Experiment* (London: Hutchinson, 1973) codified the methodology for valid experimentation. In his second book Coles describes hundreds of successful experiments in chapters that focus on voyages, subsistence, settlement, arts and crafts, and, finally, daily life and death. *Experimental Archaeology* is essentially a critical history, well illustrated, well documented, and definitive. Coles's prose is free of technical jargon, and his book as fast paced as a novel.

Kon-Tiki by Thor Heyerdahl. Chicago: Rand McNally, 1950.

Heyerdahl's account of his forty-three-hundred mile crossing of the eastern Pacific on a raft is a classic. Although few archaeologists accept his thesis today, Heyerdahl nevertheless is recognized as an innovative scholar, a pioneer in the field of experimental archaeology, and a courageous and ethical man. *Kon-Tiki* was a best-seller throughout the world, and a rereading of it reminds you of why: Heyerdahl is a gifted storyteller whose style at once captures the reader's imagination. The seventh person on the raft with Heyerdahl and his five companions is the reader.

Hokule'a: The Way to Tahiti by Ben Finney. New York: Dodd, Mead, 1979.

Finney, a Harvard-educated professor of anthropology at the University of Hawaii, in 1976 sailed a reconstruction of an ancient double-hulled Polynesian canoe from Hawaii to Tahiti and back—six thousand miles in all. The voyage proved without doubt that Polynesians could deliberately have sailed throughout the Pacific, transplanting their culture to its many archipelagoes. *Hokule'a* is a record of Finney's voyage and the effect the trip had on modern Hawaii and native Hawaiians. The book is a case study in experimental and applied anthropology. Although Finney's theory of Pacific migrations contradicts Heyerdahl's, *Hokule'a,* like *Kon-Tiki,* is a thought-provoking, exciting book.

The Ra Expeditions by Thor Heyerdahl. New York: Doubleday, 1971.

Thor Heyerdahl is a unique blend of academic archaeologist, project manager, daredevil, and sage teller of tales. His books reflect his personality—they are thought provoking, inspiring, awesome, and readable. We may question his premises but never his honesty and courage. The purpose of the Ra

SIX MEN CROSS THE PACIFIC ON A RAFT

KON-TIKI

By THOR HEYERDAHL

WITH EIGHTY PHOTOGRAPHS OF THE VOYAGE

Kon-Tiki, Thor Heyerdahl's epic 1947 voyage across the Pacific on a raft. —*Photograph by Sharli Powell*

expeditions was to prove that the civilizations of ancient Egypt and the Americas could have been linked by the sea. To accomplish this goal, Heyerdahl and his crew (representing half a dozen different nationalities) constructed and sailed a papyrus-reed ship across the Atlantic from Morocco to the West Indies. *Ra I* sank, but a more authentic *Ra II* succeeded. After fifty-seven days and more than thirty-five-hundred miles of open sea, Heyerdahl once again demonstrated the validity of simulation as a research tool. As in the case of *Kon-Tiki*, Heyerdahl makes you believe you are on board his ship.

The Tigris Expedition: In Search of Our Beginnings by Thor Heyerdahl. New York: Doubleday, 1981.

Like Heyerdahl's previous voyages, *Kon-Tiki* and *Ra I* and *Ra II*, the *Tigris* expedition generated data to answer a theoretical question. Could the Sumerians, who developed one of the world's earliest civilizations in Mesopotamia (now Iraq), have sailed around the Persian Gulf, the Arabian Sea, and the Indian Ocean, setting up a trading empire? In 1977 Heyerdahl constructed a thirty-ton reed vessel similar to *Ra II* and sailed it for 144 days, covering almost four thousand miles. *Tigris* negotiated the dangerous Gulf and Strait of Hormuz and ventured well out into the Arabian Sea. Only political circumstances brought the expedition to an end off the coast of Somalia, in northeast Africa. From an archaeological and historical point of view, *Tigris* was Heyerdahl's most successful voyage, since he proved without a doubt the navigational potential of large reed ships. This book, like Heyerdahl's other two, is a gripping chronicle of a complex project and a daring adventure.

The Sinbad Voyage by Tim Severin. New York: G. P. Putnam's Sons, 1983.

Four years after crossing the Atlantic in the *Brendan,* Severin undertook another voyage, this one inspired by the medieval epic of Sinbad, *The Thousand and One Nights.* He wanted to retrace the Arab explorer's voyage from the Arabian Peninsula to China. After exhaustive research on the nature of Arab ship design and navigational principles, Severin built a replica of an early ninth-century ship. Named the *Sohar,* after Sinbad's home port in modern Oman, the ship was unusual in that its hull was constructed of fitted planks sewn together with coconut fiber rope. Few observers thought it would complete the voyage, but in 1980–1981, Severin sailed it more than six thousand miles to Canton, China. *The Sinbad Voyage* documents, step by step, every stage of the *Sohar* project: design, construction, and testing of this extraordinary floating historical laboratory. For Severin, the intellectual and sensual experiences of the trip provided significant clues in the elusive search for a more complete understanding of the many real sailors who more than one thousand years ago plied the trade routes of the Indian Ocean and the South China Sea.

I Built A Stone Age House by Hans-Ole Hansen. New York: John Day, 1964.

In 1956, with the help of teenage friends, Hans-Ole Hansen, a seventeen-year-old Dane, built his first "Stone Age" house. It took ten days to complete the job. Nine tons of clay were used for the walls, two thousand willows and hazel rods for the wattle, seventy-two poles for uprights and rafters, and 220 bundles of reed for thatching. They tied everything together with elm bark and avoided using modern tools and methods throughout the experiment. Hansen and his friends then lived in the house from time to time over the next several years until it accidentally burned down. In this charmingly youthful and enthusiastic book Hansen relates his experiences with "experimental archaeology." *I Built a Stone Age House* is characterized by an attention to detail, clear thinking, curiosity, and modesty, qualities that helped Hansen when he later founded the Lejre Historical-Archaeological Center outside Copenhagen.

Iron Age Farm by Peter Reynolds. London: British Museum, 1979.

The only published study of an experimental farm, Reynolds's volume is a remarkable report that draws the serious reader into the everyday life of Iron Age England by its careful reexamination of the ordinary farmer's home, outbuildings, livestock, crops, crafts, food, and seasonal work patterns. Reynolds's portrait is based on data generated by Butser Ancient Farm Research Project, one of the most complex experimental archaeological programs to date. Reynolds writes for both scholar and layman in the clear-headed prose that characterizes the best British interpretations of modern science.

Living in the Past by John Percival. London: British Broadcasting Corporation, 1980.

After a visit to Denmark's Lejre Center, John Percival, a BBC television producer and an amateur archaeologist, decided to produce a documentary that would show more than the usual "backsides of diggers and chattering archaeologists." The result was a twelve-part series of half-hour color films called "Living in the Past" which focused on the attempt by fifteen volunteers to live for a year like Celts in the first century B.C. Isolated in a thirty-five-acre forest in the south of England, they built and ran a re-created Iron Age farm. They grew authentic crops, cared for livestock, gathered wild foods, and rested from their labors around the hearth fire. The television series was a hit. Modern Britons were fascinated by the experiment. Percival's book is a straightforward account of the project. I found it absolutely riveting. Percival explores the experiment in depth month by month in a way the television series couldn't. He gives the reader the sense of actually living in the village, working side by side with its modern Celts, and for a brief period transcending the invisible wall of time that separates us from our forebears.

The Brendan Voyage by Tim Severin. New York: McGraw-Hill, 1978.

A geographer and medieval scholar educated at Oxford and Harvard, Tim Severin built a large leather curragh and sailed it from Ireland to Newfoundland in 1976–1977. He sought to retrace the fifth-century voyage of Saint Brendan. Severin's account of the re-creation of the curragh and the harrowing voyage across the North Atlantic in it is reminiscent of *Kon-Tiki*—exciting, yet modest, well written and carefully considered. In addition to the narrative, Severin, an experienced sailor, provides a scholarly appendix on the design, manufacture, and performance of his craft.

The Second Mayflower Adventure by Warwick Charlton. Boston: Little, Brown, 1957.

This is the official account of the *Mayflower II* experiment by the originator of the project. Charlton takes readers through all stages of the venture: planning, research, construction, and the voyage itself. The author's enthusiasm is boundless as he describes his initial fund-raising efforts, William Baker's quest for an authentic design, Stuart Upham's two-hundred-year-old shipyard where *Mayflower II* took shape, and Alan Villiers's colorful and skillful captain-

In this book, Tim
Severin sails across
the North Atlantic in
a leather curragh,
retracing St.
Brendan's legendary
sixth-century
voyage. —*Photograph
by Sharli Powell*

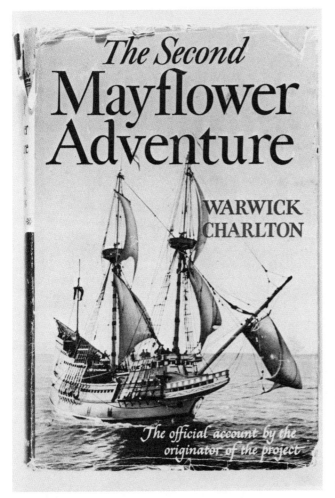

The Second Mayflower Adventure

WARWICK CHARLTON

The official account by the originator of the project

In 1957 *Mayflower II* reenacted the Pilgrims' journey to New England. The replica is now part of Plimoth Plantation. — *Photograph by Sharli Powell*

ing of the ship as she plied her way across the Atlantic in the spring of 1957. A natural storyteller, Charlton records the project's difficult and humorous moments, its gay times and solemn occasions, and most important, the thoughts and feelings of *Mayflower II*'s crew as they successfully carried out one of living history's most notable events.

The New Mayflower by Alan Villiers. New York: Charles Scribner's Sons, 1958.

Alan Villiers, who captained *Mayflower II*, wrote this book about the entire project for children. It's just under fifty pages, full of excellent photographs, and written in Villiers's straightforward style. His more complete record of the venture was published in two articles in *National Geographic* (May and November 1957), and the official account of the entire adventure was written by Warwick Charlton in his excellent *The Second Mayflower*. Nevertheless, *The New Mayflower* is a fine book for the young sailor or historian.

The First Thanksgiving Feast by Joan Anderson. With photographs by George Ancona. New York: Clarion Books, 1984.

In this beautifully designed book for children, Joan Anderson and George Ancona tell the true story of the Pilgrims' 1621 Harvest Home, the celebration that has come to be known as the "first Thanksgiving." Photographed at Plimoth Plantation, the book looks at the feast from the point of view of the people who were actually there: the surviving Pilgrims and their invited guests, neighboring Wampanoag Indians. The text (presented as an oral history) and the many black-and-white photographs are both historically accurate and suggest the robust Jacobean atmosphere that infused the event. This is a much-

The First Thanksgiving Feast

BY JOAN ANDERSON

PHOTOGRAPHED BY GEORGE ANCONA

Plimoth Plantation's annual celebration of the Pilgrims' Harvest Feast is documented in a book for children. —*Photograph by Sharli Powell*

needed nonsexist, nonracist account of one of Americans' most misunderstood cultural events.

A Second Impression by H. Dean Campbell. Trivoli, Ill.: Campbell House, 1974.

In his privately printed diary of the tricentennial reenactment of the Marquette-Jolliet expedition, H. Dean Campbell provides the living history movement with an important record of a major experimental and interpretive project. For four months, eight reenactors retraced the three-thousand-mile route from St. Ignace on Michigan's Upper Peninsula, through the Great Lakes, down the Mississippi River, and back. The purpose of the project was, in the words of Reid Lewis, its leader, "to bring living history to the people of the Midwest" in the hope that people would become "conscious of the history of their region" and thereby interested in "preserving the natural and man-made vestiges of the past" (Reid Lewis, "Three Hundred Years Later," *Historic Preservation* 26:4, July-September 1974, p. 7). Campbell's diary is not only a factual account of the voyage but a realistic celebration of the spirit which motivates many reenactors. Campbell writes that he "hoped to make human those explorers of the past by recounting some of the everyday happenings that must have been a part of their exploits also" (p. 90). His hopes are realized in *A Second Impression.*

Serious Games by Clark Abt. New York: Viking Press, 1970.

Serious Games is the classic introduction to the philosophy of gaming. The book is grounded in Abt's experience in the U.S. Air Force, his political science studies at MIT, and his work as head of Abt Associates, a group of pure and applied scientists and humanists interested in working on modern social problems. For Abt, a "game is an activity among two or more independent decision-makers seeking to achieve their objectives in some limiting context" (p. 6). Games, he argues, have great educational potential, for they unite the "seriousness of thought and problems that require it *with* the emotional freedom of active play" (p. 11). He discusses the value of gaming for the physical and social sciences, disadvantaged groups, occupational choice and training, and government and industry. Abt also includes chapters on designing games, on evaluating their cost effectiveness, and on their potential future in a highly technological world. Many of Abt's arguments for the value of serious gaming can be applied to living history interpretation, research, and reenacting.

The Guide to Simulations: Games for Education and Training by R. E. Horn. **2 vols. 3rd ed. Cranford, N.J.: Didactic Systems, 1976.**

First published in 1970, the *Guide* is an invaluable reference tool. It is regularly updated and is without question the best source of current information and thought on games designed primarily for educational use. Its primary section, more than five hundred pages long, describes and evaluates more than five hundred simulations/games in twenty categories, including domestic politics, ecology, social studies, sociology, and history. The history chapter only slightly overlaps with the type of board game produced by Avalon Hill and Simulations Publications, Inc. Most of the *Guide's* entries deal with games suitable for classroom use. Later editions of the *Guide* also include a selection of articles ("Getting into Simulation Games," "A Basic Reference Shelf on Simulation and Gaming," "How Students Can Make Their Own Simulations"), indexes (including a list of games *not* described and the reason for their exclusion), and a reviewer's checklist and information form for adding games to the next addition. The *Guide* should be especially useful for people responsible for education programs at living history museums.

A First Book of Games and Simulation by Donald Cruickshank. Belmont, Calif.: Wadsworth Publishing, 1977.

Don Cruickshank, a professor at Ohio State University, has written a good, short introduction to designing and using simulation and nonsimulation games for instructional purposes. Especially valuable is his chapter on resources: books, journals, newsletters, and national organizations. Cruickshank is a good teacher: his instructions are clear and uncluttered with jargon and proceed step by step. He notes that "games and simulations are used more than ever where first-hand experience is not feasible or is too complex or dangerous."

Little Wars by H. G. Wells. New York: Da Capo Press, 1977 (reprint of the 1913 1st ed.).

Originally published in 1913, *Little Wars* was the first book on war games for adults. Wells, one of the twentieth century's most determined pacifists, hoped that real wars might be avoided if a suitable substitute could be found. His recommendation was simulated war games, played out with miniatures, following clearly drawn rules and regulations. Wells suggested that would-be warriors could test their knowledge of strategy, tactics, and military history with "no smashed nor sanguinary bodies, no shattered fine buildings nor devastated country sides, no petty cruelties, none of that awful universal boredom and embitterment, that tiresome delay or stoppage or embarrassment of every gracious, bold, sweet, and charming thing, that we who are old enough to remember a real modern war know to be the reality of belligerence" (p. 97). Although buffs have gone far beyond Wells's rules in the sixty years since the publication of *Little Wars* and have achieved a much greater degree of authenticity, this modest book was undeniably a first and is recognized by all simulators of history as the classic.

Battles with Toy Soldiers by Donald Featherstone. London: David and Charles, 1984 (originally published, 1970).

Don Featherstone is one of the pioneers of war gaming with miniatures and contributes regularly to the fine British monthly *Miniature Wargames*. This book is the basic primer for newcomers to the hobby and a useful reference tool for the experienced player. Featherstone first covers the history and salient characteristics of miniature gaming and then evaluates ten periods of history for their war-gaming potential. For some periods, such as the ancient and World War II, he offers basic rules. In his appendixes there are good lists of figure manufacturers, scenery makers, clubs, societies, annual events, and suggested reading.

The War Game by Peter Young. New York: E. P. Dutton, 1972.

Peter Young, founder of the English Civil War reenactors' society the Sealed Knot, had the excellent idea of re-creating with miniature soldiers ten of the world's most important battles. Included are Thermopylae (480 B.C.), Agincourt 1415, Edgehill 1642, Blenheim 1704, Lobositz 1756, Saratoga 1777, Austerlitz 1805, Waterloo 1815, Gettysburg 1863, and El Alamein 1942. Each battle is illustrated with excellent color photographs by Philip Stearns, maps, and period drawings or photographs. In addition, an appendix introduces amateur history buffs to the principles of war gaming with miniatures.

The Comprehensive Guide to Board Wargaming by Nicholas Palmer. New York: Hippocrene Books, 1977.

A British enthusiast, Palmer has written a guide that predates and nicely complements James Dunnigan's handbook. (Early on, Palmer acknowledges the help of Dunnigan and the design team at Simulations Publications, Inc.) The emphasis in this *Guide* is on actual playing. Palmer deals with strategy ("forest and trees," reserve and buildup, political and economic affairs), tactics (defensive terrain, combined arms, waves and skies), winning (short cuts, broad sweep), and simulating history on ten dollars a day—"a conducted tour of war games in print." He concludes by taking the reader through a sample game, the Battle of Nordlingen between Sweden and the Imperialists in 1634. This is not a book for the rank beginner, although Palmer's prose is a delight even if you're not exactly sure what he's explaining! And his evaluations of almost three hundred games on his "tour" are discerning and full of wit. He's plainly someone you would enjoy confronting over a game of Kingmaker or Diplomacy.

The Complete Wargames Handbook: How to Play, Design, and Find Them by James F. Dunnigan. New York: William Morrow, 1980.

This is the definitive guide to board war gaming. James Dunnigan, who was one of the founders of Simulations Publications, Inc., has designed literally hundreds of games, including the all-time best seller, PanzerBlitz. He is informed, insightful, and clearheaded. Dunnigan examines the definition and

THE COMPLETE WARGAMES HANDBOOK

HOW TO PLAY, DESIGN AND FIND THEM

James F. Dunnigan

The definitive guide to
war games by one of the
hobby's most prolific
game designers. —
*Photograph by Sharli
Powell*

history of war games, the art of playing well, computers, motives for playing, and classic games from eleven historical periods. He also provides a user's guide to war games in print and discusses the art of designing a game (with a complete example based on Patton's 1944 drive on Metz). The book's tone is informal, without a trace of condescension. Dunnigan is obviously proud of the hobby and his role in it, and his enthusiasm continually carries the reader along. This is a handbook for both the novice and the experienced player. My favorite line is his definition of a war game as "a paper time-machine."

The Dungeon Master by William Dear. Boston: Houghton Mifflin, 1984.
    William Dear is a well-known private investigator who was hired in 1979 to find the missing James Dallas Egbert III, a sixteen-year-old college student with an IQ of 180-plus who was a fanatic player of *Dungeons and Dragons.* Dear's book reads like a good mystery. He pursues Egbert and his friends through the labyrinth of tunnels beneath Michigan State University where they acted out their fantasies. Eventually Egbert is found, is returned to his parents—and, tragically, commits suicide. *The Dungeon Master* is a cautionary tale, revealing the dark side of simulation. It describes a world of people who desperately need to escape into a fantasy realm where for once they can achieve power, status, recognition, and dominion. Their story is not an attractive one and raises important questions as to what drives certain modern people into the past, albeit a past of their own imagining.

Buckskins and Black Powder: A Mountain Man's Guide to Muzzleloading by
Ken Grissom. Piscataway, N.J.: Winchester Press, 1983.

Outdoor writer for the *Houston Post*, Ken Grissom is a highly regarded
buckskinner. He calls his book a "mountain man's guide to muzzleloading."
Without question, *Buckskins and Black Powder* is the model for future living
history how-to manuals. Comprehensive, well written, and beautifully illustrated with several hundred photos and line drawings, Grissom's volume sets
the standard for the field. Grissom takes his subject seriously and examines
buckskinning in the context of contemporary American popular culture. He
also speaks with the authority of an insider, in an informal yet informed style.
In his preface, Grissom acknowledges that there is probably "no way to
duplicate, in the twentieth century, the experience of having to shift for
yourself a thousand miles deep in a vast wilderness . . . yet, if a man has the
sense to yearn for a simpler and more natural life—never mind that it's
unattainable—I say his heart is good" (p. xv).

The Complete Black Powder Handbook by Sam Fadala. Northfield, Ill.: DBI
Books, 1979.

Sam Fadala was raised in Arizona, where he took up buckskinning in the
mid-1960s. He also earned a Ph.D. at the University of Arizona. The combination of fifteen years' field experience and rigorous academic training gives *The
Complete Black Powder Handbook* a breadth and depth seldom found in other
publications. In 290 pages Fadala covers such subjects as the original buckskinners, the rendezvous—then and now—black powder organizations, a front
loader's library, a directory of black powder companies, a glossary of terms
("Mountain Man Talk"), and, most important firearms. He covers just about

BUCKSKINS AND BLACK POWDER

A Mountain Man's Guide to Muzzleloading

KEN GRISSOM

DAN BREWER
(BUFFLER) 87

A complete, illustrated handbook of the mountain man's skills and equipment—
for the muzzleloading shooter who wants to be a true buckskinner

Guides such as Ken Grissom's excellent *Buckskins and Black Powder* are models for shorter, more specific sketchbooks. — *Photograph by Sharli Powell*

every aspect of black powder shooting. Fadala has a fine sense of history and a critical, careful attitude toward the craft of manufacturing and toward using, caring for, and evaluating black powder firearms. His handbook tells of the many experiments he has conducted with rifles, pistols, shotguns, black powder, and projectiles and describes other aspects of the hobby. His methods are rigorous and scientific—models for experimental archaeologists and historians—yet his work is not arcane. Fadala writes well, in a clear, economical, almost conversational style.

War Games by Anthony Price. Garden City: Doubleday, 1977.

Anthony Price is a journalist who reviewed mystery novels for the *Oxford Mail* before getting the fiction-writing bug. He has produced a series of first-rate espionage novels which reflect his personal interest in military history and archaeology. *War Games* demonstrates his knowledge of the contemporary British reenactment scene. It is essentially a spy story in which the "Double R Society," a fictional English Civil War living history organization, figures significantly. The novel opens with a superb description of the Battle of Swine Brook Field, a fictitious but very realistic reenactment. *War Games* plays games with the Sealed Knot, King's Army, and Roundhead Association, all admirable reenactment groups.

The Best of Enemies by Nancy Bond. New York: Atheneum, 1978.

The Best of Enemies, a book for young people, is set in Concord, Massachusetts, during the Bicentennial. The plot is intriguing: a teenager, Charlotte Paige, finds herself involved in an explosive confrontation between American reenactors, for whom living history is recreation, and an odd assortment of British troops, who seem bent on refighting the Revolutionary War. The result is a highly original mystery that deals with one of living history's primary themes—the line between fantasy and reality. Bond won the Newbery Honor Award for her earlier *A String in the Harp*, a book that also explores the theme of time travel.

4. Articles

SOMETIMES on an off day, generally in the dead of an Iowa winter, Ron Westphal used to give me a call. He now heads TVA's excellent living history farm, The Homeplace—1850, but in the late 1970s he worked at Iowa's Living History Farms. "If you're not doing anything critical," he'd say, "let's go into Des Moines and get some supplies." I jumped at the chance, for "supplies" meant a bowl of chili at "George, the Chili King" and the latest issue of *Military Modelling,* a British history buffs' magazine focusing on toy soldiers, miniature war gaming, and reenacting. The magazine included articles on British organizations such as the Sealed Knot, the group which re-creates English Civil War battles; color plates illustrating stories on the uniforms of exotic late Victorian regiments straight out of Kipling; and technical discussions of the problems of "war-gaming" conflicts fought long ago and far away. Such articles opened our eyes to a world of historical simulation beyond the living history museum.

Articles in magazines and journals have captured the variety and vitality of the living history movement better than any other medium. For every good book, there are at least a dozen fine articles. Perhaps it's because most of the individuals involved in living history are working full time in museums or have other regular jobs and seldom have the luxury of a sabbatical or even a small chunk of free time in which to write anything approaching a book. Putting together a selection from the many really excellent articles specifically about living history was a far easier task than compiling a list of books, but it involved establishing tough criteria.

I decided to omit articles that provided practical information of the kind offered in sketchbooks. There were simply far too many available. I also excluded newspaper features and show-and-tell descriptions of museums and events. I did include articles by many of the living history movement's pioneers and current leaders, including Jim Deetz, Darwin Kelsey, Ed Hawes, and Cary Carson. There are also historical and theoretical pieces which argue the case for reconstructed buildings, the use of facsimiles, and role playing. Finally, I wanted to include selections from as many of the serious small journals as possible. Often these publications don't receive the attention given to national journals such as *Museum News* or *Historic Preservation*, but they are important outlets for the living history movement.

The articles are grouped in five categories: history and background of the living history movement, museums, experimental archaeology, reenacting, and simulation gaming. Taken all together, these entries could serve as an introduction to the field of historical simulation in all its guises.

"Every Man His Own Historian" by Carl Becker. In *Every Man His Own Historian*. New York: F. S. Crofts, 1935.

Carl Becker, who coined the term "living history" in his 1931 presidential address to the American Historical Society, raised the issue of vitality. He suggested that each generation must "imaginatively" put forward a "living history." Becker noted, "The history that lies inert in unread books does no work in the world. The history that does work in the world, the history that influences the course of history, is living history, that pattern of remembered events, whether true or false, that enlarges and enriches [society's] collective specious present" (p. 252). The function of a "living history" is to help society ("the tribe, the nation, or all mankind") evaluate and judge its actions "in light of what is has done and what is hopes to do" (p. 248). For history to be of value, it must reach the people and move them both emotionally and intellectually.

"Living History: Simulating Everyday Life in Living Museums" by Jay Anderson. *American Quarterly* 34 (Fall 1982).

This is the first published article to treat all aspects of living history — "an attempt to simulate life in another time" — as a unit. The author suggests three primary motivations for simulating history: interpretation, research, and

A Wichita newspaper editor ponders the news that is fit to print at Old Cowtown Museum. — *Self-portrait by R. Tim McGill*

serious play. Many examples are given of these branches of the living history movement.

"The Idea of Nostalgia" by Jean Starobinski. *Diogenes* 54 (Summer 1966).

Commentators on the living history movement often note the importance of nostalgia as a motivating force. In this carefully researched article, Starobinski traces the history of the idea of nostalgia. Although the term was first used in 1688 to denote the disease of homesickness, nostalgia was later considered a frequently fatal illness, especially for soldiers. By the nineteenth century, however, nostalgia had come to mean a deep longing for the feelings or scenes of childhood.

"A Short Natural History of Nostalgia" by Anthony Brandt. *Atlantic Monthly,* December 1978.

After outlining the history of nostalgia as a "disease," Brandt examines its impact on the development of "museum villages" and "historic restorations" in America. Brandt especially notes the motivation of Henry Ford in restoring the Wayside Inn and creating his Edison Institute. Colonial Williamsburg, Sleepy Hollow Restorations, Old Sturbridge Village, Mystic Seaport, and both Disneyland and Disney World are built on a foundation of nostalgia, Brandt argues. He does not mean that they are not needed; rather he contends that, "as islands of feeling in a largely unfeeling present, they provide a kind of relief we may need to keep our sanity. They represent values which, however unlikely it is that they were ever embodied in the actual past, at least attest to the endurance in us of a vision, a dream of an alternative way of life, quieter, more contented, in the fullest sense of the word, gentler" (p. 63).

Nostalgia at Old Sturbridge Village's Summershops Program. —*Old Sturbridge Village; photograph by Robert S. Arnold*

"Past Time, Present Place: Landscape and Memory" by David Lowenthal.
   Geographic Review **45:1 (January 1975).**

For more than twenty years, David Lowenthal has been examining the function of the "past" in our present culture. An eclectic scholar, he is remarkably free from the biases of particular disciplines; his approach reflects an understanding of history, geography, literature, and other schools of research which can help us better understand the relationship between then and now. In "Past Time, Present Place," he looks especially hard at how we "remake the past" to serve our needs. About historical reconstruction, he writes: "Even when we strive for fidelity to the past we create something new that reflects our habits and preferences. . . . As we erode and alter the inherited past, we more and more contrive our own. Creatures of historical processes beyond our control, we shape landscapes and artifacts to conform with illusory histories, public and private, that gratify our tastes. All the lineaments of the present are historical, yet they are continuously reborn in the minds of every culture and of every generation" (p. 36).

"The American Way of History" by David Lowenthal. *Columbia University*
   Forum **9 (1966).**

A professor of geography at University College, London, Lowenthal was one of the first scholars to examine critically the American way of "imaginatively creating" history at outdoor museums or "History Lands." In this article, he challenges Americans with the observation that "what is old is looked at as special, 'historic,' different. Not wanting to be different, Americans anathematize the past. In the process, they become conscious of antiquity as a separate realm. And as the past was cut away from the present, history emerged

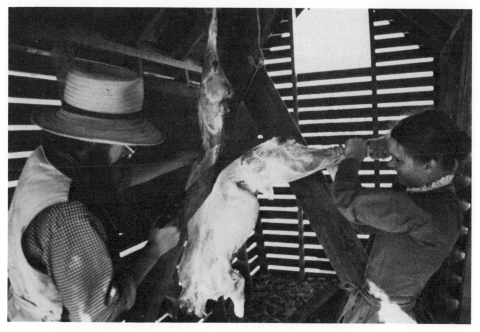

"The American way of history" includes butchering a lamb in the corn crib. —*Oliver H. Kelley Farm, Minnesota Historical Society*

as an isolated object of reverence and pleasure. For all its deliberate relevance, History Land remains detached, remote, and essentially lifeless" (p. 32).

"Visiting the Past: History Museums in the United States" by Michael Wallace. *Radical History Review* 25 (1981).

A revisionist historian, Wallace seeks to demonstrate that from "the mid-nineteenth century, most history museums were constructed by members of dominant classes, and embodied interpretations that supported their sponsors' privileged positions." Wallace argues that although most living history museums had abandoned the "American Heritage" notion of history for a "more pluralistic conception of the U.S. past," still they "shied away from politics and struggle: slave culture was one thing, slave revolts another" (p. 87). Wallace feels museums have failed "to explore the ways the present evolved out of the past." Williamsburg, he believes, fails to "explain the connections between eighteenth-century slavery and twentieth-century racism (or black nationalism). Admitting the realities of exploitation contradicted the ideals of liberty was only a first step" (p. 87). Wallace sees hope in the living historical farms movement developed by a "new generation of historians and educators concerned to explore work and family life with even higher standards of accuracy, and in some cases, with an eye to modern parallels" (p. 86).

"Living Museums of Everyman's History" by Cary Carson. *Harvard Magazine,* Summer 1981.

Carson, director of research for Colonial Williamsburg, sees living museums as a way of taking "history directly to the people." And the "history" that Carson has in mind is the "new social history." He argues that, as living

Rite of passage for a soldier at Fort Snelling. — *Fort Snelling, Minnesota Historical Society*

After a morning of stoking the furnace, a worker enjoys his dinner in a tenant house at Hopewell Village. —*Hopewell Village; photograph provided by the National Park Service*

museums, "collections of ordinary, everyday activities re-created the basic life experiences that serve as focal points for the new social history—birth, education, work, marriage, diet, disease, and the provision of clothing, housing, and material possessions" (p. 22). Carson concludes: "Like it or not, museums are forums, not attics. Their visitors' enthusiasm for thoughtful history has gone far to assuage the misgivings of attic-loving professionals" (p. 32).

Primer for Preservation by Kenneth Chorley and Louis Jones. Technical Leaflet 19. Nashville: American Association for State and Local History, 1955.

Based on a paper presented in a seminar at Cooperstown, Chorley and Jones's technical leaflet is a very early and persuasive argument for living history interpretation. Chorley argues that, if historical preservation is to be valid, a site must be of substantial historical or cultural importance, well researched, clear in its goals, and most important, powerfully presented and interpreted. For him, Cooperstown's interpreters and their message are as important as the museum's artifacts. Jones follows up this statement with a populist plea. "It's a fine thing to exhibit the aesthetic best out of the past but it can be equally important to interpret the ways men and women worked and created and played. I want to see more gun shops, millineries, schoolhouses, covered bridges, taverns, and foundries preserved for our people. Let's speak to Americans in terms that add meaning to their own everyday lives, that place their jobs, their responsibilities as citizens and parents, in historic context so that they see their present problems not as exceptions, but as continuations of the challenges faced by their forefathers" (p. 4).

The reality of women's folklife, as interpreted at Old World Wisconsin. —*Old World Wisconsin, State Historical Society of Wisconsin*

"The Relationship between Artifacts and the Public in Outdoor History Museums" by Mark Leone. New York Academy of Science *Annals* (1981).

Mark Leone, an archaeologist at the University of Maryland who often applies Marxist interpretation to contemporary museums, visited Shakertown at Pleasant Hill, Kentucky, and used the experience to suggest that our history museums could be evaluated as complex artifacts that promote a particular ideology. "For instead of being warehouses of artifacts needing further analysis or as neutral masses of potential information, such museum presentations can be seen as fully operating parts of modern American culture. . . . [museums] can be a clue to the ideological part of our own society, in this case our conception and use of the past and its relationship to the present" (pp. 305–306).

"Thoughts on the Re-creation and Interpretation of Historical Environments" by John Fortier. *Schedule and Papers, the Third International Congress of Maritime Museums.* Mystic Seaport, Conn., 1978.

Drawing on his experience as superintendent of the Fortress of Louisbourg, John Fortier presents a clearly reasoned, delightfully expressed essay on the potential of living history as a "personal approach to understanding the past." He introduces the concept of role playing: "If the goal of a museum village is to re-create a real place, it follows that the lives of the original people, as well as the landscapes and furnishings they knew, are relevant and deserve to be recalled" (p. 5). But Fortier also counts the costs and cites Louisbourg as a case study in what to do and what not to do when undertaking a serious living history program. "Historical reality," he notes, is

The Homeplace 1850's extended family interprets social history on the way to market. —*The Homeplace 1850, T.V.A.'s Land Between the Lakes*

"elusive and momentary. It may exist in its ideal form only for as long as the swing of a door, or the moment it takes for a costumed figure to disappear around a street corner. Yet that moment can bring a sense of timelessness, a realization of the humanity we share with our ancestors, that will not be like anything else you can experience" (p. 17).

"Harvests of History" by Darwin Kelsey. *Historic Preservation* 28 (1976).

Kelsey, a cultural geographer and former director of museum administration at Old Sturbridge Village, argues that the living historical farm is a new hybrid variety of historic site that seeks to preserve material and nonmaterial culture in context and in process. The simulated environments of living historical farms are not only unique institutions for preserving cultural intangibles but also effective experimental laboratories for teaching subjects that previous scholars had written off as "best left to the imagination." Living historical farms provide, Kelsey argues, "in addition to strict intellection and cognition, experimental modes of knowing—knowing through sight, sound, smell, touch, taste" (p. 24).

"The Living Historical Farm in North America: New Directions in Research and Interpretation" by Edward Hawes. *Annual of the Association for Living Historical Farms and Agricultural Museums* 2 (1976).

A professor of history at Sangamon State University in Springfield, Illinois, Hawes wrote the first full-scale academic analysis of the living historical farm. His audience was the international open air museum community, and this paper was later delivered at a congress of agricultural museum officials held in Prague. In it Hawes examines the history and theory underlying living

A farm laborer plies his craft in nineteenth-century Ontario. —*Black Creek Pioneer Village*

historical farms and discusses their research and their educational, interpretive, and preservation functions. He examines the problems that living
historical farms are facing and predicts the directions they may take in the
future.

**"The Use of Artifacts and Folk Art in the Folk Museums" by J. Geraint
Jenkins. In *Folklore and Folklife,* edited by Richard Dorson. Chicago:
University of Chicago Press, 1972.**

Jenkins was keeper at the Welsh Folk Museum near Cardiff, Wales, one of
Europe's finest open air museums. In this excellent article, he outlines the
history of folklife museums and suggests that their purpose is "to take the visitor
out of his present-day environment and straight to the people that lived in
some bygone age" (p. 510). Jenkins argues that reerected buildings should
capture the "atmosphere and character of the original," for the "purpose of a
folk museum is to create a picture of national or regional personality" (p. 498).
Such museums help provide a "key to the world of ordinary people; [they] throw
light on their astonishingly ill-documented day-to-day life. It was the prophet
Esdras who said, 'It is not in our minds to be curious of the high things, but of
such as pass by us daily.' That is the theme of folklife studies" (ibid.).

**"Things Unspoken: Learning Social History from Artifacts" by Barbara
Carson and Cary Carson. In *Ordinary People and Everyday Life,* edited
by James Gardner and George Rollie Adams. Nashville: American
Association for State and Local History, 1983.**

In this thoughtful article Barbara and Cary Carson persuasively argue that
a "community's physical form is basic to its self-identification" (p. 192). The

student can, therefore, learn a great deal about the social history of a particular place, period, or people by studying its material culture. When visiting a historic site, they suggest we ask, "What was this place? . . . What activities normally occurred here? Who performed them? How did those people work together to accomplish their tasks or make the activities happen?" (p. 195). By turning attention from artifacts to people and their relationships, "the mind is spurred on beyond mere looking and naming to contemplate the social bonds that formed the basic building blocks of community life" (p. 195).

"The Reality of the Pilgrim Fathers" by James Deetz. *Natural History* 56:6 (November 1969).

The former director of research at Plimoth Plantation, archaeologist James Deetz contends that "a step into the time capsule of re-created Plimoth evokes a living community of Pilgrims—its smoky odors, animal noises, and household clutter—and dispels our misconceptions about colony life" (p. 32). His article describes the research base and mode of interpretation that make Plimoth Plantation a powerful experiment in the presentation of history to the general public.

"A Sense of Another World: History Museums and Cultural Change" by James Deetz. *Museum News* 59 (May-June 1980).

This is one of the first articles to identify the interpretive potential of "full-scale community re-creations, such as Colonial Williamsburg, Old Sturbridge Village, Conner Prairie and Plimoth Plantation. Deetz argues that "a community re-creation can immerse the visitor in the entire world of the past, or at least some approximation of it" (p. 44). He suggests that re-created "communities have the potential of conveying the strongest sense of change in America since its early years, but, at the same time, the highest possibility of failure if not done with skill and a feeling for the time that is being represented" (p. 45).

"The Link from Object to Person to Concept" by James Deetz. In *Museums, Adults, and the Humanities,* edited by Zipporah W. Collins. Washington, D.C.: American Association of Museums, 1981.

In this short article, Deetz relates living history to contemporary anthropological theory in much the same way that Carson connects it with the new social history. Deetz notes that living history museums have the potential to interpret not only material culture, but culture itself, the concepts underlying the objects. Visitors to such museums might be viewed as "anthropological fieldworkers going in to experience a community and elicit from it what they could" (p. 32). Museum interpreters then become "informants" who can share an insider's view of past cultures.

"History Lives." *Museum News* 53:3 (November 1974).

With this issue of the journal of the American Association of Museums, living history became respectable as a mode of interpretation. In a series of articles by William T. Alderson ("Answering the Challenge"), Peter Cook ("The Craft of Demonstration"), Robert Ronsheim ("Is the Past Dead?"), and Holly Sidford ("Stepping into History"), *Museum News* presented the strengths and weaknesses of living history. Ronsheim's cautionary essay was especially prophetic in a Bicentennial era that saw living history becoming a fad.

Involvement with the past—one of living history's primary characteristics. —*Sainte-Marie among the Hurons, Huronia Historical Parks, Ontario Ministry of Tourism and Recreation*

The Interpreter: A Journal for Environmental Communicators 12:2 (Spring 1981).

During the early 1970s, living history programs at National Park Service sites flourished. A 1976 pamphlet, *Living History in the National Park System*, described seventy-one significant programs nationwide. In the late 1970s and early 1980s, however, budgetary restrictions and the reordering of priorities within the National Park Service reduced the number of living history programs. Individual interpreters and sites were encouraged to use their own initiative and to develop limited but effective programs. This issue of *The Interpreter* describes three modest programs at Sequoia and Kings Canyon in southern California, Fort Yellowstone, Wyoming, and Wind Cave, South Dakota. Each program is described by its initiator. The varying interpretive themes of each program are analyzed, as are their particular problems and successes. None of these programs approaches the complex re-created communities described by James Deetz. In their own limited way, however, they are *great* successes.

"Teaching History in Three-D: The History Museum as Educator" by Thomas Weinland. *Connecticut Antiquarian* 30:1 (1978).

A professor of history education at the University of Connecticut, Weinland takes a critical look at living history. "Most museums practicing 'living history' are really practicing craft demonstration. We see the smith smithing, the potter potting, or the farmer farming, and we are made conscious of individual skills we don't have. The consciousness, together with the ambience of old buildings and the misty glow of the good-old-days, can delude us into thinking we have seen history come alive and that we know how it really was" (p. 13). Weinland argues that "such living history may be entertaining . . . , but it is also non-history if not non-sense" (ibid.). His remedy (the "three D's") is demonstration combined with doing it (live-in involvement) and dialogue. He recalls, "In only one museum that I've visited, Colonial Pennsylvania Plantation, is there a clear request to visitors to ask questions. As at Lejre, the staff at Colonial Pennsylvania Plantation has done a great deal of 'live-in' work on its own in an attempt to better understand and interpret life at the farm" (p. 15). Weinland's article was one of the first by an educator to recommend an experimental approach to learning, using living museums as historical laboratories.

"Very Didactic Simulation: Workshops in the Plains Pioneer Experience at the Stuhr Museum" by Roger Welsch. *History Teacher* 7:3 (May 1974).

During the summers of 1973 and 1974, Roger Welsch taught adult workshops in Great Plains folklife at the Stuhr Museum in Grand Island, Nebraska. His classes consisted primarily of secondary school teachers and college students interested in the history and literature of the Great Plains. Welsch felt that the realistic late nineteenth-century atmosphere of Stuhr, with its re-created railroad town and cottonwood log farm was more "didactically stimulating" than an air-conditioned classroom in Lincoln. Long hours were spent not only in talking about the Plains pioneer experience, about which Willa Cather and other people had so eloquently written, but also in reliving it—cooking biscuits over a corncob fire, sleeping in the open, getting the feel of a sod house. The living history movement now has many fine adult live-ins. Roger Welsch's Stuhr workshops were some of the first and are happily among the best documented.

Learning by doing at Colonial Williamsburg. —*Colonial Williamsburg Foundation*

Candle dipping in an authentic, nineteenth-century New England context. —*Old Sturbridge Village; photograph by Robert S. Arnold*

"Experience in History — A Museum Time Machine for Teaching History"
by Bob McQuarie. *Social Education* (January 1981).

Bob McQuarie describes an intensive summer program for children which was developed at Littleton Historical Museum in Littleton, Colorado. "Is it really possible for a seven-, nine-, or eleven-year-old child to assume the role of an adult in the late nineteenth century and actually become skilled enough to hammer out a weather vane, set type for a newspaper, build a baby cradle, or place a dozen bales of hay in the second-story loft of a barn? And can a museum be used to teach the whys of history instead of just who, how, what, where and when?" (p. 57). His answer, based on the experience of the children using the museum's seven-acre living history farm, log schoolhouse, and blacksmith as an outdoor classroom, is "yes, it is possible." This article analyzes the program's development by his interpretation staff. While there are similar living history programs for children in many American and Canadian museums, few have been described as carefully.

"It Wasn't That Simple" by Thomas Schlereth. *Museum News* 56:1 (January-February 1978).

Thomas Schlereth, head of the American studies program at Notre Dame, compares history texts with outdoor museums and finds both lacking. Museums often present "wrong-headed accounts of the past" that are elitist, chauvinistic, rigidly periodized, sexist, and naive. "Historical museum villages are still, with a few exceptions, remarkably peaceable kingdoms, planned communities with over-manicured landscapes or idyllic small towns where the entire populace lives in harmony. . . . The visitor . . . comes away from the museum village with a romanticized, even utopian perspective of the popularly

Old and young together make lard. — *Black Creek Pioneer Village*

acclaimed 'good old days'" (p. 39). Schlereth is particularly bothered by the "homogeneity" of museum villages. He notes that "villages are still largely populated by white, Anglo-Saxon, nondenominational Protestant males" (p. 40). Schlereth suggests that museum curators should become better historians.

"Behind the Scenes at Living History Farms" by Betty Doak Elder. *History News* 34:12 (December 1979).

This entire issue of *History News* was devoted to Elder's story about Pope John Paul II's visit with 340,000 people at Living History Farms on October 4, 1979. According to Jerry George, the director of AASLH, Elder got two stories: "One was the story I sent her for, about what happens to a museum staff and facility when suddenly hundreds of thousands of people are descending on it for such an unprecedented event as a Pope's presence. But also, there's the story she saw when she got there, about how the visit brought out what such a museum and the historical experience it presents can mean for the human spirit" (p. 330). For many, that Thursday in October was one of living history's finest and most publicized hours. Elder's piece captures the excitement and the inner meaning of that day.

"Experimental Archaeology" by Robert Asher. *American Anthropologist* 63 (1961).

Asher's "Experimental Archaeology" is a historic publication—the first scholarly article on its topic. Asher, a Cornell professor, reviews the history of the term, adds a new concept of his own—"imitative experiment"—to the literature, suggests the characteristics needed for valid experiments, and evaluates five case studies of previous experiments worth consideration. Asher's

Interpreting the frustration of frontier life—a rare scene at outdoor museums. —*Historic Fort Wayne*

article laid the foundation for John Coles's two books, *Archaeology by Experiment* (1973) and *Experimental Archaeology* (1979). Together, these two creative and rigorous scholars legitimatized the field of research by simulation.

"Immaterial Material Culture: The Implication of Experimental Research for Folklife Museums" by Jay Anderson. In *Material Culture Studies in America,* edited by Thomas J. Schlereth. Nashville: American Association for State and Local History, 1982.

The author, who at the time of writing was chief of research and interpretation at Living History Farms in Des Moines, Iowa, suggests that experimental archaeology as practiced at Butser Hill and Lejre might be used by living history museums. He argues that, in addition to "correcting our perception of the past, experimental archaeology can also teach us much about contemporary postindustrial cultural behavior and the mental and physical distance we have put between our forefathers and ourselves" (p. 312). Museums such as Plimoth Plantation and the Colonial Pennsylvania Plantation are not only "repositories for the material culture of the past, but also catalysts for questioning one's own culture. . . . they have the potential to become powerful mediums for encouraging in visitors the habit of disciplined self-analysis" (p. 313).

"We Sailed the Columbus Ship" by Robert Marx. *Saturday Evening Post* January 26, 1963.

Robert Marx, the well-known underwater archaeologist, joined a crew of Spanish reenactors in 1962 and sailed a replica of Columbus's *Niña* across the Atlantic. The voyage was a perilous one. The expedition had "no motor, no

An itinerant peddler brings her wares on burro-back. —*Old Cienega Village Museum*

radio, no modern lifesaving equipment, no provisions except roughly the same as Columbus had carried" (p. 26). Quite literally, the only concession made to the modern world was a ration of tobacco for each of the nine men. A major storm blew them almost to the coast of Africa, where they were becalmed for seventeen days and came close to starvation. But they kept sailing. Marx wrote: "To the world outside our small ship, this must seem a foolish dedication to the idea of authenticity. But to the crew of the *Niña II* it was important. We had endured great peril for a historical principle" (p. 36).

"Three Hundred Years Later" by Reid Lewis. *Historic Preservation* 26:4 (July-September 1974).

One of the living history world's most indefatigable reenactors, Reid Lewis documents in this article the 1973 reenactment of the 1673 Jolliet-Marquette voyage. This expedition set a high standard for the many reenactments that followed during the Bicentennial years. And Lewis himself subsequently led a number of voyageur-period voyages throughout the upper Midwest. The 1973 voyage had its high and low moments. "We felt a sense of invigoration and freedom that must have approximated the experience of the original explorers," Lewis wrote. "Beautiful white sand beaches backed by dark pine forests evoked [in us] the fleeting impression of being the first white men to pass that way" (p. 7). But later "raw sewage in the water and an occasional junked car on the bank were grim reminders that we were back in civilization" (p. 9). Lewis captures the ecstasy and depression that infuse and surround so many reenactments.

Mayflower II, one of the best-known projects to use historical simulation as a research and interpretive tool. — *Plimoth Plantation, Inc.*

"Reliving the Past: Experimental Archaeology in Pennsylvania" by Don Callender. *Archaeology* 29:3 (July 1976).

Don Callender was research director of the Colonial Pennsylvania Plantation, a 1770s living historical farm outside Philadelphia. In this important article, he wrote: "The Plantation is not conceived as an open-air museum (such as Colonial Williamsburg, Old Sturbridge Village, or Plimoth Plantation), but as a laboratory in which serious investigators testing their understanding of a colonial farm by seeking to re-create its original environment . . . using the kinds of tools and techniques that were standard in the eighteenth century are doing many of the daily tasks which were performed by colonial husbandmen. . . . In many cases this leads to more questions than answers" (p. 174). Callender goes on to document a number of "imitative experiments" carried out at the plantation during 1974–1975.

"Getting Started in Historical Miniatures" by Tony Adams. *Adventure Gaming* 1:3 (September 1981).

This is a deceptively simple article on the rudiments of the miniature side of adventure gaming. Adams deals with motivation, figures, rules, amassing armies, battlefield terrains, finding kindred spirits, and making converts to the hobby. Much of what he says about miniature gaming applies to reenacting. On motivation, for example, Adams writes: "Every time I read a book or see a movie on a historical battle my mind races as to how it would look as a miniatures game. . . . There are many in the hobby that claim that you don't need to know anything about history to play the games. That is admittedly true. But one of the advantages of war gaming over chess and checkers is the involvement and the color and flavor of a historical period that the player is able to participate in. If you don't know anything about the figures you are moving on the table, then it becomes just another game of chess, and we are aiming for something more than that here" (p. 6).

"Renaissance Fair: Can History Survive the Anachronisms?" by Carol Deakin. *Living History* 1:2 (Fall 1983).

This short but probing review of the Seventh Annual Maryland Renaissance Festival, held outside Washington, D.C., in the autumn of 1983, is typical of the many tough-minded evaluations of living history events that appear regularly in buff magazines. Articles such as Carol Deakin's illustrate the living history movement's growing maturity and willingness to engage in constructive criticism of its own historical simulations. In this particular case, Deakin, who has more than a decade of experience with living history programs involving professionally run museums and serious reenactment organizations, finds the festival lacking. Its promotors see it as "entertainment" first and "a little dose of history" second. Deakin concludes that their "dose of history is so small it is hardly noticeable." Still, she feels many historians could profit from the festival's example "by adding more visitor participation to their living history programs" (p. 30).

"War Games" by Betty Doak Elder. *History News* 36:8 (August 1981).

As the Bicentennial celebration was winding down, Betty Elder asked, "What, if anything, do reenactments have to do with American history?" (p. 8). She went on to cite the opinions of a number of leaders in the living history and historical interpretation field—including Ben Levy, acting chief historian for the National Park Service, and William Brown, who had extensive experience as both a reenactor and a government official. The article ends with a checklist of basic rules necessary to prevent reenactments from becoming "farbfests." This issue of *History News* also contained articles on identifying American military uniforms (1775–1840) and on making authentic reproductions of soldier's clothing that will "pass inspection."

"Yorktown '81" by Thomas Deakin. *Living History* 1:1 (Summer 1983).

The first article in the first issue of *Living History* was devoted to the two hundredth anniversary of the siege of Yorktown. The event was one of the grandest in living history "history," eventually involving four thousand participants and achieving a high level of verisimilitude. Tom Deakin, editor of *Living History* magazine, was a logical choice to tell Yorktown '81's story, since he was overall commander of the re-created armies and spent almost three years planning the event. His report doesn't shy away from the difficult problems the reenactors faced with the National Park Service, which had adopted a policy against reenactments. Deakin describes in some detail the intricate politicking that went on. His evaluation of the entire event ought to be required reading for everyone in the living history movement.

"Battle on Snowshoes" by George Geiger. *F & I War* 2:1 (June 1983).

Serious reenactors are increasingly aware of the research potential of experimental living history projects. A good example is documented by George Geiger in this article. A reenactment unit, Boat Number 17 of Rogers's Rangers, simulated two skirmishes originally fought in January 1757 and March 1758 against the French. The modern unit wanted to test Rogers's original tactics, which included a long winter march on snowshoes, an ambush, a firefight with flintlocks, and a subsequent retreat and winter encampment. Geiger records what his unit learned during its authentic 1983 experiment. As he modestly notes, it both answered and raised questions about military life during the French and Indian War period.

"Pageantry and Tradition: The Reenactment Scene in England" by David Chandler. *Living History Magazine* **1:4 (Summer 1984).**

David Chandler is head of the military history department at Sandhurst, the royal military academy. A professional soldier, scholar, and experienced reenactor, he presents an erudite, comprehensive view of the large reenactment scene in Europe generally and in England in particular. Chandler outlines the history of traditional folk celebrations of history (for example, the Palio in Sienna, U-Helly-Aa Nordic festival in the Shetlands), then describes the many contemporary reenactment organizations and their activities. He continually draws comparisons with North American units and celebrates the positive value of living history as "a war without an enemy."

5. Magazines

W HEN I worked at Living History Farms in Des Moines, Iowa, we had a vintage oak hand-cranked telephone on the kitchen wall of the 1900 farmhouse. Older visitors would spot it immediately and would often share with us their memories of rural party lines. The telephone, they'd say, literally tied the community together. And that was a blessing.

The living history movement is continental in scope and encompasses thousands of museums, reenacting units, black powder clubs, period organizations, specialized associations, craftsmen and suppliers, scholars, and buffs. Publications, especially newsletters, bulletins, journals, and magazines, abound, and like the old rural telephone system, they help to tie this very loose community of historical simulators together.

One of the salient characteristics of living history groups is the importance of face-to-face interaction. Much activity is at the local level, and newcomers generally learn what they need to know by word of mouth and example. Most groups are fiercely democratic, are devoted to developing and enforcing standards of authenticity that would make a graduate student in history blanch, and are antagonistic toward farbs ("polyester soldiers") and toward academics, who are perceived as snooty.

Magazines are a maturing force. They help to break down provincialism, let individuals know what others are doing, suggest new and better ways of practicing historical simulation, and assist in overcoming the defensiveness that marred the early years of the living history movement.

In selecting living history publications for inclusion in this book, I omitted newsletters. There are simply too many, and their audience is usually limited. I did include the journals of umbrella organizations such as the National Muzzle Loading Rifle Association and the magazines that focus on a particular period or theme, especially the Civil War or buckskinning. Many of these publications were started in the 1960s and 1970s, but new ones appear regularly, particularly when a heretofore neglected period or subject (such as the late nineteenth-century Indian wars) is "discovered." The best way to find out about new magazines is to read older ones, which generally carry advertisements for the greenhorn publications.

A typical living history magazine or journal is crammed with a variety of information. It often includes a calendar of upcoming events and reviews of previous ones; features about museums, units, and programs; scholarly articles about historical subjects;

regular columns on period clothing and equipment; debates about authenticity or interpretation; reviews of books, games, and new reproductions; lots of advertisements for events, museums, suppliers, and new units needing recruits; and, most enjoyable, letters from readers. If you really want to find out what's on the minds of people involved in living history, the letters will tell you. They are filled with humor as well as criticism, but most of all they radiate enthusiasm for historical simulation.

Living History Magazine • Circulation, P.O. Box 2309, Reston, Virginia 22090 • Quarterly

This new magazine is the only one that addresses the entire world of living history and seeks as its audience all serious living history reenactors and interpreters. The magazine is a heavily illustrated glossy quarterly and runs to more than fifty pages.

The first issue, published in summer 1983, contained six articles of about two thousand words each and dealt with the 1981 bicentennial of the siege of Yorktown; programs aboard the U.S. *Constellation* in Baltimore, a National Park Service weekend in Fort McHenry in 1861; reports on the reenactment of Saylor's Creek, the last major battle of the Civil War; and the fifth annual Great War re-creation in Pennsylvania. In addition, the magazine includes book reviews, a calendar of events (such as Plimoth Plantation's 1621 Harvest Home and the fortieth anniversary of the D-Day landings), notes on equipage and clothing, profiles of model units, and interviews with leaders in the living history field.

Living History Magazine, the first publication devoted solely to live historical simulation. — *Photograph by Sharli Powell*

Living Historical Farms Bulletin • Association for Living Historical Farms and Agricultural Museums, Smithsonian Institution, Washington, D.C. 20560 • Bimonthly

Now in its fifteenth year, the bulletin contains "ALHFAMiana;" information about regional living history workshops, seminars, and conferences; descriptions of new living museums, programs, and organizations; book reviews, and thumbnail sketches of new publications. The bulletin's focus is primarily on outdoor museums and its audience of professional interpreters.

Living History Journal • Living History Association, Inc., Box 578, Wilmington, Vermont 05363 • Bimonthly

The successor to the association's tabloid-format *Catamount Chronicle,* the *Journal* is a modest bimonthly about twenty pages long and containing an assortment of short articles, book reviews, press releases, news stories, letters, and ads for living history events. Its geographic focus is primarily on the Northeast—from Pennsylvania and New Jersey up. Most of its entries deal with the Revolutionary War period, although recently it has included a short piece on the use and abuse of history in Ireland, a World War II diary, and a review of a book on black soldiers in the Civil War.

Clearinghouse Newsletter • Interp Central, Inc., P.O. Box 28, Chelsea, Michigan 48118 • Bimonthly

This useful bimonthly newsletter has been published by Interp Central, for organizations, individuals, and institutions concerned with interpretation, since 1978. It is North American in scope and contains six regular sections: news bulletins, literature update, employment opportunities, training oppor-

CALENDAR

NOTE: Most of the events listed here are held by invitation only and participants must register with the event sponsor. Names and addresses are given so that you may write for further information.

To list an event in this column send notices to Living History Events, P.O. Box 2309, Reston, VA 22090.

17th Century

September 3, PLYMOUTH, MA. Plimoth Plantation. Militia Muster. Drill, living history. Write to Rosemary Carrol, Plimoth Plantation, P.O. Box 1620, Plymouth, MA 02360.

October 6-7, ST. MARY'S CITY. Maryland's 350th Anniversary Celebration. Militia muster, drill, living history. Write to St. Marie's City, P.O. Box 39. St. Mary's City, MD 20686.

French & Indian War

October 13-14, LIGIONEER, PA. Ft. Ligioneer Days. Encampment, tactical demonstrations, living history. Authentics only. Write to Martin West, Director, Ft. Ligioneer, St. Market St., Ligioneer, PA 15658.

December 2, JEANNETTE, PA. Bushy Run Battlefield. "From the Skin Side Out." 18th century clothing and lifestyles. Write to Jack Leighow, Bushy Run Battlefield, Jeannette, PA 15644.

June 15-16, 1985, JEANNETTE, PA. Bushy Run Battlefield. 4th Annual Assembly. Information Exchange. Tactical demonstration, encampment. Write to Jack Leighow, Bushy Run Battlefield, Jeannette, PA 15644.

July 6-7, 1985, FT. NIAGARA, YOUNGSTOWN, NY. Annual Encampment. Write to Brian Dunnigan,

Ft. Niagara, P.O. Box 169, Youngstown, NY 14174.

Revolutionary War

September 8-9, FT. WAYNE, IN. Military Focus. Encampment, living history. Write to Historic Ft. Wayne, 107 South Clinton St., Ft. Wayne, IN 46802.

September 22-23, WEATHERSFIELD, CT. Battle, living history. American victory. Write to Ken Siegel, 27 Grant St. Needham, MA 02192.

October 6-7, SALISBURY, MD. Pemberton Hall. Battles, encampment. History of soldier program. Write to Dick Van Gelder, 1709 Emerson Ave., Salisbury, MD 21801.

October 20-21, FT. NIAGARA YOUNGSTOWN, NY. Revolutionary War Fall Encampment. A less formal event open to Revolutionary War

Living History Magazine's "Calendar," one of the publication's most avidly read features. — Photograph by Sharli Powell

tunities, want ads, and products. About one-quarter of its entries deal with living history interpretation. Organizations and individuals may submit, free of charge, copy for possible inclusion in the newsletter. Subscribers include outdoor museums and historic sites in thirty states and seven provinces. The newsletter certainly fills a need and could be a useful medium of communication for living history interpreters and institutions.

Tournaments Illuminated • Society for Creative Anachronism, Office of the Registry, P.O. Box 743, Milpitas, California 95035 • Quarterly
Published quarterly by the Society for Creative Anachronism, *Tournaments Illuminated* runs to more than forty pages dense with information. Seventy numbers have appeared since 1965. Generally issues include some twenty short articles of about 1,500 words each. Their range is fascinating. Recent articles have examined the brewing of sake, the manufacture of safe combat arrows, a discussion of the actual duration of the Middle Ages, sigillographica (or the craft of seals), dancing Christmas carols, and books for children. *Tournaments Illustrated* contains much artwork, especially schematic drawings and cartoons, many of which will delight seasoned knights and their ladies.

F & I War • Eighteenth Century Society, R.D. 1, Box 264, New Alexandria, Pennsylvania 15670 • Quarterly
Published by the Eighteenth Century Society, *F & I War* emphasizes the 1750–1763 period but contains articles on the prerevolutionary and Revolutionary War periods (1764–1783) as well. Edited by Ray Washlaski, an experienced reenactor, the magazine is heavily illustrated, runs to about seventy

pages, and generally carries eight articles, all focusing on living history concerns. Recent topics included the problems of establishing authentic camps, an experimental winter campaign on snowshoes, a report on the Fort de Chartres Rendezvous, and blanket-style leggings. *F & I War* can be described as a "pure" living history magazine, of interest primarily to the very serious buff. It's in its fourth year.

The American Star • P.O. Box 1837, San Antonio, Texas 78296 • Bimonthly

The American Star is published by the Society of Mexican War Historians. Tightly focused on the 1830–1849 period, *The American Star* runs to about sixteen pages and contains articles on subjects such as military insignia of the 1840s, infantry uniforms and equipment of the Mexican War, and reviews of books and even articles in other journals. The editor is Kevin Young, one of a new generation of living historians. ("I haven't fired a shot in mock anger for four years," he once remarked.)

The American Rendezvous Magazine • P.O. Box 657, Los Altos, California 94023-0657 • Bimonthly

Printed on heavy coated stock and lavishly illustrated with four-color illustrations, *American Rendezvous* is to buckskinners what *Antiques* is to collectors. Founded in 1983, the magazine runs to more than sixty pages and contains excellent articles on all aspects of the western living scene. Recently it has discussed Sutter's Fort, historical research for the buckskinner, the well-dressed mountain man, and Fort Bridger. The magazine carries regular features on period clothing, open fire cooking, fur trade history, modern rendezvous, and especially art. Painters who specialize in portraying western folklife are given flattering attention in *American Rendezvous,* and there are frequently in-depth studies of well-known artists, such as David Wright and Betty Billups, who base their work on years of experience reenacting western history. The magazine also carries a twelve-page "Gazette" which both previews and reviews the many rendezvous held annually in the West.

Muzzle Blasts • **National Muzzle Loading Rifle Association, P.O. Box 67, Friendship, Indiana 47021 • Monthly**

One of the oldest of the magazines dealing with living history, *Muzzle Blasts* has been published by the National Muzzle Loading Rifle Association since 1939. The magazine often has several hundred advertisements per issue and announcements from clubs throughout the nation. It is a no-nonsense publication of obvious value to the individual seriously interested in black powder rifles, and many subscribers are also living history buffs. It runs to about seventy pages.

Then and Now • **P.O. Box 842, Mount Vernon, Washington 98273 • Bimonthly**

For ten years *Black Powder Times* was read by the black powder enthusiast with a bias toward living history. In 1984, to avoid confusion with *Black Powder Report* and *Blackpowder Annual,* Fred Holder changed the name of his magazine to *Then and Now.* Happily, it's still the same expert amalgam of expertly written articles on living museums, muzzle loading, reproduction crafts, reenactment units, black powder club news, book reviews, and happenings in the world of today's rendezvous. *Then and Now* runs to forty pages and is appropriately illustrated.

Muzzle Blasts celebrates the National Muzzle Loading Rifle Association's 50th anniversary. — *Photograph by Sharli Powell*

***Black Powder Report* • P.O. Box 789, Big Timber, Montana 59011 • Monthly**

Formerly the *Buckskin Report*, *Black Powder Report* runs to sixty pages and is published "by buckskinners for buckskinners." John D. Baird, its editor, is also a founder of the National Association of Primitive Riflemen, whom *Black Powder Report* addresses.

Each month about twenty feature articles discuss living history subjects such as pemmican, buckskin clothing, winter camping, the problems of authenticity, and—of course—muzzle loaders. Rendezvous of primitive riflemen are announced and reviewed regularly, as are books on the fur trade period. *Black Powder Report* is in its twelfth year of publication.

***Muzzleloader* • Rebel Publishing Company, Route 5, Box 347M, Texarkana, Texas 75503 • Bimonthly**

Similar to *Black Powder Report*, but with a more eastern focus, is *Muzzleloader*. Published since 1971 by Oran Scurlock, *Muzzleloader* runs to seventy pages. A high proportion of its articles have a historical bent: "Plains Indian Art of the Fur Trade Era," "Germanic Flintlock Rifles," and "Fort Niagara Falls Again" are examples. A regular feature for women by Shari Wanemacher indicates *Muzzleloader*'s interest in attracting the family trade.

***The Backwoodsman* • Route 8, Box 576, Livingston, Texas 77351 • Bimonthly**

Charlie Ritchie has been putting out his magazine since 1979. In its sixty pages Ritchie and his field editors present a wide spectrum of articles on every aspect of buckskinning. Their features are clearly the work of experienced muzzle loaders, reenactors, and backwoodsmen. The May-June 1984 issue contained, for example, articles on Gohn Brothers (the Amish supply house in Indiana), experiments in Indian shield making, gourd craft, an evaluation of recent reproduction products, "Hawkenizing" a rifle, the second part on a feature on the chemistry of black powder, and a reprint from an 1867 issue of *Harper's* on "a stage ride to Colorado." *The Backwoodsman* also has a rich classified section and many notes on smaller suppliers.

Blackpowder Annual • Pioneer Press, P.O. Box 684, Union City, Tennessee 38261

Blackpowder Annual is published by Dixie Gun Works of Union City, Tennessee, one of the oldest of the living history sutlers. It runs to more than a hundred glossy pages and contains a mixture of twenty articles reflecting the varied interests of blackpowder advocates. The second issue (1984) included articles entitled "Survival of a Revival: The NMLRA's First Fifty Years," "Time-Tripping into the Eighteenth Century," "Blackpowder Turkey Tactics," and "In Search of Beaver Tail Stew."

Editor Sharon Cunningham notes that her readers prefer features on black powder hunting and historical and nostalgia pieces.

Civil War Monitor • Box 1862, Centreville, Virginia 22020 • Bimonthly

The *Monitor* surveys about seventy current periodicals that cover the Civil War period. It includes sections on research sources, nonliterary sources, and military, naval, geographic, political, economic, and cultural history as well as biography. The *Monitor* generally contains about one hundred fifty entries, many of which deal with living history. Most of these are included in the nonliterary sources section. The editor is Joseph Harsh, professor of history at George Mason University.

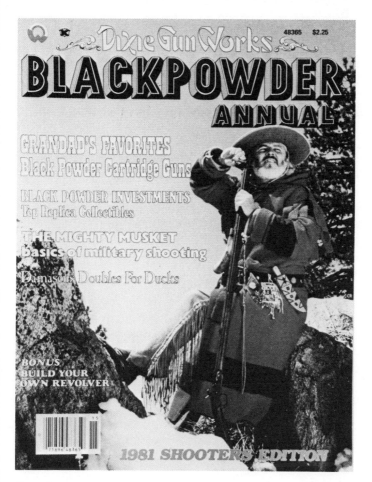

One of many blackpowder magazines. — *Photograph by Sharli Powell*

Blue and Gray • P.O. Box 28685, Columbus, Ohio 43228 • Bimonthly

David and Robin Roth broke new ground in 1983 with their attractive publication, *Blue and Gray*. They included not only the usual articles on Civil War history ("Escape! Confederate John Hunt Morgan's Escape from the Ohio Penitentiary in 1863") but also sections on reenacting and living history, board games, collectibles, tours of seldom visited battlefields, relic collecting, and the home front. The Roths packaged this fascinating variety of articles in a glossy, well-illustrated, and well-designed magazine. It has proved a success, reaching a broad audience that includes not only the usual male reenactor but also simulation game players, the growing number of women interested in the civilian aspect of the war, and buffs who enjoy traveling to battlefields equipped with a well-thought-out interpretive tour.

Camp Chase Gazette • Chase Publishing, 3984 Cinn-Zanesville Road, N.E., Lancaster, Ohio 43130 • Monthly

One of the oldest magazines published solely for Civil War buffs, *Camp Chase Gazette* is edited by William Keitz, who began the *Gazette* in 1972 in an effort to improve interpretation of the Civil War period. In its thirty-six pages, the *Gazette* generally presents five features. A recent representative issue contained a Civil War diary, a Christmas letter from the front, instructions for making authentic Confederate oilcloth, and some thoughts on "the past campaign year" and the difficulty of truly "reliving history." The magazine also contains detailed announcements of upcoming campaigns, critiques of specific events, and an excellent letter section called "Camp Gossip."

The Skirmish Line, first published in 1955, is one of living history's oldest magazines. — *Photograph by Sharli Powell*

The Skirmish Line • North-South Skirmish Association, 9700 Royerton Drive, Richmond, Virginia 23228 • Bimonthly

The journal of one of living history's oldest organizations, *Skirmish Line* is a first-rate publication. First published in 1955, it runs to about thirty pages and contains articles on the association's comings and goings, events, association "teams" or serious units, reviews of reproduction firearms, and a good selection of advertisements from sutlers specializing in the Civil War period. The journal is a model for similar organizations.

Muzzeloading Artilleryman • Century Publications, Inc., 4 Water Street, Arlington, Massachusetts 02174 • Quarterly

The publishers of *The Muzzleloading Artilleryman* suggest that it's "for everyone interested in cannons." Actually, their excellent magazine should be read by all serious reenactors. First published in 1979, this quarterly is thoroughly professional and is a good advertisement for the living history field in general. It runs to forty pages and contains features on exceptional reenactment units and places to visit—usually forts, museums, and battlefields— as well as reviews of serious living history events, short reports, evaluations of reproduction cannons, guides to suppliers, book reviews, letters from serious buffs, and good historical notes. *The Muzzleloading Artilleryman* is printed on a good heavy stock, is well designed, and contains excellent photographs.

THE POINT

SEPTEMBER/OCTOBER 1983   Volume 9   Number 5

WORLD WAR TWO HISTORICAL REENACTMENT SOCIETY, INC.

First published in 1974, *The Point* chronicles World War II reenactments. —*Photograph by Sharli Powell*

Regimental Observer • 6 Lambert Lane, Springfield, Illinois 62704 • Quarterly

Edited and published by Captain John Satterlee, an experienced reenactor, this Civil War magazine includes short pieces on Civil War soldiers, battles, and events, notes on the activities of reenactment units—primarily midwestern, reproductions of period newspaper articles, and a good selection of Satterlee's well-seasoned thoughts on the living history scene, particularly in and around "Lincoln Land." The *Observer* runs to about twenty-four pages and is always a good read. 1984 was its fourth year of publication.

Ladies Victorian Revue • c/o Camp Chase Gazette, 3984 Cinn-Zanesville Road, N.E., Lancaster, Ohio 43130 • Monthly

Pamela Keitz, editor of the *Revue*, hopes to make it a forum for female and male civilian reenactors and not just a publication that reprints original articles from women's magazines of the period. At present it is primarily the latter, but many of the documents it reproduces are fascinating. Recent examples include selections from *Harper's* and *Godey's* for the early Civil War months, letters from women to their husbands at the front, and period cartoons. Nevertheless, the *Revue* will probably evolve into a civilian version of *Camp Chase Gazette*, which most reenactors would agree is definitely needed. The social and cultural history of the 1861–1865 period is not being adequately covered by living history publications, despite the growing interest in nonmilitary folklife.

The Point • 3448 Tedmar Avenue, St. Louis, Missouri 63139 • Bimonthly

First published in 1974, *The Point* is the journal of the World War II Historical Reenactment Society. Each issue is about thirty pages long and consists entirely of reports from individual units and advertisements submitted by members and World War II suppliers. In addition, there are informal features by members on such topics as the conversion of World War II U.S. garrison caps into mock Russian "pilotka" or the possibility of joining with European units in a reenacted D-Day campaign.

Military Modelling • U.S. subscription agent: Joseph Daileda, 4314 West 238th Street, Torrance, California 90505 • Monthly

A folio-sized British monthly, _Military Modelling_ began publishing in 1970. It is the only serious magazine that covers _all_ aspects of military gaming and modeling. For the living history interpreter or reenactor, this is the best introduction to the hobby. A typical issue contains eighty pages, is heavily illustrated, and can usually be purchased at good craft shops which carry war games and modeling supplies. The magazine regularly carries features on historic regiments, period uniforms, modeling suggestions, reviews of new modeling products and war games, book reviews, monthly club news, letters, notes on the reenactment scene (for example, the Sealed Knot), and hundreds of advertisements for every facet of the hobby. _Military Modelling_ often contains special long features on subjects such as microcomputer war gaming. Few history buffs can resist this magazine; Americans find it turns them into instant Anglophiles! Every year the publishers also put out an extra edition dealing with a particular subject, such as miniature war gaming. Called the _Manual,_ it delves into one aspect of the hobby in particular depth.

World leader for Wargamers & Modelmakers

Military Modelling

FEBRUARY 1984 85p

M.A.P. MODEL MAGAZINE

FREE
MILITARY BOOKS
COMPETITION
INSIDE!

VEHICLES
Hungarian WW2 AFVs
Half Tonne Land Rovers
Plans & Colour

WARGAMES
Building A
Balanced Force

FIGURES
Modelling
Marshal Mannerheim

FLAGS
Confederate
Flags In Colour

FREE Pull-Out
"A-Z Of Figure Modelling"
Supplement

Military Modelling, the only magazine covering all aspects of military gaming and modeling. — *Photograph by Sharli Powell*

Campaigns • Combined Book Service, P.O. Box 577, Conshohocken, Pennsylvania 19428 • Bimonthly

First published in 1976, *Campaigns* is similar to the excellent British magazine *Military Modelling* in that it covers all aspects of the military gaming and modeling hobby. It runs to about sixty-four pages and generally contains four or five long features plus columns on new products, club news, military subjects, book reviews ("the good, the pretty good, and the fairly decent"), modeling, and events. *Campaigns* is a glossy magazine, rich with color illustrations and written with verve and wit. It is a reminder that people pursue a serious hobby not only to satisfy a deep curiosity but also to have fun. A recent issue contained articles on the history of military music, U.S. Army headgear, 1851–1902, uniforms of the "Raj," and the pike as a tactical weapon.

Miniature Wargames • A. E. Morgan Publications, Ltd., Stanley House, 9 West Street, Epsom, Surrey, KT18 7RL • Monthly

First published in 1982, *Miniature Wargames* is a folio-sized glossy magazine roughly fifty pages long that is devoted entirely to the miniatures end of the war game hobby. It's a good complement to *Military Modelling,* which it resembles in format and approach. A typical issue contains about twenty feature articles covering subjects such as the history of miniature war gaming, debates ("Are Toy Soldiers Really Redundant?" "Making a Case for Toy Soldiers," and so forth), particular wars ("Zulu Wars," "World War I in the Adriatic"), reviews of figures (new lines of miniatures) and books, news of clubs and events, and in-depth discussions of tactics ("Command in Early Medieval Warfare"). Articles are interspersed with advertisements.

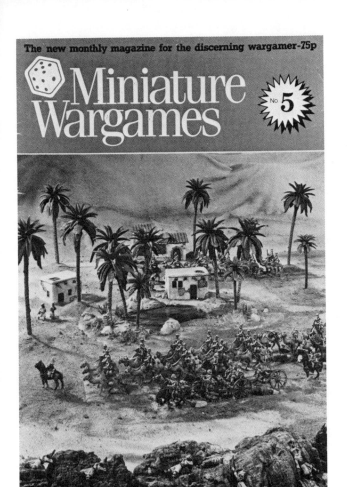

The new monthly magazine for the discerning wargamer-75p

Miniature Wargames

No 5

A British magazine, *Miniature Wargames,* focuses on the toy soldier. — *Photograph by Sharli Powell*

The Courier • Box 1878, Brockton, Massachusetts 02403 • **Bimonthly**

The Courier began publication in 1979 and has won the H. G. Wells Award for best miniature gaming magazine every year since. It is a bimonthly about sixty-four pages long and usually contains eight feature articles. Some are historical essays on various wars or battles ("The Sudan, 1855–1899,"- "Die Katastrophe von 1806"). Others review rule systems for particular miniature war games ("The Riot Wargame," "The Battle of Camden"); discuss the tactics used in a particular historical period; comment on conventions; and review historical films ("Film and the Zulu War"). Regular departments provide news of the hobby, evaluations of new products, and, most extraordinary, a form for rating all aspects of *The Courier* itself. (On a scale of 1 to 9, with 9 being "great," readers generally rate each issue of the magazine about 7.)

Military Digest • **McCoy Publishing Enterprises, Inc., P.O. Box 5526, Madison, Wisconsin 53705** • **Monthly**

One of the older magazines in the war game hobby, the *Digest* first appeared in 1973. Like its British counterpart, *Miniature Wargames,* it deals solely with the miniature side of the avocation. A typical month's issue contains about four very serious features (for example, "Use of Cavalry in the Napoleonic Period," "Wargame Rules for the Second Punic War," "Battle of Gazala," "Napoleonic Wargaming at West Point"); shorter pieces on new products; club news from the United States and Canada; notes on conventions, game fests, and so forth; and advertisements for rules, standard series of miniatures, and retailers. The editor, Gene McCoy, is an old tank man, so the *Digest* is rich in war games that feature armor.

Strategy and Tactics • Simulations Publications, Inc., Dragon Publishing, P.O. Box 72089, Chicago, Illinois 60609 • Bimonthly

First published independently in 1967, *Strategy and Tactics* was purchased by Simulations Publications, Inc., two years later. (It is now owned by TSR.) It's a bimonthly, runs to about sixty-four pages, and contains in four of its six issues a war game (complete with map, counters, rules, historical background, and so forth). *Strategy and Tactics* also contains historical features on particular battles, campaigns, and periods; long evaluations of important new board games; interviews with designers; reviews of current games and books; letters; and a "feedback" section that allows readers to rate the issue's contents as well as current and proposed games. *Strategy and Tactics* is to board games what *The Courier* is to miniatures.

Fire and Movement • Baron Publishing Company, P.O. Box 820, La Puente, California 91747 • Bimonthly

One index of the maturity of the war gamer's hobby is *Fire and Movement*, a magazine of reviews. Since 1979 it has provided in-depth evaluations of major board games. The number of games in print reached 4,000 in 1985, so a magazine of reviews is almost a necessity. *Fire and Movement* also prints interviews with designers such as James Dunnigan and lengthy letters from readers in a section called "Crossfire" (it really is!). In addition the magazine provides a forum for discussion of the hobby in general. *Fire and Movement* provides good illustrations, especially of the maps of games reviewed.

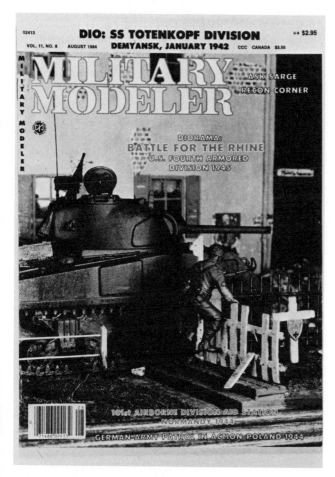

Military Modeler caters to the interests of enthusiasts who build historical dioramas that simulate military scenes. — *Photograph by Sharli Powell*

Military Modeler • 10968 Via Frontera, San Diego, California 92127 •
Monthly

As its name implies, *Military Modeler* will be of interest to the model
enthusiast who specializes in military figures and scenes. (The same publisher
also puts out *Scale Ship Modeler* and *Scale Modeler.*) The museum interpreter
and living history reenactor will be impressed by the magazine's emphasis on
historical authenticity. A typical issue will generally evaluate four or five
dioramas depicting historical scenes. Frequently, these scenes have great
emotional impact and convey in visual terms an important interpretive
theme. A recent issue discussed a diorama in which a German army patrol
attacked a Polish "safe house" for Jewish resistance fighters. Much of the
article dealt with the historical background of Jewish military activities on
the Eastern Front. *Military Modeler* runs to about seventy-four pages, is
heavily illustrated, and carries regular reviews of new products, books, and
conventions.

PART III.
SUITING UP

6. Organizations

THE first living history unit to which I belonged was the Washington Boulevard Confederates. You won't find anything like them in Frank Leslie's *Illustrated History of the Civil War*, and the Daughters of the Confederacy never erected a statue in their honor. We were an original circa 1949. Washington Boulevard—being more of a neighborhood than a street—also raised a Union contingent. Every Saturday and for much of the summer the two ragtag but very enthusiastic outfits refought the Civil War. We roamed the nearby fields and forests like a pack of half-trained puppies. Crayoned battle flags flew, firecrackers snapped, and Rebel yells pierced the Pennsylvania landscape—in falsetto. We were all in boy heaven.

Twenty-five years later, upward of a hundred thousand adults enjoy living history, as a hobby or as a vocation. Since the 1930s, when the National Muzzle Loading Rifle Association was founded, each new generation has added a new "army" of reenactors. At first it was just the buckskinners and black powder riflemen. Then the Civil War centennial of the 1960s and the Bicentennial of the 1970s and early 1980s called to arms thousands of "reactivated" units. Recent decades have also seen a resurgence of interest in the mountain men, the voyageurs, and the "neglected" American wars: the French and Indian, 1812–1814, the Mexican, that on the Indian frontier, and World Wars I and II.

Continentally, the living history scene is kaleidoscopic, with new organizations and units forming and re-forming continually. Many serious buffs are not content to join just one unit but develop various characters, or "impressions," in several groups. And if they can't find a group they like, they simply go out and start a new organization. (On the notice board of Asgard, a shop near me in Bowling Green, Kentucky, which sells miniatures and board games and serves as an informal headquarters for reenactors, there are currently advertisements for half a dozen new groups interested in simulating the Middle Ages, the Black Hawk War, the Civil War, and, most astounding, the Napoleonic period and the Zulu wars in South Africa. Six months from now there will be another batch of recruiting posters.)

In assembling this chapter I've steered clear of individual living history *units*—regiments, clubs, and other organizations re-creating a specific historical entity. These units number in the thousands and are best located through the directories published annually by magazines such as *F & I War* and the *Camp Chase Gazette*. Many other publications issue updated lists of organized units, often by state. *Muzzle Blasts* does so for the National Muzzle Loading Rifle Association, and recently Beau Jacques (P. C. House) listed 500 regional and state black powder clubs in *The Muzzle Loaders Source Book*. In short, the living history movement's publications are the best guide to specific groups.

Here I have described the "umbrella" organizations, often national or regional in scope, that provide a stable network for living history museums, interpreters, and reenacting units. The majority of these selections have been active for ten years or more. The granddaddy is the National Muzzle Loading Rifle Association, which celebrated its fiftieth anniversary in 1983. Others, such as the North-South Skirmish Association and the Brigade of the American Revolution, have been active since the 1950s and early 1960s. Still, many important coordinating organizations, such as the Association for Living Historical Farms and Agricultural Museums and the Eighteenth Century Society, are comparatively young but have nevertheless been included because of their significance.

Association for Living Historical Farms and Agricultural Museums • Room 5035, National Museum of American History, Smithsonian Institution, Washington, D.C. 20650

Mercifully dubbed ALHFAM ("Al'fam"), the association was founded in 1970 and is based in the Smithsonian Institution. It was the first group actually to use the term "living history" in its title. ALHFAM has about 250 active institutional and individual members. Most are associated with outdoor museums. It publishes a bimonthly *Bulletin* and a record of its yearly meeting, the *Annual.* In addition to its annual conference, usually held in June at a major North American museum, ALHFAM regularly sponsors regional workshops that emphasize practical instruction in living history interpretation. ALHFAM has recently sought to attract as members museums and organizations that are not necessarily agriculturally oriented.

Intermuseum Cooperation Committee • c/o Association for Living Historical Farms and Agricultural Museums, Room 5035, National Museum of American History, Smithsonian Institution, Washington, D.C. 20650

Spurred on by the success of the Midwest Open Air Museum Coordinating Council, ALHFAM in 1981 established seven regional units. They include New England, the Northeast, the Southeast, the Midwest, the Mountain-plains, the Western, and Canada (all provinces). Each functions as a clearinghouse and network. Most hold regular workshops on living history interpretation. Some publish newsletters, like *The Kudzu*—"we cover the South." The obvious result of the various units' work has been to strengthen the movement toward professional standards in living history museums large and small.

Midwest Open Air Museums Coordinating Council • c/o Lincoln Log Cabin, R.R. 2, Lerna, Illinois 62440

The council was formed in 1978 by a number of young professionals from various outdoor museums and historic sites in the Midwest. Most were active members of the Association for Living Historical Farms and Agricultural Museums and felt the need for a regional network by which they could exchange ideas on research, interpretation, collections, and issues facing living museums. The council has proved a smashing success. It publishes a monthly newsletter, sponsors a two-three day annual meeting, organizes seminars, and facilitates exchanges of museum staff. Both individuals and institutions are members.

The 1983 and 1984 interpreter seminars held at Greenfield Village in Dearborn drew more than one hundred serious participants from all segments of the living history movement and were described by one museum professional of long standing as "two of the most enjoyable, rigorous, and useful meetings on historical interpretation I've attended — ever."

Living History Association, Inc. • P.O. Box 578, Wilmington, Vermont 05363

Incorporated in 1980, the association is essentially a "chamber of commerce" for reenactors in the Northeast. Its membership is more than three hundred, including many sutlers, units, and corporate sponsors. While the association thus far has focused primarily on the colonial period, it welcomes people involved in other periods as well. From the start, its founders have sought to foster cooperation between serious reenactors and museums, historic sites, and educational institutions. Its goal is to "enhance authentic interpretations of our American heritage" by encouraging interaction between full-time and volunteer true believers in living history.

The Living History Association publishes the bimonthly *Living History Journal,* an attractive successor to the earlier tabloid *Catamount Chronicle.* Both the earlier and later publications mix information on regional events, letters from buffs, articles on social history and many, many advertisements from suppliers and historic sites.

Interpretation Canada • Box 2667, Postal Station D, Ottawa, Ontario K1P 5W7

Interpretation Canada was established in 1975 as a national organization of interpreters. "Separated by geography, bureaucracy and academic discipline," Canadian interpreters realized that they needed to "stay in touch, develop their art and to pursue a common goal." The organization welcomes historic guides, naturalists, visitor service officers—anyone, in fact, whose job is "telling the story of our land and its people." It unites interpreters from museums, historic sites, schools, wildlife centers, zoos, and a variety of national, provincial, and municipal parks.

The organization publishes a quarterly magazine, *Interpretation Canada,* and newsletters for each of its five sections: Atlantic, Ontario, Central, Alberta, and British Columbia. Interpretation Canada is without question one reason for the widespread use of serious living history interpretation in Canadian museums and historic sites.

"Grumpk d'Bohun," a Kansas member of the Society for Creative Anachronism. — *Photograph by R. Tim McGill*

Reenactment of a Revolutionary War period court-martial at Colonial Williamsburg, one of the many living history museums working cooperatively with reenactors. —*Colonial Williamsburg Foundation*

National Muzzle Loading Rifle Association • P.O. Box 67, Friendship, Indiana 47021

Established in 1933, the National Muzzle Loading Rifle Association now numbers more than twenty-five thousand members. While an all-pervading interest in muzzle-loading rifles, both antique and reproduced, is the chief characteristic of the association and its monthly journal, *Muzzle Blasts,* members have from the start shown a concurrent enthusiasm for the pioneers and soldiers who once used these firearms. Members speak of their participation in association events as an "experience in heritage." Twice a year, in spring and fall, more than ten thousand members convene at Friendship, Indiana, for a week of sharpshooting and fellowship. Recently, a "primitive camp" has been established at these matches for the several thousand members who wish to rendezvous more authentically.

Society for Creative Anachronism • P.O. Box 743, Milpitas, California 95035

The Society for Creative Anachronism was founded in 1966 at Berkeley, California, and has grown to include approximately fifteen thousand active members. It is highly organized along feudal lines into shires, baronies, and kingdoms. Frequent tournaments and courts are held at the local and regional level. Once a year, more than six thousand members gather for a week to fight the Pennsic Wars in a meadow outside Slippery Rock, Pennsylvania. The Society publishes a quarterly, *Tournaments Illuminated,* and a variety of other guides and manuals. The Society for Creative Anachronism differs from most other living history organizations in that it has, from the start, encouraged membership from both sexes.

Williamsburg interpreters confer with members of the Brigade of the American Revolution at the Colonial Fair. —*Colonial Williamsburg Foundation*

The Eighteenth Century Society • Box 264, R.D. 1, New Alexandria, Pennsylvania 15670

A comparatively young organization, the Eighteenth Century Society was formed in 1981. Its focus is on the 1750s and 1760s, but it counts as members both individuals and units interested in interpeting early and later periods in the eighteenth century. The society has more than a thousand members scattered over North America, with a concentration in the Northeast and Midwest. Annual events include a seminar at the Bushy Run Battlefield outside Pittsburgh and a rendezvous at Fort de Chartres, Illinois, and Friendship, Indiana. Associated with the society is an umbrella military reenactment organization, the Forces of Montcalm and Wolfe. The society publishes *F & I War.*

North American Voyageur Conference • 1756 Orchard Street, Des Plaines, Illinois 60018

The conference serves as a clearinghouse for the approximately two hundred organized brigades which re-create the life of the voyageur and *coureur de bois.* Most of these brigades are independent, but an increasing number are associated with historic sites, especially those concerned with the period of the fur trade and the French and Indian War.

Members receive a *Voyageur Newsletter,* published quarterly and containing a directory, a calendar of rendezvous and related events, glossaries of terms, and notes on foodways, period clothing, history, folklore, and current brigade activities.

The North American Voyageur Conference holds its annual meeting the first week in November, usually at a midwestern historic site, and organizes a major canoe trip or two each year.

Brigade of the American Revolution • c/o Adjutant John Muller, 7 Crescent Place, Ho-Ho-Kus, New Jersey 07423

Founded in 1962, the Brigade of the American Revolution has more than a thousand members enrolled in approximately 125 units. Membership is limited to units—British, Loyalist, Hessian, French, Spanish, and Continental—but many women, children, and craftsmen join the Brigade's Civilian Corps. The brigade's standards of authenticity are extremely high. Brigade units sponsor about two events a month, as well as an annual cantonment in New Windsor, Connecticut, and a spring School of the Soldier, an advanced workshop in living history interpretation. The brigade also publishes a fine magazine, *The Dispatch.*

Northwest Department, Brigade of the American Revolution • 576 Carolyn Drive, Brunswick, Ohio 44212

In 1972, ten years after the Brigade of the American Revolution was founded, it became obvious to many of its midwestern members that a regional branch in the Old Northwest was necessary. Propinquity, not politics, was the reason for being. With the Bicentennial rapidly approaching, midwesterners felt that western reenactments could be more easily organized by a regional organization.

The department has stood the test of time. Since 1977, it has published an excellent quarterly newsletter, the *BAR Shot,* which carries news and reviews of events in the Old Northwest, notes on new offerings from sutlers, letters, and policy discussions which reflect the brigade's continuing concern with high standards of authenticity.

The Northwest Department has about three hundred active individual

N.W.T.A. Courier

Volume VII No. 8

October 1983

Oh, Lord help me, how I do love them army beans

(or 40 years under pressure) see page 2

The Northwest Territory Alliance's newsletter, *Courier*. — *Photograph by Sharli Powell*

Two members of the Charleston (Illinois) Guard enjoy the 1840's militia muster at Lincoln Log Cabin. —*Lincoln Log Cabin State Historic Site*

members and twenty-two units, primarily based on historic regiments, militia, and so forth, which originally served in the western theater of the Revolutionary War.

North West Territory Alliance • c/o *The Courier,* 380 Hawthorn, Glen Ellen, Illinois 60137

A midwestern organization, the North West Territory Alliance was founded in 1974 in Racine, Wisconsin. The alliance concentrates on the Revolutionary War period (1776–1783) and limits membership to serious units interpreting the history of that era. It is unusually active and sponsors demonstrations, concerts, fashion shows, and encampments at numerous midwestern rendezvous and festivals. The largest is the Feast of the Hunter's Moon, held at Fort Ouiatenon, outside Lafayette, Indiana. The alliance publishes *The Courier,* an excellent newsletter. It encourages serious interpretation of camp life and has a high percentage of women members.

American Mountain Men • Box 259, Lakeside, California 92042

The American Mountain Men began in 1968 and now numbers more than a thousand active members. The organization focuses on the period from 1800 to 1840 and stresses authenticity. Requirements for membership are difficult; this is the Marine Corps of black powder groups. It solicits "men who are willing to step back in time and live life as man was meant to live it, a Free Individual, a true Son of the Wilderness." Members are loosely organized and participate in seasonal rendezvous, often under strenuous conditions. It takes at least a year for a "pilgrim" to qualify for full membership.

Muskets fire on Militia Day at Old Sturbridge Village. —*Old Sturbridge Village; photograph by Robert S. Arnold*

National Association of Primitive Riflemen • P.O. Box 789, Big Timber, Montana 59011

Founded a decade ago by John Baird, editor of *The Black Powder Report*, the National Association of Primitive Riflemen has grown to 6,500 members. They rendezvous yearly at a wilderness site somewhere in the West. In 1983, more than three thousand members camped fifty miles inside a national forest near Glacier National Park, along the Canadian border. The association covers a wide period of history—from prerevolutionary days to the period when cartridge guns were popular for buffalo hunting. It uses old-time rules for its matches—offhand shooting, open sites, loading from the pouch, and so forth—and charcoal-drawn targets. Although the association encourages living history, it doesn't limit itself to purists. Rather, its events stress informal enjoyment of history and old-fashioned shooting.

1840s Living History Association • c/o Kevin Young, P.O. Box 1837, San Antonio, Texas 78296

Typical of many new organizations that focus on a specific period and stress authenticity, the 1840s Living History Association has several hundred members, primarily in the Southwest. They specialize in the social and military history of the period from 1830 to 1850. The association puts out a modest journal, *American Star*, and sponsors encampments at a variety of sites associated with the Mexican War.

Members of the Richmond Grays bivouac at the Meadow Farm. —*Photograph by Patti Ferguson*

North-South Skirmish Association • 9700 Royerton Drive, Richmond, Virginia 23228

One of the oldest of the living history organizations, the North-South Skirmish Association was founded in 1950 to provide a vehicle for competition with Civil War firearms. It now has more than 175 units and three thousand individual members. Twice yearly, the association holds a national skirmish at its 250-acre home range, Fort Shenandoah, in Virginia. Most members are military buffs, collectors, and marksmen. The association has published a bimonthly journal, *Skirmish Line,* since 1955. While the organization focuses on target shooting, the majority of its units are authentically uniformed and equipped, and the camp life aspects of its events have become progressively more accurate historically.

Missouri Civil War Reenactors Association • c/o Bob Talbott, 4405 South Cottage, Independence, Missouri 64055

Established in the early 1980s, the MCWRA is an excellent example of a regional association. It is the Civil War analogue of the North West Territory Alliance or the Northwest Department of the Brigade of the American Revolution. It draws its members—reenactors of both sexes—primarily from Missouri and the surrounding states.

Every year in August or September, the association stages a major Civil War living history/battle reenactment at one of the three Civil War sites administered by the Missouri Division of Parks and Historic Preservation. The events rotate, so in 1985 the Battle of Lexington will be simulated, in 1986 Pilot Knob, and in 1987 Athens. Participation in each event is by invitation only and attains a high level of authenticity. Pilot Knob in 1983 drew four hundred serious reenactors.

Perhaps most significant about the association and similar groups is their success in winning the support of national, state, and local historical agencies. This recent development indicates an increasing acceptance of both buffs and living history interpretation on the part of the public history establishment.

American Living History Association • P.O. Box 7355, Austin, Texas 78712

A slightly older counterpart of the 1840s Association is the American Living History Association. It focuses on the period 1830 to 1870, especially the Civil War years. Michael Moore, one of its founders, calls the association a "museum without a site." The several hundred members are unapologetic purists who consider themselves living history interpreters, not reenactors. The organization began publishing *Phoenix*, a quarterly, in 1980. It runs to about thirty pages and provides members with information about various aspects of living history. The association has recently worked closely with the National Park Service in providing interpretive encampments at both Gettysburg and Vicksburg.

General Miles Marching and Chowder Society • c/o John Sutton, Box 345, Fort Davis, Texas 79734

Named after General Miles of the Fifth U.S. Infantry, a popular hero of the Indian Wars, the society was founded in 1978 by professional and amateur historians interested in the post–Civil War Indian War campaigns. Many of

In a quiet moment in camp, five experienced reenactors from the 98th New York pose for a modern Matthew Brady. —*Photograph by Richard Cheatham*

its members have been front-line living history interpreters with the National Park Service, with state historical societies, or with regional museums in the West. The society gives them an opportunity to keep in touch with the nonprofessional but equally serious buff. Together they participate in a week-long, extremely rigorous annual encampment. Recent campaigns have taken them from the Chiracahua Mountains of Arizona and the West Texas Plains to the 100th Meridian at Fort Hartsuff, Nebraska. All members represent regular U.S. Army regiments that saw service west of the Mississippi from 1867 to 1891. Admission is limited to serious reenactors who demonstrate an interest in better understanding the daily life of these earlier neglected G.I. Joes of the West. Great store is set by using living history as a research tool to "get it right."

The California Bounty Hunters • c/o Gary and Carol Helms, 1707 Bates Court, Thousand Oaks, California 91362

Based in Thousand Oaks, just west of Los Angeles, the Bounty Hunters have been presenting carefully scripted vignettes of the Old West (1865–1885) for regional audiences since 1967. A nonprofit institution, they belong to that branch of the living history movement which thrives on a mixture of hard-nosed research and creative interpretation.

Each member develops impressions of "real" rather than stereotypical western types. These include dirt farmers, sheepherders, drummers (traveling merchants), temperance advocates, widows in a male-oriented society, and more. Although their presentations often include scenes of violence, the group takes pains to place such episodes in historical context.

The Bounty Hunters attack head-on one of living history's most per-

Glory days for the 12th Virginia, Company G. — *Photograph by Richard Cheatham*

sistent problems: a confusion in the minds of the public that reenactors belong in theme parks, ersatz historical tourist traps, or grade B movies. So far, this California group has been successful in reeducating its public regarding reenactors' concern with understanding and presenting historically accurate accounts of the past.

Great War Association • c/o Brian Pohanka, 425 Queen Street, Alexandria, Virginia 22314

The nucleus of the Great War Association was formed in 1976 when a small number of historians and experienced reenactors constructed a trench line near Emmitsburg, Maryland, and spent several days simulating World War I trench warfare. Their primary motivation was research—all participants wanted to understand more fully the physical environment of the Western Front, where, as Wilfred Owen wrote, "death becomes absurd and life absurder." In 1979, the association was formally established, and its annual campaign moved to a permanent "battlefield" near Shrimpstown, Pennsylvania. The battle is normally held in October. Both the participants and outside observers have been impressed by its terrible authenticity. One of the association's founders has written of members' awareness that "all war is hell, but surely no war was more hellish to the common soldier than World War I" (Brian Pohanka, "Gasmasks, Grenades, and Barbed Wire," *Living History Magazine* 1:3 [Spring 1984], p. 23).

At present, the association is divided into United States, French, British, and German contingents, each with about half a dozen very authentic units. With the centennial of the "war to end all wars" less than thirty years away, interest in simulating this period is rapidly growing.

Second Kansas Light Artillery, Indian Wars. —*Photograph by R. Tim McGill*

Second Kansas Light Artillery, World War I. —*Photograph by R. Tim McGill*

World War II Historical Federation • c/o George A. Peterson, 7904 "F" Yarnwood Court, Springfield, Virginia 22530

The federation is a "sister" organization to the World War II Historical Reenactment Society. It was formed in 1980 and consists mainly of reenactors from the eastern third of the United States. The federation insists on realism in "personal appearance, uniform, haircuts, vehicles, and equipment." It sponsors an annual winter battle at Fort Indian Town Gap in eastern Pennsylvania as well as other events in training areas at Fort George Meade, Maryland; Fort Belvoir, Virginia; and the U.S. Marine Corps base at Quantico, Virginia. Members freely cooperate with events organized by the World War II Historical Reenactment Society and the Military Vehicles Collectors' Club. The federation publishes a newsletter, "The Front Line."

World War II Historical Reenactment Society • c/o John Ong, 3432 Sunset Drive, Madison, Wisconsin 53705

The World War II Historical Reenactment Society was incorporated in 1976 and has sponsored more than one hundred battle reenactments. It holds an annual national battle in mid-October. Membership is more than fifty units and nearly a thousand individuals. The society has published a bimonthly magazine, *The Point*, since 1974. It contains unit reports, announcements of upcoming campaigns, and advertisements. Although the society has increasingly provided demonstrations or impressions for the public, often at military bases, the majority of its events are closed, carefully supervised battle reenactments.

7. Suppliers

AS a nine-year-old aspiring reenactor, I once tried to make a Confederate kepi out of a baseball cap. You can imagine the result. The visor was cut down with scissors and painted black, and a tin can top was put into the crown to give it a rakish overhang. It didn't quite succeed, but there was no alternative. You couldn't buy a reproduction from anyone—at least not for a few years. Then, as if by the will of Robert E. Lee, pseudo-kepis flooded the market. Some were poor imitations made of cheap pressed felt with the texture of a couple of slices of Wonder bread. But later you could buy something that approached the real article—a rough wool *hat* that shed rain like a duck, felt heavy on the head, and looked just like Audie Murphy's in *The Red Badge of Courage*.

Today you can order a kepi from probably a hundred sutlers and be fairly certain of receiving an authentic reproduction. The living history movement has come a long way in the last thirty-five years, and many museum interpreters and reenactors will argue persuasively that this progress is due in large measure to the availability of historically accurate reproductions. If you are going to simulate life in the past, authentic reproductions of clothing, equipment, firearms, and other parts of material culture are crucial. They are the tools of the living historian's trade, for historical simulation is bound up with the artifact more than with the word. And the artifact must be a reproduction. The ethics of the movement dictate that originals must be used only as part of study collections. No self-respecting reenactor would campaign with antiques.

Of all the chapters in my sourcebook, this one was the most difficult to compose. There are hundreds of dedicated suppliers, sutlers, and manufacturers of quality reproductions. I limited my selection almost exclusively to suppliers who have been in the business for many years and who have earned a reputation for truly caring about the authenticity of their products. Their reproductions are based on verifiable original artifacts, often in documented museum collections. These are representatives of a growing comunity of serious "quartermasters."

I also have included a number of sourcebooks, guides, and annotated lists of suppliers. These have been compiled by such reputable organizations as the Association of Living Historical Farms and Agricultural Museums, *Old House Journal,* and *Early American Life.* One of these guides, P. C. House's *The Muzzle Loaders Source Book* (1984), contains a list of more than two thousand individual suppliers. Many of these are craftsmen who specialize in fabricating a specific line of traditional items. I don't attempt to list these tinsmiths, coopers, blacksmiths, gunsmiths, and other specialists in here because they are so many—and I didn't want to duplicate the work of other compilers.

The "catalog culture" that has transformed marketing in our modern society has also affected the reproduction business. Most suppliers will take mail orders, and many send out informative, illustrated, and often glossy catalogs. Fortunately, serious sutlers are still an integral part of the living history scene and are a regular feature of reenactments, fairs, and events.

The Early American Life Sourcebook • The Early American Society, P.O. Box 1831, Harrisburg, Pennsylvania 17105

The third edition of the *Sourcebook*, published in 1980, is a valuable reference tool. About 350 companies are included. The publishers note that "only those [firms] of good reputation who we feel will promptly and satisfactorily handle your order" are included. The *Sourcebook* is also limited to "companies who specialize in the hard-to-find products specifically for the do-it-yourself home restorers and decorators." There is an excellent index with very carefully prepared entries. A section organized by categories lists building supplies, ornamental and architectural detailing, prepackaged homes,

Every man his own historian. — *Photograph by R. Tim McGill*

paints, finishes and preservatives, tools, hardware, bath fixtures and accessories, fireplace equipment, woodstoves, lighting fixtures, decorating supplies, crafts, furniture, fabrics, floor coverings, wall coverings, window hangings and fixtures, gardening materials and supplies, and building inspection, custom design, and restoration services.

Historical Reproduction and Replica Source List • **Association for Living Historical Farms and Agricultural Museums, c/o The Alonzo Wood Homestead, Box 111, East Winthrop, Maine 04343**

Compiled in 1983 as a "grassroots volunteer effort in the best tradition of the ALHFamily," the source list is twenty-five pages long and includes more than two hundred entries. The ALHFAM replica committee which compiled the list is already working on a revised and expanded version. Entries are placed in sixteen categories: living history museums, general merchandise, general directories, basketmaking, blacksmithing, equine accoutrements, housewares, military reenactment supplies and firearms, native American arts and crafts, pottery, printing, textiles, tinware, tools and hardware, woodworking, and "miscellaneous" (toleware, painted cutwork). Each entry is annotated, and a reasonable attempt is made to evaluate the goods offered by the suppliers. This ALHFAM project is an important effort of particular value to the small living history museum or historic site. The committee welcomes suggestions and plans to distribute an updated edition in 1986.

Reproductions in the 1870 general store at Iowa Living History Farms. —*Photograph by Mimi Dunlap*

The Muzzle Loaders Source Book • R. C. House, Editor/Publisher. Beau Jacques Enterprises 1984, P.O. Box 122, La Canada, California 91011.

For more than a quarter century, Dick "Beau Jacques" House has been seriously involved in living history. In the early 1960s he belonged to Loomis Battery, a Civil War artillery unit, and participated in many Civil War centennial reenactments. Later, after moving to California, Dick became an avid buckskinner. He wrote the introductory "philosophical" chapter in *The Book of Buckskinning*. His *Source Book* is more than seventy pages long and contains three sections. The first covers fourteen major topics (publications, cleaners, clothing, gun collectors, black powder supplies, cases and cabinets, gunsmiths, gunsmith supplies and tools, knives, muzzle-loading guns and parts, Indian crafts, tipis and tents, leather goods and furs, and good powder horns and hornware) and eighty-one minor categories. Under each subject is a list of all the suppliers who indicated to "Beau Jacques" that this item was one of their major specialties. The second section is an alphabetical list of almost two thousand suppliers. (Most are cottage industries, small businesses, or single craftspeople.) Finally, the *Source Book's* third part enumerates by state both these suppliers and more than five hundred black powder societies and clubs. Although the *Source Book* is not annotated, it is nevertheless an invaluable aid for anyone who is trying to understand the world of muzzle loaders.

The Old-House Journal Catalog • c/o *The Old-House Journal,* 69A Seventh Avenue, Brooklyn, New York 11217

Compiled and edited by the staff of the *Old-House Journal,* this catalog is an invaluable directory of resources for anyone restoring and furnishing houses built before 1939. The catalog covers building materials—exterior ornament and architectural details, hardware, and ironwork; interior decorative supplies, hardware, plumbing, and fittings; heating systems, fireplaces, and stoves; lighting fixtures and parts; paints, finishes, and removers; antique and recycled house parts; renovation and restoration supply stores; and restoration and decorating services. There are roughly one hundred pages of advertisements plus directories by company, state, and products, and entries for more than fifteen hundred firms.

Amazon Drygoods • 2218 East Eleventh Street, Davenport, Iowa 52803

Janet Burgess's complete name for her company is the Amazon Drygoods, Vinegar and Pickling Works. She is "purveyor of items for the nineteenth-century impression, and also serves the owners of old homes, the history buff, the staffs of historic homes, the multicentennials of small towns, and lovers of Victoriana . . . with the heaviest emphasis on the hoop skirt era and the bustle eras." There isn't a firearm in the Amazon catalog. Rather, it brims with domestic items: there are parasols, hand-crocheted mitts, Edwardian underthings, and pages of yard goods.

Avalon Forge • 409 Gun Road, Baltimore, Maryland 21227

John White joined a Revolutionary War regiment and was disillusioned by the lack of suitable accoutrements. In 1975, he and his wife, Kay, started

Avalon Forge, first as a hobby, now as a part-time job. Their goal is to provide well-researched and well-documented reproductions of goods of the period 1760 to 1780. The forge's clientele is about 60 percent buffs, with the remainder being museums and historic sites with living history programs. The twenty-five-page catalog of eighteenth-century military and camp equipment documents virtually all listings.

The Black Powder Shop • Box 231, Suburban Route, Rapid City, South Dakota 57701

Dave Steinberg's Black Powder Shop sells only high-quality reproduction black powder firearms, shooting equipment, and buckskinner's accessories. His sixty-page catalog takes pains to stress safety. He also includes a wry definition of a muzzle loader: "How to become a muzzle loading nut: Fill one pocket full of marbles and the other pocket full of money. Buy muzzle loading gun and accessories. Every time you buy one, take one marble out of your pocket and throw it away. When you have spent all your money and lost all your marbles, you have become a first-class muzzle-loader!!"

Britannic Arms • 692 Maple Drive, West Webster, New York 14580

Michael Grenier specializes in reproduction muskets and rifles, pistols, swords and bayonets, powder horns, tomahawks, commonly needed firearms parts and accessories, bullets and molds, and superb metal castings. His line of Loren Lillis's brass and bronze castings is impressive. Made from molds fashioned directly from original verifiable artifacts, the castings include shoe, knee, cartridge box, waist vest, sling, and stock buckles; buttons, scabbard parts, badges, medals and crucifixes, and clasps. Britannic Arms does custom metal work as well and carries fabrics made from natural fiber.

Buffalo Enterprises • 308 West King Street, East Berlin, Pennsylvania 17316

Carole Roberson and Raymond Moore began their cottage industry in 1972. As living history impressionists, they always dreamed of starting a living history farm but instead "ended up developing the business." Buffalo Enterprises is a full-time enterprise best known for period clothing from the French and Indian, Revolutionary, and Civil War eras. The owners like to emphasize that they make and sell *clothing,* not costumes. Their seventy-page catalog is both charming and informative. The enterprise is an excellent example of the much higher standard of historical accuracy that the new, serious sutlers are attempting.

C & D Jarnagin Company • Route 3, Box 217, Corinth, Mississippi 38834

The Jarnagins have done for the Civil War reenactor what Godwin has accomplished for the Revolutionary War era: theirs is the standard against which other suppliers of Civil War uniforms and equipment are judged. Their thirty-page catalog, really just a price list, abounds with evidence of authenticity. The reader needs to be very knowledgeable about military uniforms just to peruse it intelligently.

The Calico Corner • 513 East Bowman Street, South Bend, Indiana 46613

When Kathleen York and her husband, Dave, became active in Civil War reenacting in 1975, Kathleen was surprised at the scarcity of historically accurate clothing for women. She opened a shop to supply both dressmaking materials and finished articles, and wrote the excellent Civil War Ladies Sketchbook. Recently she has also begun buying and selling used clothing. "If you are new to reenacting or leaving the hobby, outgrowing your clothes or switching armies, please telephone me at home or visit me at Midwest reenactments in the sutler camp." York heralds a new and welcome day in the world of living history: the marketing of army and civilian *surplus* reproductions!

Colonial Williamsburg Foundation • Post Office Box C, Williamsburg, Virginia 23187

Williamsburg has since the 1930s recruited and employed craftsmen who specialize in reproducing eighteenth-century artifacts. Some are sold in the nine shops in the town's historic area. These replicas serve both an economic and an interpretive function: they help support the foundation and provide authentic "props" for the shops' living history activities. (Many other products are made in small quantities exclusively for the museum's other interpretation programs.) Some of the categories of historically accurate reproductions fashioned at Williamsburg include baskets, printed matter (broadsides, maps, newspapers, and so forth), clothing, nonperishable food, ceramics (salt glaze, red earthenware, porcelain, Queensware, delft) teas, coffees, herbs and spices, horn, glass wine bottles, brass, pewter, wrought and cast iron, silver, jewelry, hats, music and musical instruments, ribbons, soaps, stationery and writing equipment, textiles, tobacco, toys, cooper's items, and other wooden objects. A museum or serious living history group may contact the products manager of the historic area and inquire about the specific products that can be purchased or commissioned.

Cumberland General Store • Route 3, Crossville, Tennessee 38555

The Cumberland General Store seems to have been in business forever. Like the Dixie Gun Works, it is a Tennessee—and American—institution. The 1984 catalog is its 184th number. The thousands of goods offered in its 260 pages could equip a late Victorian town and its surrounding farms. The range of its cooking utensils, agricultural equipment, household furnishings, hardware and tools, clothes, dry goods, tonics, and toys is astounding. Even more interesting, however, is that most of the items are not reproductions. They are the products of firms that have continued to manufacture lines of merchandise once commonplace in the nineteenth and early twentieth century. These goods constitute a historic enclave in our post–1984, high-tech world. The store calls its catalog a "wish-and-want book." For many living history farms and historic sites that wisely choose *not* to animate their programs with antiques, the Cumberland General Store offers many realistic and reasonable alternatives.

Dixie Gun Works • Gunpowder Lane, Union City, Tennessee 38261

For almost thirty years Turner Kirkland's Dixie Gun Works has been selling antique guns and replicas and muzzle-loading supplies from its headquarters in Union City, Tennessee. Its annual catalog is as thick as a big city telephone directory and is almost six hundred pages long. Almost every item

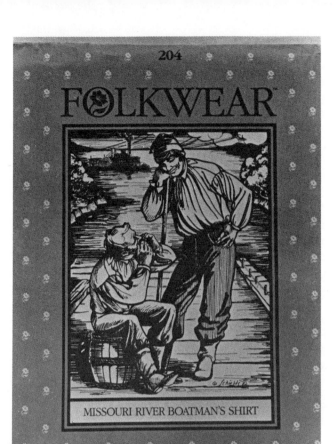

204

F⦾LKWEAR™

MISSOURI RIVER BOATMAN'S SHIRT

Two of Folkwear's most
popular patterns. —
*Photographs by Sharli
Powell*

Folkwear.

PATTERNS FROM
TIMES PAST

201

© Folkwear 1978

PRAIRIE DRESS

PATTERN • SEWING INSTRUCTIONS • FEATHERSTITCHED APRON

is illustrated and described in detail. While the works at first catered primarily to muzzle-loader enthusiasts and buckskinners, its inventory has now expanded to include artifacts such as hot air balloon kits, armor helmets, and nearly five hundred books. The works is a highly professional but nevertheless down-home operation. Most of its employees are delightfully pictured in the catalog, often wearing a voyageur cap or holding a long rifle.

Eagle Feather Trading Post, Inc. • 760 West Riverdale Road, Ogden, Utah 84403

For many Native Americans, the Eagle Feather Trading Post is a sensitive source of supplies. Its goods will be used by Indians not as part of living history programs that simulate life in the past but rather as equipment for living in a traditional Indian manner. Like the Gohn Brothers, who help supply the Amish and Mennonite communities, the post assists Native Americans. Many peole who are not Indians will find the catalog a useful resource for hard-to-obtain materials to help re-create and interpret western folklife. Buckskinners will find it especially useful. The post's 1984 catalog listed in its eighty pages hundreds of items, from patterns, kits, beads, and blankets to buckskin, feathers, and leather to shells, trade clothes and silver, and other essential materials. The post offers discounts to Native American craftpersons and is willing to trade finished products for raw materials. The post is *not* to be confused with the many other suppliers who market primarily to hobbyists who have gotten, in their own words, the "Red Indian bug."

NEW COLUMBIA

Nineteenth Century American Clothing
by

~JOSEPH S. COVAIS~

SERVING

MEN, WOMEN & CHILDREN
THE WORLD OVER

Serious suppliers of period clothing attempt the realism found in historical photographs. —*Photograph by Sharli Powell*

Past Patterns truthfully advertises that it is a "historical pattern company devoted to authenticity."—*Photograph by Sharli Powell*

Folkwear Patterns • P.O. Box 3859, San Rafael, California 94912

Founded in 1975, Folkwear is one of the most creative small companies in the United States. It sells patterns for modern variants of antique and ethnic clothing. The selection—more than seventy patterns are available—is appetizing: Kinsale cloaks, tea frocks, Palm Beach pants, English smocks, Tibetan panel coats, Bolivian milkmaid's jackets. Afghani nomad dresses, and Hong Kong cheongsams. Some packets, such as "Shirts of Russia and the Ukraine" (no. 116), contain pages of notes on the pattern's history, lore, and cultural significance. All patterns are made from authenticated garments, sized for the modern figure, tested, and drawn up. Many items contain directions for both modern and more traditional versions. Instructions are clear, obviously evaluated by experienced sewers, and free from errors. And are they all romantic! Folkwear unabashedly caters to the nostalgic urge in modern man and woman, and its patterns are both promoted and packaged with élan.

Gohn Brothers • Box 111, Middlebury, Indiana 46540-0111

From the tiny northern Indiana town of Middlebury (population 1,665), the Gohn family have for decades been supplying the Amish, Mennonite, and other Plain People with clothing and dry goods. Their legal-size, eight-page catalog contains more than 350 items which are symbolically acceptable to religious communities that require plain clothing. Since most plain people are also farmers, the Gohns take care to purvey products which are of the highest quality yet remarkable inexpensive. Their catalog is the dry goods counterpart of a good Lancaster County farmers' market. For reenactors and interpreters at nineteenth-century living museums, especially living history farms, Gohn Brothers is a crucial source of goods which are grounded stylistically in the mid-nineteenth century. Gohns sells 100 percent wool black suits with a frock coat, pre-1849 gray denim broadfall trousers, a variety of wide-brimmed, low-crown fur felt hats, bonnet board, melton short coats, 100 percent Australian wool drawers and shirts and all-cotton red union suits, black wool shawls in Berwick squares and doubles, and more.

Green River Forge • P.O. Box 715, Roosevelt, Utah 84066

The Forge has an extensive selection of patterns from various periods in American history. They include military uniforms, civilian men's and women's clothing, and Indian outfits. Their patterns do not include the usual scholarly information found in the packets of Folkwear or Past Patterns, for example, and their directions are scant. A thorough knowledge of the clothing tradition that the pattern represents is a prerequisite to any purchase.

The Hawken Shop • 3028 North Lindbergh, St. Louis, Missouri 63074

Art Ressel, a serious collector, acquired the famous Hawken-Gemmer gun factory, which had closed in 1915, and reopened the company in 1971 as the Hawken Shop. Ressel began making production guns that were absolutely authentic. They are weapons with both "show and blow." Ressel also supplies a variety of accessories, forged items, clothing, and trade silver—all interesting to the muzzle loader.

James & Son, Military Clothier • 1230 Arch Street, Philadelphia, Pennsylvania 19107

An old family business that began by providing the costumes for Philadelphia's mummers and, later, for stage actors, James and Son branched out during the Bicentennial and began to outfit serious historical reenactors. The firm now manufactures "authentic military clothing from World War II and back." Its scope includes some of the lesser-studied periods, such as World War I, the Spanish-American War, the Indian campaigns, and the War of 1812. Much of the company's business is done with overseas reenactors, especially in Germany.

James Townsend & Son • P.O. Box 677, Winona Lake, Indiana 46590

Townsend's is located in the northern Indiana lake country near the Tippecanoe River. It's a family business, begun in 1973 by James Townsend, an experienced reenactor. His wife and son, Francis, continue to help with the firm, which specializes in the period roughly covered by units in the North West Territory Alliance: French and Indian War, Revolutionary War, and fur trade. The thirty-page catalog carries a good selection of reproduction artifacts, each annotated with a brief historical note. Included are military and civilian firearms, books, eighteenth- and early nineteenth-century clothing, patterns, trade silver, camp equipment, tents, and Townsend's specialty, tin lanterns.

Kit Ravenshear, Craftsman Armourer • Ashland, Pennsylvania 17921

You are likely to see Kit's replicas of original flintlock guns in historic sites and outdoor museums that seriously attempt to simulate the past. His firearms look and feel authentic and lack the "shine and squareness" of many mass-produced items. His muskets, fowlers, fusils, and pistols capture the character of their periods. Like really good living history programs at museums such as the Fortress of Louisbourg and Sainte-Marie among the Hurons, his firearms have stood the test of time. They are classics. Ravenshear has striven to distance his work from "modern misinterpretations" of historic guns. A good place to see his line is at Dixon's Muzzleloading Gunshop (R.D. 1, Kempton, Pennsylvania 19529) in the "gay" Dutch country at the foot of the Blue Mountains.

La Pelleterie • P.O. Box 127, Highway 41, Arrow Rock, Missouri 65320

La Pelleterie was founded by Pat and Karalee Tearney a decade ago. Both were living history professionals, as their superb ninety-page catalog indicated. Pat passed away in 1984, but his wife, Karalee, carries on, providing "custom-tailored historic reproductions and re-creations of historic costume" from the eighteenth and nineteenth centuries. The catalog includes both historical headnotes and photographs of all items. The result is a handy guide to historic clothing for both the layman and the experienced reenactor.

The Ladies Companion • Cassandra Zaharias, P.O. Box 31152, St. Louis, Missouri 62131

Cassandra Zaharias specializes in Civil War–period clothing and accessories for ladies. Her modest catalog includes such items as petticoats, drawers, chemises and other undergarments, camp and day dresses, plain and fancy ballgowns, snoods, aprons, nightclothes (gowns, caps, bed sacks, and so forth), capes, cloaks, lace-up shoes, and stockings. All her reproductions are made from documented patterns and/or original specimens. Complementing The Ladies Companion is John Zaharias' Sutlers, which is famous for its "haversack stuffers": eating utensils, muslin tobacco bags, "soldier's house-wives" (needles, pins, heavy brown thread, assorted buttons, and so forth), straight razors, writing equipment, period envelopes, period manufacturing labels, and more.

Log Cabin Shop • P.O. Box 275, Lodi, Ohio 44254

For more than forty years, the Log Cabin Shop has been supplying muzzle loaders with the tools of their hobby. The shop's 220-page catalog reflects the company's long experience. Almost every item is illustrated with a photograph. You see exactly what you are getting. The shop offers a comprehensive line of replica arms, kits, firearm parts, accessories, knives, tomahawks, clothing, patterns, and books. Some categories, such as tomahawks, are especially well represented. The shop carries twenty-three different tomahawk heads, for example, and offers the same variety in rifle parts and kits.

Mediaeval Miscellanea • 7006 Raleigh Road, Annandale, Virginia 22003

Mediaeval Miscellanea sells, as its name implies, a variety of items of interest primarily to members of the Society for Creative Anachronism. These goods include a line of period patterns for Tudor undergarments, gowns, headdresses, medieval military garments, bags, purses, pouches, and even pavilions and tents, as well as books, puzzles, and games, and various paper products—posters, paper castles, stationery, and so forth. The modest twenty-four page catalog notes that the firm is dedicated to bringing people interested in the European Middle Ages and the Renaissance "useful, unusual, and hard to find items."

Mountain State Muzzleloading Supplies • Williamstown, West Virginia 26187

For more than a decade, Mountain State Muzzleloading Supplies has been selling "everything for the muzzleloading shooter and builder." Its 150-page catalog does cover a wide variety of goods, ranging from firearms to patterns, from books to "primitive paraphernalia." The 1984–1985 edition even lists The Last Rendezvous, a board game for buckskinning families.

Navy Arms Company • 689 Bergen Boulevard, Ridgefield, New Jersey 07657

Val Forgett, founder of Navy Arms, began serious marketing of modern mass-produced replica black powder firearms in 1957. An experienced member of the North-South Skirmish Association, Forgett wanted to purvey a line of replicas both authentic and safe. His thirty-page catalog is a glossy wish list for the serious reenactor.

Ne Shutsa Traders • Box 186, Haven, Kansas 67543

Rick and Cathy Banman's thirty-page catalog opens with an informal note: "If ye want something unusual or hard to come by, drop us a line and we'll send ye some smoke or what we can do . . . make it—get it—look for it—or send ye a source for it. Remember—WE TRADE." Hand drawn and hand written, their catalog is friendly and spirited and does indeed contain a variety of buckskinner's goods seldom seen elsewhere: mirror boards, swivel

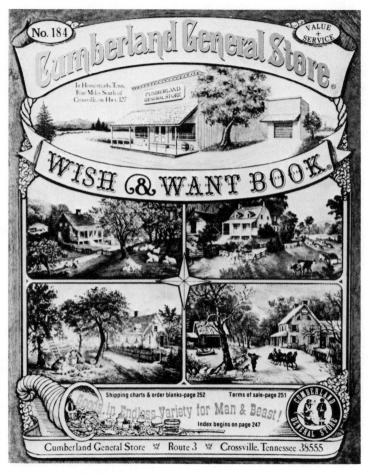

For reenactors, suppliers' catalogs are indeed "wish-and-want books."—
Photograph by Sharli Powell

guns, brain tan clothing, a reproduction 1750 brass sundial compass, elk rawhide parfleches, buffalo bladders, 1830-period saddles, jewelers' pewter, trade silver facsimiles, kaibabs, tobacco twists, canvas capes, and a large selection of patterns and books. And they note, "all of it is as authentic and researched as mortal man can do."

New Columbia • P.O. Box 524, Charleston, Illinois 61920

Joseph Covais's firm provides an extensive line of authentic period clothing. His catalog is especially strong in men's and women's civilian clothing from the nineteenth century and military uniforms from all of America's wars in the nineteenth and twentieth centuries (1812, Mexican, Civil, Indian, Spanish, and World Wars I and II). The patterns, composition, and methods of construction of Covais's reproductions are all taken from original examples. His method is to examine, photograph, and carefully study several examples of each type of clothing before attempting a reproduction. New Columbia regularly supplies period clothing to some of the most discerning living history museums and historic sites, such as Fort Snelling and Cincinnati Fire Museum. Especially impressive are Covais's German and Russian uniforms for this century's two world wars.

Old Sturbridge Village • Sturbridge, Massachusetts 05166-0200

Old Sturbridge Village, one of the finest living history museums in North America, has many craftsmen who produce a small surplus of reproduction artifacts representative of the goods available in New England between 1790 and 1840. The items that Sturbridge sells in limited numbers include tinware (lighting devices, household utensils, and dairy equipment),

An aura of realism and nostalgia colors many of the buckskinner's
catalogs. — *Photograph by Sharli Powell*

ironware (nails, cranes, toasting forks, and so forth), hand-dipped candles, wool rollags and batting, broadsides, copy books, leather pocketbooks and shoes, pottery (redware pots, bowls, churns, cups, jars, pitchers, ink wells, and the like), pounded black ash splint baskets, brooms, and bound blank ledgers. Sturbridge also does custom cabinet work and cooperage for other museums. In addition to these craft reproductions, the museum has an excellent line of teaching materials (curriculum kits, audiovisuals, realia, and so forth). A catalog for these materials is available from the mail order department of the museum gift shop.

Past Patterns • 2017 Eastern, S.E., Grand Rapids, Michigan 49507

Past Patterns, owned by Saundra Rox Altman, sets the standard for historical patterns. Altman's work is admirable. Her catalogs contain more than one hundred patterns from the early Victorian period (1850s) through the 1930s. Most are based on actual authenticated outfits. Others are copied from period tailor's books (for example, the 1903 American Garment Cutters) or from "brown paper copies" of original patterns for professional seamstresses and tailors. Her catalog entries are carefully footnoted, and she also supplies thirteen of the best available books on historical clothing and takes the trouble to explain just exactly why each is a definitive text in its area. Since all of Altman's patterns are for women or civilian men and she targets the post–Civil War world for special attention, her work fills a void not covered by sketchbooks. One final but important note: Altman's "past patterns" are remarkably free from printing errors, and her instructions and diagrams are unusually clear. The experienced sewer will find them eminently sewable.

A slow time at the rendezvous for two young blanket traders. —*Photograph by Ken Grissom*

Patterns of History • The State Historical Society of Wisconsin, 816 State Street, Madison, Wisconsin 53706

This line of patterns was one of the first based on authenticated originals. Drafted from examples in the collection of the State Historical Society of Wisconsin, the series covers every major style change in women's clothes for the period 1835 to 1899. The patterns are well documented with considerable commentary from period fashion magazines. Information on suitable accessories is also given. Some early problems with the "sewability" of the patterns themselves are being corrected.

Pegee: Costumes of Williamsburg • P.O. Box 127, Williamsburg, Virginia 23187-0127

For nearly fifteen years Pegee Miller has been developing a limited line of "patterns from historie." Her selection now numbers fourteen, ranges from 1608 to 1910, and includes clothing for both sexes. Each pattern is meticulously researched and includes suggestions for fabric, color, and so forth, with good historical background notes.

George A. Peterson, National Capitol Historical Sales, Inc. • 7904 "F," Yarnwood Court, Fullerton Industrial Park, Springfield, Virginia 22153

From his Virginia store, George Peterson sells a full line of World War II and American reenactment uniforms, headgear, field equipment, insignias, medals, and related material. Ironically, this is not old army surplus, the stuff that, as kids and—later—as students, we used to buy cheap. Peterson sells brand-new, mint condition accurate reproductions to reenactors, many of whom have studied originals in museums and are therefore sticklers for authenticity. An experienced buff, Peterson does handle genuine surplus for all of America's twentieth-century wars, since his clientele includes collectors as well as reenactors, but few reenactors would commit the curatorial sin of campaigning in antiques!

The Quartermaster Shop • 3115 Nokomis Trail, Port Huron, Michigan 48060

Jeff O'Donnell has been making accurate replicas of 1850–1865 clothing for a decade. An experienced reenactor, he is careful to base his clothing and uniforms on documented originals. The shop's twenty-page catalog contains a basis selection of military kepis, caps, coats, jackets, greatcoats, trousers, vests, chevrons, service and trouser stripes, suspenders, and buttons, as well as a smaller collection of civilian clothing—frock, tails, sack coats, vests, trousers, and a shirt. O'Donnell also includes fabric samples.

The Regimental Quartermaster • P.O. Box 553, Hatboro, Pennsylvania 19040

The Regimental Quartermaster supplies a variety of reproduction Civil War goods. These include supplies for black powder guns (cartridge cases, bullet molds, front sights, tompions, and so forth); leather goods such as cartridge boxes, cap pouches, belts, straps, frogs, and scabbards; brass buckles, buttons, plates, and insignia; camp equipment and accessories; specialized books; and a limited line of clothing. Authenticity is a priority.

Salish House, Inc. • P.O. Box 280, Somers, Montana 59932

The original Salish House, located near the present site of Thompson Falls, Montana, was a North West Company trading post. Here in the foothills of the Cabinet Mountains, west of Flathead Lake, David Thompson carried out extensive fur trade activities from a series of outposts. The type of merchandise originally sold by Thompson is supplied by Salish House, Inc., today. Mike Coston, the proprietor, specializes in leather clothing made from rough split elk and deer skin. His basic patterns and designs are based on museum pieces, authenticated artifacts, and drawings, paintings, and eyewitness descriptions from the fur trade period. All of his reproductions have the look of authenticity. His recent catalog includes a variety of women's dresses, leggings, and belts plus shirts, pants, coats, breechclouts, aprons, coats, headgear, and capotes for men. Salish House also makes moccasins, gun covers, shooting bags, and accessories. Mike also custom makes museum-quality items for institutions and individuals who demand "complete" authenticity.

Spencer Firearms, Inc. • 5 South Main Street, Sullivan, Illinois 61951

Since 1949, George Spencer has been manufacturing museum-quality reproductions of Civil War weapons, insignia, and equipment. His "Soldier's Catalogue" is a trove of unusual items, including wooden ID tags, sharpshooter's scopes, rosettes, breastplates, forage bags, shoulder knots, Kinikinic tobacco, officer's tin desk sets, playing cards, and a wide assortment of accessories, firearms, buckles, buttons, and mess tinware. Before he went into the reproduction business, Spencer was a collector of Civil War and Indian War artifacts; his originals form the basis of his facsimiles.

The Sutler of Mount Misery • c/o G. Gedney Godwin, Inc., Box 100, Valley Forge, Pennsylvania 19481

Legend has it that G. Gedney Godwin, Inc., was given permission to erect his tent at any and all Brigade of the American Revolution encampments. His reputation for historical accuracy is well established, and his seventy-six page catalog covering the French and Indian and Revolutionary war periods is a textbook on correctness.

Tecumseh's Frontier Trading Post • Box 369, Shartlesville, Pennsylvania 19554

Jerry Fick's post is located just south of the Appalachian Trail in historic Berks County. Since 1964 Fick has been collecting original fur trade artifacts, participating in serious buckskinning, and making buckskin clothing by hand. He combines the role of historian, hobbyist, and craftsman. His modest twenty-page catalog carries a good basic selection of old-style northern plains shirts, coats, bags, and pouches; frontier and riflemen's capotes; and accessories.

Track of the Wolf • Box Y, Osseo, Minnesota 55369

A good example of the many new companies devoted to the buckskin trade is Track of the Wolf. It publishes a 150-page catalog that lists books, kits for historical clothing, rendezvous equipment, and a good selection of firearms.

The American Historical Supply Catalogue by Alan Wellikoff. New York: Schocken Books, 1984.

Alan Wellikoff's carefully annotated catalog contains more than 175 recommended manufacturers and suppliers of nineteenth-century replica and reproduction artifacts. He covers twenty-five categories of material culture and includes sections on structures and plans, building supplies, furniture and housewares, dry goods, timepieces, vehicles and harness, food and drink, wearing apparel, military goods, books, photographic goods, musical instruments, toys and games, remedies and toilet articles, pipes and tobacco, and Christmas paraphernalia. Wellikoff illustrates more than 350 items with photos, line drawings, or period advertisements and provides both general and subject indexes. An excellent general sourcebook, especially for the enthusiast who has recently become interested in living history as a hobby.

8. Sketchbooks

I DON'T know if this story is true, but a friend of mine who is an experienced reenactor and the director of a famous outdoor museum swears it is. He says that at a reenactment of a battle on World War II's Eastern Front, the competition got pretty rough—not between the Germans and the Russians, but between the authentics and the super-authentics. The latter group included a West Point professor who awed his associates by producing, at the appropriate moment, a packet of Nazi toilet paper.

If sketchbooks can't make us super-authentics, at least they can help prevent us from becoming farbs. Sketchbooks are *the* unique living history publication. They are a secondary source of primary importance. Written by and for historical simulators, sketchbooks focus on material culture—the clothing, accessories, and equipment every reenactor or interpreter needs to slip out of the present and into the past. The best sketchbooks base their descriptions on authenticated artifacts. It is a comfort, for example, to note at the bottom of an illustration in James Hanson and Kathryn Wilson's *The Mountain Man's Sketch Book*

19th Century Buckskin Hunting Shirt/Jacket

By William L. Brown, III

In 1819, Titian Ramsay Peale, son of the famous American artist, naturalist, and museum operator Charles Willson Peale, joined the Major Stephen H. Long expedition as assistant naturalist. The expedition left from Pittsburgh and reached the Rocky Mountains, returning to the East in late 1820. Peale had this hunting jacket/shirt made for him over the winter of 1819-1820 probably by an Indian woman near Council Bluffs, Iowa.

It is smoked, tanned buckskin, all sinew sewn. Hunting shirt/jackets are very rare today. It is unfortunate that most garmets used as everyday wear have a low survival rate.

The hunting shirt had its beginning in Europe as a simple peasant smock; brought to America it continued as a pullover smock, the working man's garment, usually made of tow or

coarse linen. By the time of the French & Indian War we find an offshoot called the hunting shirt, jacket, or coat. One description of the militia at the Battle of Point Pleasant in 1773 describes the militia as wearing "hunting shirt, many reaching to their ankles, various colors. As the leaves turn in autumn."

We know of one surviving linen hunting shirt of the Revolutionary era; it is now at the Washington's Headquarters Museum, Newburgh, New York.

This garment, chronologically, is the next earliest one surviving, that I know about. Hollywood would have us believe that American soldiers of the 18th century were wearing buckskin hunting shirts, but we can find no evidence for it, all the facts point to linen and no paintings or sketches show buckskin hunting coats. But in the 1830's and 1840's we have a great deal of graphic sources showing buckskin garments in use in the West.

This coat, made during the winter of 1819-20 on the Missouri River in the present State of Iowa, might be the earliest buckskin hunting shirt that survives.

There are some features that should be noted, particularly to those readers who might wish to reproduce this garment:

1. All of the seams have a welt sewn in them.

2. While it is a simple garment, the sleeves conform to the fashion of the period—fairly tight, pinched at the wrist, flaring to the cuff.

3. The belts, crossing in the back, then tying in front, are an interesting and unusual feature.

4. Titian Peale, then 19, was of

Feature articles on historic material culture in publications such as *Living History Magazine* often set high standards for sketchbooks to emulate. — *Photograph by Sharli Powell*

that their "work shirt" is taken from a "Caleb Bingham painting and example in Royal Ontario Museum" (vol. 1, p. 32). Also reassuring is a good relevant bibliography of primary sources. Recently authors have been providing, in addition to descriptions of material culture, honest historical backgrounds for their subjects. It's not enough to know what Rogers's Rangers wore; you've got to understand who they were, what they were about, and what it must have been like to be one of them. A good sketchbook attempts to answer these questions. It's not only what you wear; it's also what you know.

Of the approximately twenty good sketchbooks that have been published, most of them understandably deal with those historical periods favored by reenactors: the buckskinning era, the French and Indian and Revolutionary wars, and recently— and perhaps surprisingly—the ladies' side of the Civil War. There are some huge gaps: at least six major wars, male civilian clothing from the last half of the nineteenth century, and the dress of ethnic groups which was brought over from the Old World as "cultural baggage."

In the future I hope we will see more sketchbooks that go beyond an individual's "kit." Comprehensive bibliographies of primary and secondary sources are needed for all the groups that reenactors portray. And we could also use material culture "background studies" of particular periods—books that describe the mercantile scene and include information on the factors which influenced the development and nature of textiles, firearms, equipment, foodways, and so on. Many of these studies will undoubtedly come from living history museums.

For the present, however, we're fortunate to have a basic shelf of valuable sketchbooks, a good selection of which I've described here.

The Known World Handboke. 1979. Society for Creative Anachronism, Box 743, Milpitas, California 95035

A two-hundred-page compendium assembled by several dozen experienced members of the Society for Creative Anachronism, *The Known World Handboke* is the ideal introduction to the society and its activities. The *Handboke* contains four sections on medieval etiquette, arts and sciences, life in the "current" middle ages, and fighting. All in all, there are fifty short chapters on subjects such as choosing a persona, speaking forsoothly, practical herbalism, costumes constructed from patterns, pavilion design, an anachronist's "basic-basic" reading list, waggon-loading for the compleat idiot, gaming medievally, Society publications, combat conventions, swords, shields, banned weapons, and maps of the "Known [SCA] World." Delightful illustrations and cartoons pepper the text, which is joyful in tone.

The Pleasure Book by Rodena de Rohan and Sir Raymond, Baron al-Barran. 1979. Raymond's Quiet Press, 6336 Leslie, N.E., Albuquerque, New Mexico 87109

This 190-page guide complements the official Society publication the *Known World Handboke*. It covers the society's organizational structure and events, combat, armor, calligraphy, cookery, costuming, dancing, decorative banners, games and amusements, heraldry, pavilions, ballads, and books. It also has useful chapters on the philosophy behind creative anachronism, the motivations of members, getting started, and moving up in the society. The *Pleasure Book* makes great use of photographs as well as illustrations that look as if they had come from a medieval manuscript. As the book's title indicates, its focus is more on the pacific aspects of creative anachronism. Rodena and Raymond's guide is more appropriate in the revel tent than on the field of battle.

The Fighter's Handbook by Earl Kevin Perigrynne (Philip McDown). Rev. ed., 1978. Society for Creative Anachronism, Box 743, Milpitas, California 95035

Philip McDown spent four years preparing this handbook with the assistance of thirty-two other Society members. The revised handbook runs to 150 pages, divided into five sections: equipment construction, weapons, equipment and other standards, field behavior (rules of the lists and conventions of combat), a primer on tourney fighting, and appendixes and supplements.

The Society notes that its members "build weapons, armor, and shields—and fight with them." McDown tells you how in richly detailed chapters on padding and flexible armor, shield and armor inspection, field etiquette, melees and wars, field first aid, and tournament dying. He includes a bibliography on source documents. The 148 illustrations are clear and helpful. McDown's resources are virtually all secondary sources written by other Society members. Future fighters will no doubt be interested in the primary sources that underlie the Society's activities.

Historic Colonial French Dress by Mary Moyers Johnson with Judy Forbes and Kathy Delaney. 1982. Ouabache Press, P.O. Box 2076, West Lafayette, Indiana 47906

The authors have given the living history movement a fine introduction to the fashions and fabrics worn by French-American colonists in New France during the period from 1710 to 1760. Their focus is primarily on the ordinary farmers, soldiers, traders, artisans, voyageurs, and women who constituted the vast majority of the European population in what is now southern Canada and the midwestern United States. Solidly based on primary sources which are cited in the references and notes, *Historic Colonial French Dress* includes sections on the fashion and fabric of France, on women's and men's dress, on colonial roles, and on the craft of re-creating eighteenth-century French period clothing. This 138-page sketchbook also contains a useful glossary and a bibliography of secondary sources on historical clothing in general; the index spans both the text and the book's forty-eight patterns. The numerous illustrations have a Gallic flavor, and the pattern directions are admirably clear. In every way, this is a model guide to re-creating North American French clothing.

Reenactors perfect their "impressions" of British soldiers at Meadow Farm's Colonial Muster. — *Meadow Farm Museum; photograph by Katherine Wetzel*

The Voyageur's Sketchbook by James A. Hanson. 1981. The Fur Press, Box 604, Chadron, Nebraska 69337

Dedicated the "les Moongasses," or greenhorns, whose "eager questions and unbounded enthusiasm have prompted me to write this books," Hanson's *Voyageur's Sketchbook* is admirable and dovetails with *Historic Colonial French Dress*. Solid research and imaginative interpretation are conspicuous in all of Hanson's Sketchbooks. As a museum curator and experienced reenactor, Hanson understands the importance to the living history movement of reliable guides. This sketchbook is a good example. Hanson covers all the primary artifacts which collectively made up the voyageur's material culture: canoe, cassette (trunks), hats and tuques, trousers, sashes, shirts, capotes, moccasins and other footwear, knives, axes, hardware, traps, firearms, powder horns and flasks, hunting pouches, tobacco and smoking paraphernalia, cooking and eating utensils and food containers, silver, and checkerboards. Each item is documented, and illustrations picture actual authenticated museum pieces. Hanson also provides a bibliography. The sketchbook is forty-eight pages long.

The French Marines (Sketch Book 56, vol. 2) by Ted Spring. 1984. The Brandy Press, P.O. Box 2076, St. Louis, Missouri 63123.

This is the second of a series of sketchbooks that Ted Spring has written on the French and Indian War period. It provides a complement to *Historic Colonial French Dress*. In addition to material on the French marine's material culture (weapons, tools, various seasonal uniforms, and so forth), Spring gives us information on the marine's daily life, cuisine, working conditions, and discipline. The artwork is forthright, and there is a short section of recommended reading.

Buckskinning generates more how-to-do-it publications than
any other branch of living history. —*Photograph by Sharli Powell*

Rogers' Rangers (Sketch Book 56, vol. 1) by Ted Spring. 1984. The Brandy Press, P.O. Box 2076, St. Louis, Missouri 63123

The "56" in *Sketch Book* stands for 1756, the year when the French and Indian War officially broke out. Ted Spring plans a series of sketchbooks dealing with this event. *Rogers' Rangers* is the first to appear. It runs to sixty-four pages and contains information on Robert Rogers's Rangers. He mixes in historical information with descriptions of uniforms, accoutrements, and arms. The formation of the unit, development of its tactics, the "Battle on Snow Shoes," and the Abenaki raid are covered.

The Longhunter's Sketchbook by James A. Hanson. 1983. The Fur Press, Box 604, Chadron, Nebraska 69337

Historically, the longhunter was a frontier hybrid, a blend of Dutch *boschloper* and French *coureur de bois*, Anglo-Celt and native American. Longhunters flourished in the eighteenth and early nineteenth centuries. They pioneered half a continent, marched with George Rogers Clark, and died at the Alamo. Davy Crockett is perhaps the best-known example. Hanson's guide thoroughly communicates the material aspects of the long-hunter's life. Included are illustrated studies of head-gear, the coonskin cap, breeches, trousers and drawers, Indian and "white man's" leggings, moc-casins, buckskin shirts, eighteenth- and nineteenth-century hunting shirts, George Rogers Clark's coat, the Kentucky pistol, longarms, hunting pouches, firearm accessories, knives and sheaths, tomahawks, hatchets and axes, fire-making and smoking equipment, foodways materials, personal items, com-passes, beaver traps, and a bee box. As with all Hanson's work, each artifact is authenticated and the choice of examples is absolutely apt.

Authentic military units such as the Fort Henry Guard demand first-rate historical research. — *Fort Henry, St. Lawrence Parks Commission*

Sketchbook '76 by Robert Klinger and Richard Wilder. 1974 (reprint of 1967 ed.). Pioneer Press, Box 684, Union City, Tennessee 38261

This superb fifty-three-page book was a first. Originally published privately in 1967, *Sketchbook '76* provided Revolutionary War–period reenactors and interpreters with sketches, notes, and patterns of historically accurate uniforms and equipment originally used by the American foot soldier between 1775 and 1781. Klinger and Wilder based the examples used in their book on original artifacts, thereby establishing a model for authenticity that was followed by thousands of living history buffs during the Bicentennial years. *Sketchbook '76* was quickly followed by several dozen other similar guides to the material culture of particular periods. Klinger and Wilder helped "professionalize" the field of living history.

Distaff Sketch Book by Robert L. Klinger. 1974. Pioneer Press, Box 684, Union City, Tennessee 38261

Robert Klinger followed up his pioneering *Sketchbook '76* with *Distaff Sketch Book*. With the assistance of a number of clothing scholars, reenactors, museums, and sutlers, he introduced a generation of living history buffs to the argument that the American Revolutionary War period (1774–1783) couldn't be validly interpreted or celebrated if the significant role of women in the late eighteenth century was neglected. Drawing on museum artifacts and contemporary writings, drawings, and paintings, Klinger outfitted the colonial women. His book describes just about every article of clothing, including aprons, bonnets, chemises, dresses, jackets, petticoats, skirts, stockings, and working dress. In sixty-one pages, he actually covers forty-three categories of apparel or accessory. Illustrations are many—often four or five per page—and helpful. Most important, Klinger raised an important, complex subject and challenged buffs and interpreters to include in their studies the distaff point of view.

Rural Pennsylvania Clothing by Ellen J. Gehret. 1976. Liberty Cap Press, R.D. 7, York, Pennsylvania 17402

This exceptional study of rural Pennsylvania German and English clothing is not technically a sketchbook. It runs to more than three hundred pages, is a beautifully designed and printed hardback, and contains 315 illustrations, many of which are detailed photographs of original garments. *Rural Pennsylvania Clothing* is really a model that every writer of sketchbooks should study before undertaking the task of describing the material culture of a historic group. Gehret notes that her volume "is a source-book to be used when making reproduction everyday rural clothing of the type worn in southeastern Pennsylvania, particularly between 1750 and 1820, by the farmer, the day laborer, the tradesman, their women-folk and children. Sewing instructions are derived from the measurement and analysis of Pennsylvania clothing of the period; the original garment is the only guide to use in making historically-accurate patterns" (p. 7). An experienced local historian, Gehret understands what good academic research is, and her book is thorough. She also appreciates the needs of living history museums and reenactors for practical, readable books on period wear, and *Rural Pennsylvania Clothing* meets their requirements.

The Book of Buckskinning, vol. 1 and 2, edited by William Scurlock. 1981, 1983. Rebel Publishing Company, Route 5, Box 347-M, Texarkana, Texas 75501

In volume one of *The Book of Buckskinning,* the editor asked ten experienced buckskinners to write essays on the basic components of their "sport." The result was a unique compendium containing articles on philosophy, getting started, rendezvous and shoots, guns, clothing, accoutrements and equipment, skills, crafts, the lodge, and women's activities. His choice of contributors was commendable: each was knowledgeable and articulate. The result is a highly useful manual for "pilgrims" on the road to becoming accomplished buckskinners as well as an invaluable primary source for historians of the living history movement.

Volume 2 continues along the same lines, with new articles on leather work, eighteenth-century clothing, horseback travel, design and construction of powder horns, fire making, traveling on foot and by canoe, making camp gear, and gun tune-up and care. The nine authors—including five holdovers from volume 1—are all experienced buckskinners who have done their homework. Instructions and patterns are very clear, and there are literally hundreds of illustrations. Both volumes are well worth the money.

Feminine Fur Trade Fashions by Kathryn Wilson and James Hanson. 1976. The Fur Press, Box 604, Chadron, Nebraska 69337

During the 1800–1840 period when the western fur trade was at its height, Indian and white women from Canada, the United States, and Mexico played an important role as helpmates, companions, and negotiators. *Feminine Fur Trade Fashions* provides accurate information for the many women reenactors involved in simulating the folklife of this period. Wilson and Hanson include instructions for reproducing Indian, Canadian, American, and Mexican dresses (thirteen in all), and moccasins and leggings, headgear, coats, belts, ornaments, sewing bags, parfleches, baby carriers, saddles and travois, tanning and sewing tools, and a variety of gaming paraphernalia for adults and children. Patterns are clear and historical notes fascinating.

The Frontier Scout and Buffalo Hunter's Sketch Book by James Hanson. 1980. The Fur Press, Box 604, Chadron, Nebraska 69337

In the 1850s and 1860s, the frontier scout, followed by the buffalo hunter, transformed the West. The scout made it possible for the American army to "pacify" the Indian warriors of the Great Plains, and the buffalo hunter in less than a decade killed more than twenty million bison, the foundation of the Indians' economy. The age of the hunter had ended; the epoch of the cowboy and the farmer had begun. Hanson's sketchbook illustrates the material culture of the frontier scout and buffalo hunter. He includes sections on hats, vests, leggings and trousers, shirts, jackets, coats, overcoats, caps, gauntlets, moccasins, saddles, belts, knives and holsters, and smoking gear. All Hanson's examples are authenticated. Many of his items are based on artifacts from the U.S. Military Academy Museum.

The Mountain Man's Sketch Book, vol. 1 and 2, by James Hanson and Kathryn Wilson. 1976. The Fur Press, Box 604, Chadron, Nebraska 69337

Hanson and Wilson's foreword captures the serious living historian's philosophy: "The Mountain Man era—the age when white hunters rather than Indians reaped the harvest of pelts in the Rockies—lasted about thirty

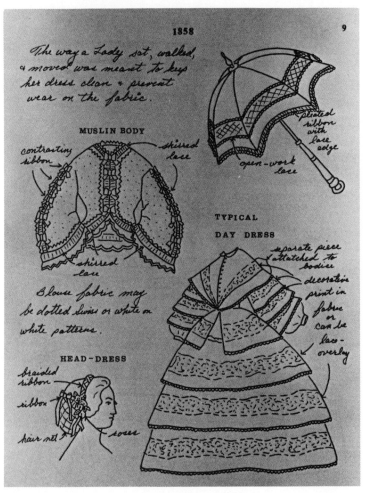

The way a Lady sat, walked, & moved was meant to keep her dress clean & prevent wear on the fabric.

MUSLIN BODY

contrasting ribbon

shirred lace

shirred lace

Blouse fabric may be dotted Swiss or white on white patterns.

pleated ribbon with lace edge

open-work lace

TYPICAL DAY DRESS

separate piece attached to bodice

decorative print in fabric or can be lace-overlay

HEAD-DRESS

braided ribbon

ribbon

hair net

roses

Civilian period clothing in the *Civil War Ladies Sketchbook.* — *Photographs by Sharli Powell*

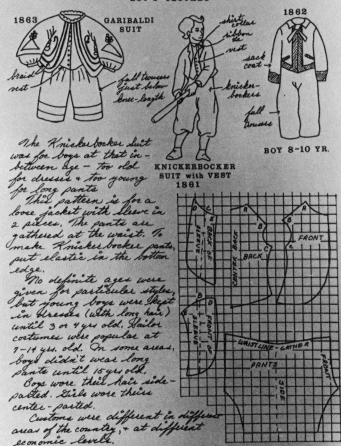

1863   GARIBALDI
               SUIT

braid
vest

fall trousers
just below
knee-length

shirt
collar
ribbon
tie
vest

sack
coat

knicker-
bockers

fall
trousers

1862

BOY 8-10 YR.

KNICKERBOCKER
SUIT with VEST
1861

The Knickerbocker Suit was for boys at that in-between age — too old for dresses & too young for long pants

This pattern is for a loose jacket with sleeve in 2 pieces. The pants are gathered at the waist. To make Knickerbocker pants, put elastic in the bottom edge.

No definite ages were given for particular styles, but young boys were kept in dresses (with long hair) until 3 or 4 yrs old. Sailor costumes were popular at 7-14 yrs. old. In some areas, boys didn't wear long pants until 15 yrs old.

Boys wore their hair side-parted. Girls wore theirs center-parted.

Customs were different in different areas of the country, & at different economic levels.

One test of a sketchbook's information—a military ball. Farbs aren't evident at this gathering at Fort Monroe, Virginia. —*Photograph by Richard Cheatham*

years, from 1810 to 1840. Trappers went in groups or brigades, and most were employees of someone else. The romantic idea of living snug in a log cabin with an Indian wife is mere fiction. This book was prompted by a deep friendship with many of today's mountain men, and the knowledge that they are sincere in wanting to have realistic costumes and equipment. Drawings herein were made from actual specimens or contemporary illustrations. We hope you enjoy reading the book as much as we did making it" (p. 3).

It's virtually impossible *not* to enjoy their richly researched study. Even though the authors essentially demystify a romantic subject, the authentic portrait they detail is far more fascinating and useful than the Hollywood version. Hanson and Wilson cover headgear, a variety of authentic capotes, coats and jackets, pants, shirts, boots, moccasins, gloves and mittens, pouches, traps, containers, trapping and fishing gear, knives, hatchets and axes, smoking equipment, saddles, carts, boats, shelters, and much more. These sketchbooks are an indispensable tool for modern mountain men, buckskinners interested in the early nineteenth century, and reenactors looking for models to study.

The Civil War Ladies Sketchbook, vol 1, 2, 3, by Kathleen York. 1980, 1981. The House of York, 32 North Union Street, Elgin, Illinois 60120

The Civil War centennial celebration (1961–1965) primarily involved men and boys. Military units were formed and battles reenacted. Recent Civil War activity has lost much of its sexist orientation as more women have taken up living history as a hobby. Kathleen York's sketchbooks both reflect and encourage this trend. (Sutlers and pattern suppliers have also been significant

Interpreting historical patterns and fabric at the 1870 general store, Iowa Living History Farms. — *Photograph by Mimi Dunlap*

forces and are discussed in the appropriate section of this book.) York's examples are based on fashion plates which appeared in ladies' magazines such as *Godey's, Harper's,* and *Peterson's* between 1856 and 1865. Her notes are useful, carefully considered but not pedantic. They are written out in script, as in so many other sketchbooks—which adds an informal charm. Volume 1 contains an "inventory" of outfits suitable for various occasions. Volume 2 contains twelve historic patterns, clearly explained and adapted by York. Included are directions for reproducing a jacket, fishu, chemisette, pantalettes, camisole, chemise, boy's jacket, girl's dress, ball gown, party dress, riding skirt, and bodices. Together the volumes constitute an excellent introduction to the clothing of women in the Civil War period.

Tim McGill, an experienced reenactor, is well turned out as a "blind date" of the 1920s. —*Photograph by Sherry Eslick Buettgenbach*

PART IV.
FUN AND GAMES

9. Films

THE historical film (I should really say the "war movie") that had the greatest impact on me when I was a budding reenactor isn't included in this chapter. I remember its plot, the weather on the Saturday when my buddies and I went to see it, how it ended, and who the good guys and the bad guys were. What I forgot and still can't track down is its title. The movie was set in the Civil War, and the heroes (Confederates) had managed to haul a cannon up a strategic mountain, thereby halting Sherman's advance into Georgia. The boys in gray valiantly held off the evil Yankee attackers until, in desperation, the old men in blue resorted to a mammoth cannon mounted on a railway carriage. Armed with advanced technology and guile, the Northerners won. In short, it was *Guns of Navarone* in reverse. Despite the ending, it was a super movie, especially if you were about ten and saw your sole purpose in life as the refighting of the Civil War.

The living history movement and historical films have obvious relationships. First, many (if not all) interpreters, reenactors, and simulation gamers are also historical film buffs.

They watch films for inspiration, for ideas, and to sharpen their critical skills. Serious historical films are often featured in museum film programs or as evening entertainment at living history events. On the night before a World War II battle reenactment, it's almost become a tradition to screen one or two old war movies, such as *Battleground* or *A Walk in the Sun*. The Stuhr Museum in Grand Island, Nebraska, schedules each winter a festival of films that deal with the history of the Great Plains (*The Grapes of Wrath, Heartland*) as a complement to the museum's interpretive program. Historical films are accounts of life in the past, and many attempt to be really believable. One way to judge both a film and a living history program is to ask yourself whether it was realistic, if you suspended disbelief. In short, is the simulation effectively carried out? Finally, films— like living history—are theatrical. They involve the use of role playing, sets, costumes, props, scripts, and scenarios. Films attempt to create a "period feel," an authentic atmosphere that is full of historically accurate details. The same is obviously true of a good living history program at a museum, reenactment, or event.

Historical films are significant in one other important way. They are historic artifacts, a "prime" primary source for evaluating how one period of history looked at another. Their bias is frequently glaring, and we can often spot the inaccuracies that characterized the films of earlier decades. Furthermore, films don't change (unless they are edited—bowdlerized for television, for example) in the way that museum programs or reenactment units do. Their prejudices are more permanent. By studying their limitations, perhaps we can more effectively identify our own failures to achieve authenticity.

Since there are so many historical films, my criteria had to be rigorous. (I have files on more than two hundred films in this genre!) I omitted documentary and nonfiction films because they are records of history, not simulations. This is a selection of "fiction" films, and it's limited to those readily available on videocassettes. You can, if you want, buy or rent copies of all these films and study them at home. I tried to stay with classics—films that critics over time have judged to be historically accuracte, rich in texture and detail, strong in period atmosphere, realistic, and serious in intent. They are all basically good movies, too. Each has captured the interest of successive generations of film critics and buffs. In short, these films aren't just "costumers." I have regretfully omitted the many fine orientation and educational films produced by living history museums such as Colonial Williamsburg and Old Sturbridge Village. I hope that many of these films will someday be available for home viewing at reasonable prices. Last, although this selection is mine, many friends with experience in reenacting looked it over and said that whenever I decided to show the films, they would bring the popcorn.

The selection is arranged chronologically by historical period except in the case of three entries that deal with time travel, *Time Bandits*, *Time after Time*, and *Westworld*, which serve as a sort of visual entree.

Time Bandits (1981). Director: Terry Gillian. Craig Warnock, John Cleese, Ian Holm, Sean Connery, David Warner, Ralph Richardson

In this disturbingly funny black comedy, Monty Python's Terry Gillian takes us on a trip through time with an English boy (Craig Warnock) and six sleazy, rude, greedy, dirty, and very amusing dwarfs—the "time bandits." Ralph Richardson plays the Supreme Being, whose blueprint of the universe has been stolen by the dwarfs. They plan to dart through its uncompleted "holes" into different times and "loot" history. They take the boy with them as they raid Napoleon (Ian Holm) after the Battle of Castiglione, Robin Hood (John Cleese), and Agamemnon (Sean Connery), all the while pursued by Evil (David Warner). History, as interpreted by Gillian, is in a disorganized, hostile mess. Progress is an empty notion and innocence forever lost. The film's closing image shows the Supreme Being rolling up his map of the universe, apparently tired of the project. *Time Bandits* suggests that both "the good old days" and history itself may ultimately prove to be an illusion.

Time after Time (1980). Director: Nicholas Meyer. Malcolm McDowell, David Warner, Mary Steenburgen

In Jack Finney's novel *Time and Time Again* (1970), the hero, Si Morley, travels back to the New York City of 1882 and decides to stay. Despite the corruption and poverty he encounters, Si prefers a world free from the collective memory of two worlds wars and a holocaust. *Time after Time* reverses this idea. Jack the Ripper (David Warner) steals the time machine from H. G. Wells (Malcolm McDowell) and travels from the Windsor of 1893 to the San Francisco of 1979. Wells, a pacifist, pursues him, fearing the machine has "turned the bloody maniac loose upon utopia." Of course they meet, and the Ripper, turning on a television set, shatters Wells by showing him a succession of late twentieth-century violent images. "You see," the Ripper boasts, "this is where I belong." Fortunately, Wells manages to blast the Ripper into infinity. *Time after Time* suggests that our "temporal ethno-centrism" may be effectively blinkering our view of today's world.

Westworld (1973). Director: Michael Crichton. Richard Benjamin, James Brolin, Yul Brynner

The subject of *Westworld* is an old one: the revolt of the robots. Michael Crichton, who both wrote and directed the film, freshens this idea by placing the robots in three historical re-creations: Romanworld, Medievalworld, and Westworld. Here, for a thousand dollars a day, visitors can satiate their vanity, lust, and aggression. The robots, actually computer-programmed humanoids, eventually tire of being broadaxed, gunned down, or sexually put upon. They act out a fanasty every interpreter at living history museums surely harbors at times: they turn on the tourists. The Black Knight in Medievalworld, the

Nubian Slaves in the Roman baths, and the gunslinger (Yul Brynner) in Westworld mercilessly eliminate their "modern" masters. Historical simulation, according to Crichton, may cost you more than money. Don't mess with history; people in the past—and by inference, people today—don't like to be exploited.

Quest for Fire (1981). Director: Jean-Jacques Annaud. Everett McGill, Ron Perlman, Nameer El Kadi, Rae Dawn Chong

Based on *La guerre de feu*, the 1909 novel that J. H. Rosny, Sr., wrote about prehistoric life, this French-Canadian film gives a naturalistic, tense, arresting, and ultimately touching account of life in the Stone Age. Filmed in the wilds of Kenya, Scotland, and Canada, the film follows three men as they search for fire. Along the way, they encounter saber-toothed tigers, mammoths, two different cultures (neo-Neanderthal and pseudo-Australian Aborigine), and some spectacular scenery. Director Jean-Jacques Annaud strove for authenticity. He hired anthropologist Desmond Morris (author of *The Naked Ape*) and linguist Anthony Burgess to re-create the language and gestures of people eighty thousand years ago. The result may readily be dismissed by experts (a review in the *American Anthropologist* particularly criticized the film's telescoping of evolution), but *Quest for Fire* remains the best fiction film about early man.

The War Lord (1965). Director: Franklin Schaffner. Charlton Heston, Richard Boone, Rosemary Forsyth, Maurice Evans, Guy Stockwell.

Historical roles are Charlton Heston's cup of mead. He has been Moses, Michelangelo, El Cid, and the mountain man Bill Tyler. In *The War Lord*,

Antonius **Block**, **the** knight, plays chess with Death in *The Seventh Seal.* —*Courtesy of Svensk Filmindustri*

Heston plays Chrysagon, a Norman knight sent by his duke to pacify a Fresian backwater somewhere along the English Channel. The time is pre-1066, and the world Heston enters is a murky one filled with druidic omens and hostile peasants. Despite the able assistance of Bors (Richard Boone) and Draco (Guy Stockwell), Heston makes a hash of his assignment. He falls in love with another man's bride, Bronwyn (Rosemary Forsyth), and demands the "right of the seignior," the privilege of sleeping with her on her wedding night. He can't bear to let her go, so naturally the Fresians storm his Norman tower. There follows some really authentic mayhem which should appeal especially to the "bop and bashers" of the Society for Creative Anachronism. *War Lord* is more entertainment than edification but it does depict a neglected period of history with reasonable accuracy.

Becket (1964). Director: Peter Glenville. Richard Burton, Peter O'Toole, John Gielgud, Donald Wolfit

This version of Jean Anouilh's play about the on-again, off-again relationship between Henry II and Thomas Becket has a rich, stately period feel. It is the twelfth century as you've always dreamed of it: sumptuous English scenery, technicolor pavilions, rippling chain mail, and ecclesiastical solemnity. The film follows Henry (Peter O'Toole) and Becket (Richard Burton) as they move from the drinking and wenching of youth to the perplexities and responsibilities of power. They have a falling out when Becket, appointed archbishop of Canterbury by Henry, gradually grows away from the king. Henry feels his love for Becket has been spurned, and the result is, as they say, history. Henry goes on to become a great, guilty king and Becket is a saint. *Becket* is first-rate historical fare.

Itinerante actors Mia, Jof, and Skat, perform as the Black Death nears. — *The Seventh Seal; courtesy of Svensk Filmindustri*

The Seventh Seal (1957). Director: Ingmar Bergman. Max Von Sydow, Gunnar Bjornstrand, Bibi Anderson

This masterful film is set in mid-fourteenth-century Sweden. A disillusioned knight (Max Von Sydow) is returing home from the Crusades with his worldly squire (Gunnar Bjornstrand). Word of the Black Death has reached Scandinavia and is terrorizing its people. Many think that Judgment Day is at hand. Flagellants roam the countryside, "witches" are burned, others snatch a little fun while they can. By playing chess with Death, the knight briefly forestalls his own demise and allows an innocent couple and their baby to escape. The atmosphere is darkly realistic, and the characters seem to have stepped out of a medieval wall painting. We meet common soldiers, traveling players, gloomy priests, and honest country folk. Their roles are drawn in subtle, almost Chaucerian tones. Anyone seriously re-creating history should study *The Seventh Seal*. Bergman especially has lessons to teach members of the Society for Creative Anachronism.

Henry V (1944). Director: Laurence Olivier. Laurence Olivier, Robert Newton, Leslie Banks, Leo Genn, Renée Asherson

Shakespeare would have enjoyed this film. Olivier re-creates the realism, exuberance, and flair for historical drama that characterize the Bard's original play. *Henry V* opens in the Globe Theater, and we are treated to a backstage view of Elizabethan stagecraft. The action then shifts back in time and across the Channel to France. The scene is Henry V's 1415 invasion of France. Olivier uses an almost naturalistic technique to capture the power, glory, and bloody horror of Agincourt. The battle sequence is rivaled only by the famous climactic engagement in *Alexander Nevsky*. Finally, against a flat, stylized

The dance of death, *The Seventh Seal*'s climactic ending. —*Courtesy of Svensk Filmindustri*

Laurence Olivier's *Henry V* cheered war-weary Britons in late 1944. —*Courtesy of Two Cities Film*

backdrop reminiscent of a medieval illumination, Henry V gently courts and wins the hand of Princess Catherine, daughter of the king of France. To create the right atmosphere, Olivier uses period music, costumes, and a cast of classical actors who seem to be born-again Elizabethans. This is a film for the head and the heart.

Kagemusha (1980). Director: Akira Kurosawa. Tatsura Nakadai, Tsutomu Yamazaki, Kenichi Hagiwara

Kurosawa is one of the greats of cinema. His *Seven Samurai* (1954) explored the human aspects of battle on a small scale; irony infuses this film about professional soldiers plying their craft. In *Kagemusha* ("The Shadow Warrior"), Kurosawa examines the grandeur and fatal attraction of war. The film takes place in feudal sixteenth-century Japan and deals with the attempt of three warlords to capture the capital city of Kyoto. One of them dies, and the others decide to keep his death a secret (shades of *el Cid*) and hire a double to impersonate him. The "volunteer" is a thief, Kagemusha, who is about to be crucified for his crimes. Rescued, he must now attempt to live up to the dead warlord's reputation, a formidable task. During the Battle of Nagashino—a superb forty-minute re-creation—he discovers his latent gifts of courage, honor, and leadership. *Kagemusha* is a magnificent tribute to tradition and Kurosawa's finest work.

The Seven Samurai (1954). Director: Akira Kurosawa. Toshiro Mifune, Takashi Shimura, Yoshio Inaba

Set in sixteenth-century Japan, Kurosawa's masterpiece is ostensibly about a farming village which hires seven professional warriors to defend it

Henry, at war, inspires his English army before Agincourt. —*Henry V; courtesy of Two Cities Film*

from forty mounted bandits. The film runs for three and one-half hours, and there is not a dull minute. No other director has approached Kurosawa's ability to combine action, violence, and human comedy realistically. The film's texture is almost palpable. Kurosawa reaches out and envelops you; disbelief is totally suspended. No other film I've seen comes closer to simulating life in the past and involving you in its context and intense drama. Medieval reenactors should especially appreciate its choreographed battle scenes, which are models of suspense, irony, and dramatic impact.

The Three Musketeers (1973). Director: Richard Lester. Oliver Reed, Michael York, Richard Chamberlain, Frank Finlay, Raquel Welch, Faye Dunaway

The Three Musketeers and its 1975 sequel *The Four Musketeers* (which was actually filmed at the same time) take place in the mid-1620s, the heart of the "Age of Kings," an extraordinarily colorful period of history. France is ruled by Louis XIII, still in his twenties, and the older, craftier Cardinal Richelieu. Richard Lester's films are definitely not history lessons, however. Based on the romantic novel of Alexander Dumas and the lighthearted screenplay of George MacDonald Frazer (creator of the Flashman novels), both *Musketeer* films are more like irreverent social histories of the French aristocracy. We see, Athos, Aramis, Porthos, D'Artagnan, and their friends and enemies feasting, loving, gambling, jousting, dueling, and sporting at the Siege of Rochelle. The period details are sumptuously rich and the action creatively choreographed. In the best slapstick tradition, the cast plays it straight, which makes the films even more amusing. The movie's interest for the living historian consists not in humor but in the enthusiastic manner in which the texture of life (albeit life at the top) is re-created.

Henry, in love, courts Kate, daughter of the king of France. —*Henry V; courtesy of Two Cities Film*

The Silent Enemy (1930). Director: H. P. Carver. Yellow Robe, Long Lance, Akawansh, Spotted Elk, Cheeka

A silent film classic that has recently been made available on videotape, *The Silent Enemy* is one of the first attempts to simulate the past on film. The producers, William Burden and William Chandler, traveled to northern Ontario and persuaded a community of Ojibwa Indians to re-create an episode in their folk history in which a younger man (Long Lance) challenged his chief (Yellow Robe) to leave their hunting base, where they were slowly being decimated by the silent enemy, hunger. It is a simple yet realistic and convincing narrative.

The photography of Marcel Le Picard makes *The Silent Enemy* a memorable film. He captures the natural beauty of the Great North Woods and its wildlife in scene after scene. The fish and game are seen from the Ojibwa point of view—as food. No attempt is made to personify them as was done in many subsequent films, such as the Disney true-life adventure series.

Native Americans are treated as human beings, not as stereotyped noble savages. Long Lance, who served in the Canadian army in World War I, and Yellow Robe deserve much of the credit for the authenticity of the final film. *The Silent Enemy* left me feeling that I had seen the Ojibwa as the Jesuits did during the first encounters in the seventeenth century.

Tom Jones (1963). Director: Tony Richardson. Albert Finney, Susannah York, Hugh Griffith, Edith Evans

Tom Jones is the wonderful exception to the rule that you can't make a great movie out of a great novel. Winner of four Academy Awards (best picture, best director, best screenplay, and best score), Tony Richardson's romp through Henry Fielding's 1740s England will continue to delight history buffs and movie buffs alike. No attempt is made to duplicate eighteenth-century style; rather Richardson uses a whole bag of modern movie tricks to pull us into Tom's world. There are slapstick chases at "silent movie" speeds, stop-camera shots in which the characters wink asides to us, a jazzy score played on a harpsicord, a droll narrator, subtitles, a deer hunt filmed from a helicopter, syncopated cuts, and more. Somehow it all works. The brilliant cast re-creates in the countryside sequences a robust tone which contrasts effectively with London scenes that seem straight out of Hogarth. The plot is similar to that in *Barry Lyndon*, the picaresque adventures of a country lad, but there the similarity ends. Tom is a lovable eighteenth-century Everyman, alive and well in England's "green and pleasant land."

Barry Lyndon (1975). Director: Stanley Kubrick. Ryan O'Neal, Marisa Berenson, Patrick Magee, narrated by Michael Hordern

For reenactors, *Barry London* is a masterpiece. Never before or since has a director taken such pains to ensure absolute authenticity. The film chronicles the adventures of an Irish knave before, during, and after the Seven Years War, 1756–1763. Based on W. M. Thackeray's 1844 novel, *Barry Lyndon* is pan-European in scale, beginning in Ireland, moving to the Continent, and ending in England. The pacing, lighting, musical score, and especially cinematography mirror the deliberate, detailed, excessively "rational" style that characterizes middle- and upper-class culture of the period. This is the film equivalent of performances of baroque music that use only period instruments and settings. Many filmgoers found *Barry Lyndon* tedious, a reaction Thackeray would have shared. For history buffs, reenactors, museum curators,

Six of *The Seven Samurai* prepare to defend a poor village from bandits. —*Courtesy of Toho Productions*

Akira Kurosawa called *The Seven Samurai* a "jidai-geki," a real period film. —*Courtesy of Toho Productions*

and art (or architectural) historians, however, Kubrick's film is a three-hour visual feast.

The Devil's Disciple (1959) Director: Guy Hamilton. Laurence Olivier, Burt Lancaster, Kirk Douglas, Harry Andrews, Basil Sydney

Set in 1777 just before General Burgoyne's defeat at Saratoga, *The Devil's Disciple* is a wry, almost camp version of George Bernard Shaw's play. In the original 1897 drama, Shaw poked fun at some of his pet targets: colonialism, war, Victorian morality, and especially man's propensity for rewriting history. In a scene toward the end of the film, "Gentlemanly Johnny" Burgoyne (Laurence Olivier) sardonically tells his major, Swindon (Harry Andrews), that the British army will soon be defeated by the American rebels. Swindon is appalled. "Impossible. I can't believe it. What will history say?" "History, sir," Burgoyne replies, "will tell lies as usual."

The tone of *The Devil's Disciple* would please the real eighteenth-century Burgoyne: it's satiric, witty, intelligent, and polished. Guy Hamilton never allows his actors to take themselves seriously. Filmed in England, the production has a proper period feel and some tongue-in-cheek performances by Olivier, Lancaster, Douglas, and a number of British character actors.

The Duellists (1977). Director: Ridley Scott. Keith Carradine, Harvey Keitel, Edward Fox, Tom Conti, Albert Finney

Adapted from Joseph Conrad's short story "The Duel," this staggeringly beautiful film is about a fifteen-year private feud between two French huzzar officers during the Napoleonic period. Their quarrel, like the very war in which they are fighting, often seems confused, meaningless, and especially

The final scene in *The Seven Samurai,* the funeral of four warriors. —*Courtesy of Toho Productions*

endless. The film's point of view is that of Lieutenant D'Hubert (Keith Carradine), a lanky, fair, sensitive aristocrat with an ironic sense of humor. His adversary, Lieutenant Ferand (Harvey Keitel), is short and dark, a peasant by birth and caught in an obsession he can't shake. Ferand is a born fighter, a "cavalry man" who views war as a "massed lot of personal contests, a sort of gregarious duelling." Ferand lives to duel and vice versa. D'Hubert can't fathom his opponent, nor can he shake him. D'Hubert simply longs for peace, a quiet life in the countryside, escape. But both men are inextricably bound to each other and to history. Fortunately for us, the historical period within which they are trapped is both pastoral and martial, and no film has ever pictured its atmosphere as effectively. The beautifully composed historical scenes in *The Duellist* seem to glow.

Jeremiah Johnson (1972). Director: Sydney Pollack. Robert Redford, Will Geer, Stephen Gierasch, Allyn Ann McLerie

If there's such a thing as a "cult classic" for buckskinners, then it's probably *Jeremiah Johnson*. Sam Fadala dedicates his *Black Powder Handbook* to both his wife Nancy *and* "Robert Redford, who resurrected Jeremiah Johnson." Many would share Fadala's admiration for the original John Johnson and the role Redford built around his legend. The film was shot in Utah's Rocky Mountains and is a stunner. It makes you want to pack up and head west. The first hour and a half of *Jeremiah Johnson* is compelling. Pollack has a good story to tell (it is based on Vardis Fisher's novel *Mountain Man*), and he does so without a lot of tricks. There is much humor (provided by Will Geer and Stephen Gierasch), scenes of great beauty and understandable horror, and an understated empathy for the mountain men and the Indians they emulate in so many ways. Redford plays his role with an unforced naturalness. He is equally good as a bumbling pilgrim and later as an experienced hivernant. The last part of the film shows Johnson successfully warding off Crow attempts to kill him. He becomes known as "Crow Killer" and enters the world of legend.

Man of Aran (1934). Director: Robert Flaherty. Coleman King, Maggie Dirrane, Mikeleen Dillane, Pat Mullen

Man of Aran, the second of Robert Flaherty's masterpieces (*Nanook of the North* preceded it in 1922), is generally considered to be a documentary about the traditional folklife of the Aran Islands off the west coast of Ireland. It was a way of life that had seemingly managed to survive unchanged into the modern world. Actually, cultural change was well on its way when Flaherty arrived with his film crew to make a feature for Gainsborough Pictures. Flaherty, a charismatic romantic, persuaded the islanders to simulate the life of their great grandparents, the age-old ways essentially discarded in the nineteenth century but still retained in the people's memory.

The result is a magnificent, memorable account of life in one of earth's inhospitable environments. Deviod of trees and soil, exposed to the open Atlantic gales, the Aran Islands are nevertheless home to a small community of farmer-fisherman. Flaherty tells the story of their fight for survival by focusing on one family—father, mother, and son—played by three islanders who were not in fact related. Still we identify immediately and totally with them and watch with fascination, fear, and empathy as they fight to stay alive.

City meets country in Tony Richardson's *Tom Jones.* Hugh Griffith and Dame Edith Evans exchange barbs. —*Courtesy of Woodfall Productions*

The Emigrants (1970) and the *The New Land* (1972). Director: Jan Troell. Max Von Sydow, Liv Ullmann, Eddie Axberg, Monica Zetterlund

Ironically, it took a Swede to make the best films ever about a theme in American history. Jan Troell's two films are masterpieces. Based on novels by Vilhelm Moberg, they chronicle the experiences of a band of Swedish emigrants in America in the mid-nineteenth century. The epic films are long, with running times of 150 and 160 minutes, respectively. In *The Emigrants*, we follow peasant farmer Karl Oskar (Max Von Sydow), his wife, Kristie (Liv Ullman), and their children and close friend from a feudal, poverty-stricken Sweden, across the Atlantic on a brutal voyage to New York, and finally by train, paddleboat, and foot to Minnesota. Then, in *The New Land*, we share their experiences in America as they create farms from forests are caught up in the tragic Sioux Rebellion that swept Minnesota in the 1860s, and, in the case of Karl Oskar's brother Robert, join in the ill-fated search throughout the West for gold. Shot on location in Sweden and America, the films powerfully evoke the texture of life for the ordinary people who saw America as the "best poor man's land."

The Red Badge of Courage (1951). Director: John Huston. Audie Murphy, Bill Mauldin, John Dierkes, Douglas Dick

The Red Badge of Courage is an almost literal rendering of Stephen Crane's classic short novel about an Ohio farm boy's encounter with the hopes, fears, terrors, and triumphs of battle. The part of "The Youth" is played by Audie Murphy, the most decorated soldier in the U.S. Army during World War II. The director, John Huston, was also a veteran of World War II; his documentary *San Pietro* is considered a classic study of battle. The film was

In *The Emigrants*, Karl and Kristie find life in Sweden unbearable and realize they must leave for America. —*Courtesy of Svensk Filmindustri*

actually shot on an isolated part of Huston's ranch, and the scenery is almost too idyllic. Nevertheless, the picture itself presents the ordinary soldier's view of war: the seemingly senseless marches and endless waiting, the vainglorious posing before battle and sheer terror afterward, and the horror of being amid the wounded and the dead. Although purists will fault the film on the accuracy of its details, the *Red Badge of Courage* is arguably one of the truest "war movies" ever to come out of Hollywood. Unfortunately, some of the more graphic sequences in the original print were heavily edited by studio censors, who worried about a negative public reaction; the film was released in 1951, during the middle of the Korean War.

Stagecoach (1939). Director: John Ford. John Wayne, Claire Trevor, Thomas Mitchell, Andy Devine, John Carradine, Donald Meek, Louise Platt

Although this film is closely associated in viewers' minds with the great outdoors, much of *Stagecoach* was actually shot on Hollywood sound stages and studio back lots. Nevertheless, *Stagecoach* has become a reference point for anyone interested in the Western as a realistic simulation of life in the past. Compared with most Westerns made earlier and later, *Stagecoach* rings true, at least to the spirit of the West.

The place is Arizona in 1885. The plot essentially follows the "ship of fools" theme. A variety of passengers travel from Tonto to Lordsburg by stagecoach during the period when Geronimo has left the Apache Reservation on the Natanes Plateau and is attempting to turn back the clock to precontact times. An alcoholic doctor (Thomas Mitchell), a timid whiskey drummer (Donald Meek), a Virginia matron (Louise Platt), a gambler (John

Carradine), an absconding banker (Berton Churchill), and a prostitute (Claire Trevor) have all been thrown out of Tonto and are traveling on. They have one adventure after another, meeting the Ringo Kid (John Wayne), Indians, U.S. Cavalry, and finally outlaws. All the good guys eventually win.

Based on a novel by Ernest Haycox, *Stagecoach* is not a realistic account of an actual historic incident retold on film. Rather it's a period piece, capturing the themes and textures of life in Arizona in the 1880s and interpreting them through drama. Unlike hundreds of other superficially similar films, this one succeeds. *Stagecoach* is regarded as a classic.

Cheyenne Autumn (1964). Director: John Ford. Richard Widmark, Carroll Baker, Edward G. Robinson, Dolores Del Rio, Gilbert Roland

Cheyenne Autumn is based on a tragic episode in American history. In 1878, the Northern Cheyenne began a two-year, fifteen-hundred-mile trek from a reservation in Oklahoma to their ancestral home along Montana's Yellowstone River Valley. Sick and straving, they had to contend with both the vicissitudes of the Great Plains' climate and harassment from a troop of U.S. Cavalry assigned to return them to the Indian territories. Their story was empathetically told by Mari Sandoz in the 1953 book from which the film takes both its name and inspiration.

John Ford is in top form here. The film is rich in period detail and atmosphere. The grandeur of the scenery the Cheyenne pass through is matched by their desperate determination to reach their homeland. There is little question where Ford's sympathies lie. In an early scene, a group of Cheyenne ride across the desert at dawn to meet a congressional delegation. It never arrives. The Cheyenne patiently wait, wrapped in their government blankets, stoic but slowly realizing that they can no longer trust Washington and must at least try to recover their land and dignity. Ford lets us accompany them on their final journey.

Buffalo Bill and the Indians; or Sitting Bull's History Lesson (1976). Director: Robert Altman. Paul Newman, Joel Grey, Kevin McCarthy, Burt Lancaster, Geraldine Chaplin, Frank Kaquitts, Will Sampson

An ironic scene comes about half-way through this film. Sitting Bull's interpreter (Will Sampson) tells Buffalo Bill (Paul Newman) that the chief wants to stage his own play as part of the Wild West Show, an 1885 "living museum" that Bill has set up in North Platte, Nebraska, to reenact the history of the West for tourists. Sitting Bull's play will show white men killing Indian women and children. Bill is naturally aghast, but Annie Oakley (Geraldine Chaplin) explains, "He just wants to show the truth to the people." Bill replies, "I have a better sense of history." That's the theme of *Buffalo Bill and the Indians*: our conflicting accounts of the past. In Altman's film, Bill's account wins out because Bill is the better showman. Like P. T. Barnum, Artur Hazelius (founder of Skansen), and Walt Disney, William Cody "invented" a new medium for interpreting history. Altman is fascinated with both the creative brashness of Cody's medium (a sort of open air museum, festival, and pageant) and Bill's egocentric-ethnocentric view of American history. The film re-creates Bill's "Historyland," animates it with an ensemble of great character actors, and allows the show to evolve. The result is a superb period piece, rich in atmosphere and detail, and full of ironic comments on man's propensity to rewrite history and sell it to a mass society craving a sense of its own past.

Hester Street (1974). Director: Joan Macklin Silver. Carol Kane, Steven Keats, Mel Howard

Resembling one of Isaac Bashevis Singer's short stories of Jewish ghetto life, *Hester Street* is a small jewel of a film. Set on New York City's lower East Side in 1896, the film tells the painful yet often comic story of Jake (Steven Keats), his wife, Gitl (Carol Kane), and their boarder, Bernstein (Mel Howard), as they are transformed from Russian immigrants into Americans. They go a long way. In an early scene, the group is picnicking in a park. Jake plays baseball with his son, and Gitl sits by a tree with Bernstein, who was a rabbinical student in the old country. The innocent wide-eyed Gitl (brilliantly played by Kane), who has never left the ghetto in either Russia or New York, asks "Are there any Gentiles in America?" She wises up fast after Jake divorces her to run off with his new American girlfriend. Gitl doesn't collapse into self-pity; rather she and Bernstein work out their own variation of the American success story.

Zulu (1964). Director: Cy Endfield. Stanley Baker, Jack Hawkins, Michael Caine, Nigel Green

A cult film for reenactors and military history buffs, *Zulu* re-creates the Battle of Rorke's Drift which was fought between the Zulus and the British in January 1879. Four thousand Zulus attacked one hundred British, who somehow managed to hold their own and to win eleven Victoria Crosses in the bargain. The British unit was the Twenty-Fourth Foot, a Welsh outfit, as Stanley Baker rather proudly notes throughout the film. Most characters are presented as types—aristocratic snobs, middle-class professionals, working-class rascals, and so forth. The real stars of *Zulu* are the Zulus themselves, who are treated with respect as a first-class fighting force. The scenery of the Natal National Park is magnificent, and the film is authentic in atmosphere and is refreshingly free of colonial jingoism. Although the story celebrates the victory of a handful of white men over a mass of blacks, the emotional climax comes when the Zulu regiments pay tribute to their enemies and give them a shield-pounding salute, soldier to soldier, man to man.

Breaker Morant (1980). Director: Bruce Beresford. Edward Woodward, Jack Thompson, John Waters, Vincent Ball

Based on *Scapegoats of Empire*, George Witton's bitter denunciation of British duplicity in the Boer War, this Australian film re-creates the trumped-up court-martial of three Australian soldiers in 1901 and the subsequent execution of two of them. Beresford leaves little doubt as to who the good and bad guys are. Your sympathies are always with Harry "Breaker" Morant (Edward Woodward) and his down-to-earth buddies who are persecuted for doing the Empire's dirty work. Nevertheless, the film raises many ethical questions about what is and isn't justifiable in war, moral dilemmas that have great relevancy in the modern post-Vietnam world. *Breaker Morant* obviously had the support of some good military historians; its details are absolutely authentic. Shot in color with some glorious scenes of the velt, it is a visual treat, a somewhat polemical but sad and ironic film about man's inhumanity to man. The theme sets *Breaker Morant* apart from most other war movies.

McCabe and Mrs. Miller (1971). Director: Robert Altman. Warren Beatty, Julie Christie, René Auberjonois, Shelley Duvall, Michael Murphy, Keith Carradine, John Schuck

Everyone involved in living history—the simulation of life in other times—dreams of re-creating a historical farm, town, camp, or event that literally transcends time. Upon entering the place, you will know immediately that this is how the past really looked. You will sense the period completely. Altman manages to break the time barrier in *McCabe and Mrs. Miller*. He does so in part by building a raw, unfinished 1902 town called Presbyterian Church in the cold, sloppy forests of Washington, just under the Canadian border. Presbyterian Church is, as they say, not the end of the world, but you can see it from there. Altman then adds a cast of incredibly realistic characters: the saloon keeper McCabe (Warren Beatty), the bordello madam (Julie Christie), and an assortment of prostitutes, miners, lumbermen, and other working types. The society is virtually all male, rough, and never quite clean, warm, or dry enough. Presbyterian Church *is* the Northwest, the last and very unheroic frontier. Somehow Altman and his actors bring this miserable little town alive. More important, the reality that *McCabe and Mrs. Miller* simulates represents the true experience of most Americans throughout our history. This film makes most other historical dramas, and Westerns in particular, seem like cheap plastic substitutes.

Heartland (1979). Director: Richard Pearce. Rip Torn, Conchata Ferrell, Barry Primus, Lilia Skala, Megan Folson

Set in 1910 Wyoming, *Heatland* deglamorizes pioneer life. Every aspect of this modest film radiates honesty. Conchata Ferrell plays a widow from

Warren Beatty blissfully bathes in *McCabe and Mrs. Miller.* —*Courtesy of Warner Brothers*

Denver who hires out as a housekeeper for a homesteading rancher (Rip Torn). Neither is a clean-cut, all-American Hollywood type; they both look as if they had stepped out of a historical photograph. Their faces, especially, have a tough, broad, peasant character: they are survivors. They have to be — winter is a killer in Wyoming. She quickly loses her dreams of going it alone, marries the dour Torn, and together they lose half the cattle and their infant son. Pearce doesn't permit an ounce of melodrama. Rather, *Heartland* takes a naturalistic point of view that's in keeping with the place, period, and realistic events depicted. Why do they stay? The land is theirs, and its beauty is a continual revelation. You are left to believe that if they can only manage to make the prairie yield a living, Wyoming will be their Eden.

Days of Heaven (1978). Director: Terrence Malick. Richard Gere, Brooke Adams, Sam Shepard, Linda Manz

The setting of *Days of Heaven* is Texas in 1916, a vast remote wheatland isolated from a world at war and on the verge of a technological revolution fueled by oil. The Oscar-winning cinematography of Nestor Alemandros captures the sun-bleached farmscapes of this land that hasn't really entered the twentieth century. The film was shot in 70 mm film, and much of its beauty will be only suggested if seen on television. Nevertheless, Terrence Malick is able to achieve a powerfully realistic sense of place and time that will awe even the viewer who sees *Days of Heaven* on a small screen. Malick's tone is laconic. Except for Sam Shepard, who plays a wealthy young farmer, most of the characters are migrant workers, emigrants from the cities of Eurpoe and the Northeast. They are tired, poor survivors, exiled from their homes and seemingly in a state of geographic shock. They haven't a clue as to how to set down roots. The viewer of course knows that those who manage to find a way to settle down will ironically be set adrift again in the dust bowl in less than a generation. *Days of Heaven* is a prophetic, realistic film, as serious as it is beautiful.

Potemkin (1925). Director: Sergi Eisenstein. Alexander Antonov, Vladimir Barsky, Grigori Alexandrov, Mikhail Goronorov

Eisenstein's first "war movie," *Potemkin* was a landmark in the history of the cinema. It re-created a significant event in Russian history and pioneered a realistic style. Although *Potemkin* is a silent film, Eisenstein's images seem to follow a visual score. You *hear* the desperate frustration and erupting anger of the Russian sailors and people as they revolt in 1905. The film lacks an overt story; Eisenstein simply pictures a meeting on the cruiser *Potemkin* in Odessa harbor during the waning days of the Russo-Japan war. His primary sources are the official ship's log and the oral histories of eyewitnesses. The hero of the film is revolution itself. All else—the ship, sailors, people of Odessa—is supporting cast. Eisenstein's style is realistic; his technique has the look of a documentary but is in fact filled with artful innovation. The ten-minute Odessa Steps sequence, the best-known movie scene of all time, is the prime example. For students of the historical film, *Potemkin* is a first. For history buffs, it is a marvel of simulation, a powerful account of the past.

Former German officer Hans von Morhart, technical adviser for *All Quiet on the Western Front*, checks John Wray's uniform with director Lewis Milestone. —*Courtesy of Universal Pictures*

All Quiet on the Western Front (1930). Director: Lewis Milestone. Lew Ayres, Slim Summerville, Russell Gleason, Bill Bakewell, John Wray, Richard Griffith

Lewis Milestone, the Ukrainian-born director of *All Quiet on the Western Front*, said that, at the opening night of the film, while the first battle scene was unfolding, two veterans who had been wounded at the front jumped out of their seats and charged the screen. "That's how close we came to the truth of the thing." Based on Erich Maria Remarque's 1929 autobiographical novel of World War I, the film follows a group of German schoolboys from home to training camp to the front and eventually to death. Along the way, they shed their romantic ideas of war, heroism, and the fatherland. As realistic as newsreel footage, *All Quiet on the Western Front* pulls you into its terrifying vortex. No film before or since has captured the horror of life in the trenches more completely. Yet despite its tragic message, the film remains a testimony to the common man, who sadly cannot avoid sacrificing himself in every new war-to-end-all-wars. This humanistic theme is one often echoed in the living history movement. It was banned in militaristic countries throughout the world, but the story of Paul, Albert, Kat, and their comrades will continue to be read, seen, and understood.

La Grande Illusion (1937). Director: Jean Renoir. Jean Gabin, Pierre Fresnay, Erich Von Stroheim, Marcel Dalio

Jean Renoir's sensitive study of French prisoners of war and their captors in World War I is one of the great films of all times. The main characters are two aristocrats, the German von Rauffenstein (Erich Von Stroheim) and his French counterpart, de Goeldieu (Pierre Fresnay); a working-class mechanic,

May, 1917.—*All Quiet on the Western Front; courtesy of Universal Pictures*

A German barracks square is magnificently re-created for the realistic film version of Eric Maria Remarque's 1929 novel, *All Quiet on the Western Front.* —*Courtesy of Universal Pictures*

Marechal (Jean Gabin); and Rosenthal, a bourgeois Jew (Marcel Dalio). Divided by nationality, class, and religion, these four are nevertheless united by their shared humanity. Renoir's message is no secret: our modern world is littered with *isms*, all of which are illusory. We must put our faith in fraternity, the brotherhood of man. Although the film's theme is deadly serious, Renoir's technique is not. *La Grande Illusion* is great entertainment. It is rich in humor, camaraderie, suspense, excitement, tragedy, and romance. The film has a great period "feel" and is filled with authentic details. Although there is not a single battle scene, not any suggestion of malevolent violence, the film is a superb interpretation of men at war.

Zelig (1983). Director: Woody Allen. Woody Allen, Mia Farrow, Patrick Hogan, Ellen Garrison

One of the games that people involved in living history like to play is a kind of photographic *trompe l'oeil*. The aim is to achieve such a high level of historical realism that a photograph taken of you or your group looks exactly like an original print, the sort you would find in an old photo album or on a stereoscope card. (This sourcebook has some fine examples.)

Woody Allen's *Zelig*, the story of a "human chameleon" with no personality of his own who takes on the physical and mental characteristics of anyone he's with, is a delightful example of the simulation game played by a master. About the only way you can be positive that you're *not* looking at a 1920s or 1930s film is to spot the puckish Allen, who plays Zelig. The degree of authenticity achieved by the filmmakers is amazing. Every detail is perfect: the clothes, sets, speech, and especially the period mannerisms.

Zelig is gentle little comedy that contrasts nicely with the run-of-the-

Paul (Lew Ayers) is in shock after killing a French soldier in the last months of World War I. —*All Quiet on the Western Front; courtesy of Universal Pictures*

mill, overblown historical spectacular. Allen's picture has little to say about modern American "history," but much to teach us about the craft of historical simulation. *Zelig* is also great fun.

The Grapes of Wrath (1940). Director: John Ford. Henry Fonda, Jane Darwell, John Carradine, Charlie Grapewin

The Grapes of Wrath, based on John Steinbeck's Pulitzer prize-winning novel, retains the book's desperate realism and has the look of a documentary. Despite its naturalistic, tragic tone, John Ford's film ranks as one of the most popular American movies ever made. Ford won an Academy Award for direction, Jane Darwell, who played Mrs. Joad, received an Oscar for best actress, and Henry Fonda made his first big splash. The film focuses on the Joads, an "Okie" family, and their desperate trek from a dust bowl farm to California. We identify completely with their plight and their struggle to survive. The film's level of authenticity is high. The scenes of Oklahoma recall James Agee's portraits of tenant farmers in *Let Us Now Praise Famous Men*. For living historical farm curators and interpreters, *Grapes of Wrath* presents a powerful challenge. Can a living museum ever hope to rival the film's re-creation of the 1930s hard times?

Das Boot (1981). Director: Wolfgang Petersen. Jurgen Prochnow, Herbert Gronemeyer, Klaus Wennemann

Based on Lothar-Guenther Buchheim's autobiographical novel of life aboard a World War II German submarine, *Das Boot* ("The Boat") is a tense, realistic, very human account of life at sea during war. Petersen, who both directed and wrote the script, filmed *Das Boot* inside an exact replica of a U-boat. The result is almost claustrophobic; you are crammed with the crew into a filthy, noisy, fragile, small, and very dangerous place. Like *All Quiet on the Western Front*, *Das Boot* captures the boredom, tension, panic, and terror of war as experienced by the ordinary man. We identify completely with the U-boat captain, a professional sailor, and his men, all of whom are presented as patriotic Germans—not fanatical Nazis. The film makes it clear that, although the crew is willing to risk their lives to kill the "English" out of a deep sense of duty, the men in fact have more in common with the Allied sailors they are torpedoing than with their Fascist leaders. In one emotional scene, the captain plays a recording of "A Long Way to Tipperary" to cheer up his men, and they all respond by singing along in English. A poignant, tragic, beautiful film about the common man at war.

Twelve O'Clock High (1949). Director: Henry King. Gregory Peck, Hugh Marlowe, Gary Merrill, Dean Jagger

Few war films do a credible job of interpreting the complex relationships that develop between officers and enlisted men. *Twelve O'Clock High* is the story of a young general (Greogry Peck) who takes command of an American bomber group in England during 1942 when daylight attacks over Germany were taking a heavy toll. He replaces a commander who has over-identified with his men and is on the verge of breakdown. Peck takes the opposite tack and enforces a stern, almost ruthless discipline. The tactic succeeds, but he, too, eventually cracks under the pressure. Everything about the film rings true—the airbase, the uniforms, the behavior of the airmen, and especially the combat with the Luftwaffe. The film lacks the usual self-conscious heroics, overwrought battle scenes, and even women. Instead, King managed

Erich von Stroheim, playing an aristocratic German officer, mocks a Jewish intellectual prisoner of war in Jean Renoir's *La Grand Illusion*. —*Courtesy of R.A.C. Productions*

Henry Fonda as Tom Joad in
The Grapes of Wrath. —
Courtesy of 20th Century Fox

to re-create the physical and emotional context of war in the air. Dean Jagger, the paunchy, middle-aged adjutant through whose memory the story unfolds, won an Academy Award.

A Walk in the Sun (1946). Director: Lewis Milestone. Dana Andrews, Richard Conte, Sterling Holloway, John Ireland, Lloyd Bridges

Although director Lewis Milestone didn't duplicate his earlier achievement with *All Quiet on the Western Front*, *Walk in the Sun* was nevertheless one of the best movies to come out of World War II. The film is based on Harry Brown's classic novel of a platoon's struggle at Salerno and begins on a landing barge as it plows toward the Italian beach. We follow the platoon as it regroups onshore after its lieutenant has been killed. The confusion of the men, their tension, fear, and final emergence as stubborn G.I.'s is graphically captured. Milestone pulls us into the picture and forces us to "walk in the sun" with them. We can't help but empathize with these ordinary soldiers. Authenticity is crucial—the film was aimed at many ex-G.I.'s who actually fought in Europe—and the cast achieves it. Dana Andrews, Richard Conte, and Lloyd Bridges went on to important movie careers. *Walk in the Sun* is one of the few films about the war to come out of Hollywood without looking like a commerical production. Rather, it has the stamp of a film made by soldiers for soldiers.

Machine versus man as the frustrated Joads attempt to save their farm. —*The Grapes of Wrath; courtesy of 20th Century Fox*

Battleground (1949). Director: William Wellman. Van Johnson, John
Holiak, Ricardo Montalban, George Murphey, Marshall Thompson

When I first saw *Battleground* as a boy, it reminded me immediately of a
book I had been reading, Bill Mauldin's *Up Front*. Both the G.I.'s in the films
and Mauldin's Willie and Joe view World War II from the foxhole, where they
wait—dirty, unshaven, uncomfortable, and eternally griping—for the war to
end. Only the Germans and the "brass" keep them from going home. Today,
the populist point of view espoused in *Battleground* is especially popular with
World War II reenactors, for whom the film is a cult favorite.

The film concerns a squad of G.I.'s from the 101st Airborne Division,
who held Bastogne during the Battle of the Bulge in late December 1944.
William Wellman presents the defenders of Bastogne not as idealized heroic
figures but as real soldiers—tired, mud-caked, and mad at having to miss
their promised Christmas furlough in Paris. The film abounds with realistic
details, for example when Johnson tries to cook eggs in his helmet. The all-
star cast, backed by a number of extras from the 101st, are cast as types but
nevertheless look and act like G.I.'s. The script won an Academy Award.

On the road to California, the Joads' promised land. — *The Grapes of Wrath; courtesy of 20th Century Fox*

10. Simulation Games

O NE of the greatest joys of my childhood was playing with toy soldiers. This activity was definitely a family tradition. My grandfather, a soft-spoken, almost saintly gentleman, refought many of Queen Victoria's little wars on his bedroom floor when he was growing up in rural Ontario. He passed on his enthusiasm and several dozen boxes of toy soldiers to my father, who in turn added to the family collection and took his place as commander-in-chief. During the early 1920s, his "ladies from hell" and "doughboys" waged trench warfare against the Hun. I grew up during World War II, and armed with Dad's soldiers, I fought my private war incessantly. My armies were replenished every Christmas with red boxes of Britains. In my memory, I can still feel the balanced weight of those wonderful boxes, with the name of the regiment printed on one end and with each soldier neatly tied in with heavy black thread. Opening a box of Britains was a delicious experience.

The pleasures of simulating both the martial and peaceful sides of history—through toy soldiers and other means—are even more widespread today than when I was young. Just up the street from my home, for example, is a veritable time machine called Asgard ("Home of the Norse Gods"). Any evening I can walk over to this game and hobby shop and see several dozen people transported into other times, other places. The medium by which they venture into the past is simulation gaming. For them, gaming is a way of playing with, learning about, and simulating history. Many of these avid gamers are also into reenacting (and vice versa). Board games and simulation games with a table full of miniature soldiers are closely related activities. In fact, one of my friends who works at a living historical farm and is an active buckskinner calls simulation gaming "a scaled-down version of living history."

Within the hobby, generally called "simulation gaming," three different activities are popular, each with its own adherents. The first is miniature gaming with toy soldiers, actually tiny scale armies that are moved about following rather complex rules. H. G. Wells's book *Little Wars* was the first to deal seriously with this aspect of the hobby. Then there are two types of board games, one in which you are just a player competing with other players—refighting the Battle of Waterloo, for example. The other type requires that the player adopt a role and develop a persona, often historical. (Dungeons and Dragons is the best-known example, but there are many historical variants, too, and I've included a number in this chapter.) Finally, there are the modelers who meticulously paint individual miniatures or re-create historical dioramas, scaled-down "accounts" of episodes in the past. The relationship of this last aspect of the hobby to indoor museum work is obvious.

Simulation gaming is a world of its own. It includes dozens of specialized magazines, numerous publishing companies which have created more than four thousand board games, manufacturers of miniature armies, tens of thousands of enthusiastic players, societies and clubs, regular conventions, special events, shops, and social centers in cities and towns throughout the world.

In several previous chapters I've touched on various aspects of gaming. There are entries for books, magazines, and articles. In this chapter I recommend board games with historical themes. My criteria for recommending these games are tough. Most of my choices are recognized classics within the hobby. They have received good reviews in magazines, and a few have sold one hundred thousand copies or more. In short, they are landmarks in the history of gaming. Each game is historically accurate and "playable." It's possible to get so caught up in these games that you actually have the illusion of being in a time warp.

Often a good game is described as an "obsession." A friend, after playing Civilization one night, said, "It was so compelling no one dared breathe!"

Finally, I tried to select games that paralleled the historical periods of greatest interest to living history interpreters and reenactors. These games would make great winter or foul weather complements to full-scale simulations, and in fact, some reenactment units and museums are already using them in this way. A simulation game can provide the player with a "bigger picture" than a tactical battle reenactment or a single historic site ever can.

Simulation gaming, like reenacting, is essentially a social activity. The best way to learn how to play and enjoy historical board games and miniature war gaming is with the help of experienced players. Hobby shops are usually centers of activity and are good places to begin. Before tackling any of the games I've mentioned here, I would first stop in at a nearby hobby shop and ask for basic information. If you already know someone who is a simulation gamer, ask that person to help you get started.

Time Master • Pacesetter, Ltd.

At the beginning of Time Master's instruction books, there are these lines from Hamlet: "The time is out of joint; O cursed spite, /That ever I was born to set it right!" It's a fitting description of this 1984 role-playing game. The setting is A.D. 7192, and the player, a Time Corps agent, must travel back in time and protect *history* against evil Demoreans who want to prevent benevolent events from happening (a variant of the same theme was used in the film *Time after Time*). Some of the "stops" include fifth-century Athens, Caesar's Rome, Angevin and Tudor England, and Napoleonic and World War II France. Included in the game's personnel are Lee, Lenin, Raleigh, Rommel, Cleopatra, Henry VIII, Hitler, Newton, and Marx. The game is great fun: you zip about on a "Chronoscooter," fight with standard period or "paranormal" weapons, and, by protecting history, get to play with it.

Sticks and Stones (10,000 B.C.) • Metagaming

Sticks and Stones is a "micro game," a slim packet that fits easily in your breast pocket or purse. Designed in 1978, the game simulates intertribal warfare in the late Stone Age, about 10,000 B.C. The battlefield is a river valley where small bands of warriors engage in raids, ritual territorial fights, and hunting expeditions. Counters stand for the warriors, dependents, domesticated or wild animals (dogs, goats, mastodons), and goods (food, skins, and so forth). Rules are simple and clear for the game's five scenarios. Authenticity is moot—during one playing session I was alternately reminded of *Quest for Fire* and the documentary *Dead Birds*, which examined ritual warfare in New Guinea. This is one of relatively few serious games to deal with prehistory.

With Bonaparte in Italy and Hood at Gettysburg—simulating history by means of board games.—
Photograph by Sharli Powell

Civilization (8000–250 B.C.) • Avalon Hill

A great game! Designed by F. G. Tresham and the Hartland Trefoil, Ltd., group, Civilization is set in the period between the agricultural revolution and the early years of Rome. The geographic locale is the classical Middle East, and players (two to seven) represent Babylon, Egypt, Assyria, Crete, Illyria, Thrace, Italy, and Asia. "Victory" is won by advancing your land's culture, economics, politics, and "civilization." There are barriers: epidemics, famine, civil disorder and war, pestilence, floods, and the odd heresy. Players quickly learn to cooperate; wars are by and large counterproductive. The emphasis is on persuading nomads and farmers, warriors and merchants, artisans and citizens to work together. Like the period that Civilization simulates, the game is a classic. It's accurate, informative, clear, attractive, and very playable.

PRESTAGS: Pre-Seventeenth-Century Tactical Game System (Chariot 3000–500 B.C.; Spartan 500–100 B.C.; Legion 100 B.C.–A.D. 700; Viking 700–1300; Yeoman 1250–1550) • Simulations Publications

Available as a "master-pack," Prestags features five "compatible" games covering the biblical, Greek, and Roman periods and the Dark and Middle Ages. All the games follow the same standard rules—modified, of course, for each period. The games focus on tactics, use rather nondescript maps, and are relatively short and easy to play. The fun comes from experimenting with the wide variety of military units the games' time span allows. You can, if you want, also fight across historical periods, for example, matching a Viking raiding party against a company of longbowmen, a Roman legion, or a Spartan rear guard. This is a good game set for people who enjoy a variety of historical experiences: rampaging elephants, stoic Saxons, Mongol cavalry, and ferocious Norsemen. In an afternoon, you can time trip from Marathon to Hastings, from Acre to Bannockburn.

Art of Siege: Tyre (585–573 B.C.); Acre (1187); Lille (1708); Sevastopol (1854–1855) • Simulations Publications

This is one of Simulations Publications's best sets—all the four siege games are faithful to their subjects and compelling to play. Tyre covers Alexander the Great's siege of Tyre, thought at the time to be impregnable. The game involves naval and land operations. Also located in the Middle East, Acre was the scene of one of the Crusades' greatest battles. Lille features as its map a period engraving of the famous Vanban fortress. Unlike most war games, Lille doesn't use hexagons or squares to regulate units. Rather, playing pieces take the form of actual siege works, giving an additional aspect of realism. Finally, Sevastopol simulates the great Crimean War siege and includes British, French, and Russian armies. All four games are first rate.

Caesar (52 B.C.) • Avalon Hill

A historically accurate, exciting simulation of the Battle of Alesia, in which Caesar defeated Vercingetorix during the Gallic Wars. The battle was a complex one, and so is the simulation. Caesar has the Gauls holed up in the fortified city of Alesia but is himself besieged by a quarter of a million Gallic reinforcements. The Romans are outnumbered six to one. Units include ten Roman legions, Germanic cavalry, Balearic slingers, and Numidian archers. There are twenty-five miles of forts and, on the part of Caesar, inspired leadership. An excellent war game dealing with a neglected period of history.

Agincourt (1415) • Simulations Publications

Designed by Jim Dunnigan in 1978, Agincourt simulates the 1415 battle in which Henry V's two thousand English longbowmen literally decimated a French army at least four times as large. One of Dunnigan's problems was the lack of solid historical information on exactly how the battle was fought. The Simulation Publications team went to work and wrote an exact history of the physical operations that occurred at Agincourt. In the process they discovered the crucial importance of fatigue, morale, and leadership—variables which are all given an important place in the game. Agincourt offers an enjoyable way to learn more about the Hundred Years War between England and France, especially if you can also include a screening of the film *Henry V*.

Kingmaker (1455–1485) • Avalon Hill

If ever a board game seemed to have been created expressly for the Society for Creative Anachronism, Kingmaker is it. Based on the Wars of the Roses, the game was originally produced by Philmar, a British company which markets the ever-popular Diplomacy. Kingmaker has the same appeal—it involves roughly half a dozen players, is heavier on chance than skill, and is great fun. Although not as historically accurate as purists would like, the game nevertheless has the kind of mad reality that characterizes a Monty Python historical epic. Local rebellions flare, plagues waste armies, pretenders pop up when least expected, and Parliament caters to the powerful. Kingmaker won the Charles Roberts Award as best strategic game in 1976.

Seventeenth-century military tactics demonstrated at Plimoth Plantation. More than one hundred board games simulate this period of history. —*Plimoth Plantation, Inc.*

A Mighty Fortress (1500–1600) • Simulations Publications

A Mighty Fortress deals with the entire Protestant Reformation. Here is history on a large scale for people who prefer forests to trees. Players take on the roles of Martin Luther, Henry VIII, Pope Clement VII, Charles V (the Holy Roman Emperor), Suleiman I (sultan of Turkey), and assorted other historical characters. Action sweeps across Europe, from Calvin's Geneva to Loyola's Spain. The Ottoman Turks capture Egypt, Magellan's expedition circumnavigates the globe, and missionaries burn. Participants in the living history movement who have trouble grasping the "big picture" will find this a useful game. (A similar game covering the 1910–1914 pre–World War I period is Diplomacy.)

Frederick the Great (1756–1759) • Simulations Publications

If you enjoyed *Barry Lyndon*, you'll like this game. It focuses on the campaign of Frederick the Great and his Prussian army during the Seven Years War. A great master of strategy, Frederick was surrounded on all sides by the independent armies of France, Russia, Sweden, and Austria, but he managed to survive. His campaign consisted of forced marching interspersed with some brilliantly fought battles such as Rossbach in 1757. This classic game captures the period's atmosphere; it's a favorite with history buffs who don't mind a lot of maneuvering and relatively little bloody action. Frederick the Great is best played over a long winter's weekend by candlelight and with a bottle of good port at hand. If there is such a thing as civilized war, this is probably it. A final note—the game places a premium on intelligence, restraint, and a respect for life. One irresponsible, ill-conceived charge and you're out.

Quebec, 1759 • Gamma Two—Columbia

French and Indian War buffs have comparatively few war games to while away the winter months. Quebec 1759 is undoubtedly the best. It borrows a good deal from the miniature traditions. The map, like the Plains of Abraham and St. Lawrence River, is long and beautiful. Units are represented by small wooden blocks and move simultaneously. Quebec 1759 also features naval units and logistical and supply variables. In short, this game is well outside the mainstream of board war games but is highly realistic and rich in period atmosphere. The game is full of suspense but nevertheless gives you a sense of total involvement in the entire engagement.

American Revolution (1775–1783) • Simulations Publications

James Dunnigan designed this strategic game in 1972, and it was a Bicentennial favorite. In contrast to miniatures and full-scale reenacting, board gaming offers the advantage of letting you simulate history at a strategic rather than tactical level. The game is a fine complement to living history activity—battle reenactments, cantonments, musters, and so forth. It helps you put your Revolutionary War site, unit, or event into perspective. Dunnigan uses large zones rather than hexes to maximize the strategic feel. While the major land campaigns are emphasized, there are naval features as well. He has also supplied a number of "what-if" factors which work well in the American Revolution. Because it's relatively easy for the British commander to sweep the board if he uses a modicum of brilliance, Dunnigan has provided some rules that prevent an unrealistic situation from developing.

Napoleonic-period warfare is popular at living history museums and with war gamers. —*Fort Snelling, Minnesota Historical Society*

La Bataille de la Moscova (1812) • Game Designers Workshop

When this massive simulation of the Battle of Borodino came out in 1973, the board-gaming world was taken aback. The game contained a virtual folio of maps, more than one thousand unit counters, and very complex rules that emphasized tactical accuracy. It was obvious that the game might take as much as a week to play. In short, in complexity and conception it was on par with Leo Tolstoy's description in *War and Peace*. Game Designers Workshop bought it from Martial Enterprises, the California group which designed it, and the game took off. It was the first of the really popular "monster" simulations and still remains a favorite in the polls.

Napoleon at Waterloo (1815) • Simulations Publications

It used to be that when you bought a subscription to Simulations Publications's magazine *Strategy and Tactics*, the publisher sent you a copy of Napoleon at Waterloo. It's a great introduction to war gaming: short (a game can easily be finished in an hour), easy to learn (there are about fifty units and simple rules), and authentically exciting. Simulations Publications added an expansion kit as a supplement to the original game; it appeals to the more experienced player. One reason for the continuing popularity of the game is its period feel: mass cavalry charges, stubborn squares, artillery bombardments, demoralization, and over all the "fog of war." The game was designed by James Dunnigan in 1971.

Wooden Ships and Iron Men (1760–1850) • Avalon Hill

This simulation of naval conflict during the Napoleonic era is one of the most popular war games ever issued and needs only two players. Like C. S.

Full-scale battles are impossible to totally re-create; there are not enough reenactors—hence, the popularity of miniature war gaming. —*Photograph by Richard Cheatham*

Forester's Horatio Hornblower historical novels, Wooden Ships and Iron Men retains its appeal year after year. The game is highly realistic and informative yet playable (always a popular combination) and rich in variables: a variety of period ships; shifts in wind; opportunities for grappling and boarding; changing amounts of ammunition, morale, and seamanship. This is not a game for beginners. Its rules are complex but clear and relatively error free. As with most classics, this game is deeply involving and has a great period feel.

Oregon Trail (1820–1860s) • Fantasy Games Unlimited

Designed in 1981 by Leonard Kanterman and Steven Ulberg, Oregon Trail is one of the few "civilian" games available. It can be played solo or with as many as eight players. Each player adopts the role of a wagon train captain and attempts to lead a party from Independence, Missouri, to various destinations in the Far West. Along the route, you encounter hideous terrain, swollen rivers, deserts and droughts, rockslides, breakdowns, and detours. You must also cope with dwindling supplies, lapses in morale, and Indians. Oregon Trail is realistic and informative but, like the way west, difficult to navigate.

Blue and Gray I and II (1862–1864) • Simulations Publications

These two four-game sets (QuadriGames) simulate eight of the Civil War's more important battles. Included are Shiloh (1862), Chickamauga (1863), and Chattanooga (1863) in the West and Fredericksburg (1862), Antietam (1862), Chancellorsville (1863), Gettysburg (1863), and the Wilderness (1864) in the East. All the games follow the clear, relatively easy-to-play system of Napoleon at Waterloo. Blue and Gray continually rates high in

Rally 'Round the Flag

**Miniature Rules For
The American
Civil War
1861-1865**
25MM and 15MM

Complex rules have been developed for miniature war gamers bent on realistically simulating the past. —*Photograph by Sharli Powell*

Painting an HO-scale
German tank in preparation
for a miniature war game. —
Photograph by Sharli Powell

polls, and no wonder. These games are very authentic, simulate some of the war's most interesting battles, and are all at the tactical level. The cast of characters includes Lee, Grant, Burnside, Hooker, Meade, McClellan, Bragg, Thomas, Rosecrans, and Johnston.

Gettysburg (1863) • Avalon Hill

This game is a golden oldie. Gettysburg first appeared in 1958, well before the Civil War centennial. More board gamers probably cut their teeth on it than on any other game. I certainly did, and today whenever I see an old copy of it, nostalgia charges in like Pickett. Experienced board gamers no longer find Gettysburg challenging. Its rules are overly simple, its balance not quite right. But it's still a great introduction to the hobby and to the Civil War and is perhaps a stepping-stone to Terrible Swift Sword, Simulation Publications's superb simulation of the same battle. An original copy of Gettysburg is something of a collector's item, as it was Avalon Hills "theme" war game to deal with a particular engagement.

Terrible Swift Sword (1863) • Simulations Publications

To gauge just how far war gaming has come in the last twenty-five years, compare Gettysburg with Terrible Swift Sword. The latter is Simulation Publications's first large-scale tactical battle along the lines of La Bataille de la Moscova. It has three highly detailed giant maps, counters at the regimental level, and rules that account for such factors as leadership, supplies, morale, prisoners, and so forth. The game is very authentic and has a true period feel. Some wags have dubbed it "Terrible Slow Sword" because you need almost as much time to play it as Meade took to beat Lee. Terrible Swift Sword in 1976 won the Charles Roberts Award as best tactical war game.

Rail Baron • Avalon Hill

This classic game simulates the halcyon days of railroading after the Civil War. Players (three to six) adopt the role of "rail barons" such as Jay Gould or Cornelius Vanderbilt and, "armed" with $20,000 and one of twenty-eight train lines, set out to accumulate the $200,000 needed to win. It's quintessential capitalism and far more realistic and informative than Monopoly. Like Diplomacy, Rail Baron has attracted a large following. It's a good complement to Oregon Trail, has a three-board map which illustrates all twenty-eight of the major railroad lines in the "Gilded Age" United States, and can be played in an evening.

Diplomacy (1910–1914) • Avalon Hill

Designed by Allan Calhammer in 1960, Diplomacy is said to "destroy friendships, ruin marriages," and "subvert true education." Naturally it's one of the most popular board games of all time. Hundreds of clubs have been formed for the express purpose of playing Diplomacy. The objective of this mania is to control Europe through double-dealing, back-stabbing, Machiavellian maneuvers, and self-serving guile. There are seven countries involved: England, Germany, Russia, Turkey, Austria-Hungary, Italy, and France. Agreements are made and abrogated, armies mobilized, fleets sailed, and diplomacy "practiced." Many serious critics question whether Diplomacy really simulates international relations as they were in the pre–World War I period: rules are primitive, negotiations villainous. For addicts, however, such quibbling is pointless: the game's the thing.

Getting ready to "push micro."—*Photograph by Sharli Powell*

A miniature war game in progress in the basement of Asgard, a hobby and gaming shop.—
Photograph by Sharli Powell

Richthofen's War (1914–1918) • Avalon Hill

An exceedingly popular game, Richthofen's War simulates aircraft combat during World War I. It's a good game to play before watching *La Grande Illusion*. The game has a great period feel and includes photoreconnaissance missions, trench strafing and bombing, dogfights, and even—shades of the *first* Battle of Britain in 1917–1918—balloon bursting. The rules are clear, the maps show ground terrain, and most of the scenarios can be played in less than an hour.

Panzerblitz (1941–1944) • Avalon Hill

This is the all-time best-selling war game. Well over a quarter of a million copies have been sold. It was designed by James Dunnigan in 1970 and covers tactical armored warfare on the Eastern Front during World War II. The three boards include a rich slice of the Russian countryside—forests, fields, riverbeds, peasant villages, dirt roads, gentle hills, and so forth—and can be fitted together. Included is a wide variety of German and Soviet armor, infantry, and weapon units. The game is highly realistic, and the very fast, complex action demands a high level of skill. A follow-up game, Panzer Leader, which deals with the Western Front and includes a beach, is also available.

Squad Leader (1942–1945) • Avalon Hill

Someone once described a sailboat as a "hole in the water you pour money into." For many people, Squad Leader is a similar obsession, a "bottomless pit you can toss years of your life into," one of my friends ruefully noted. Designed by John Hill with assistance from Don Greenwood, Squad

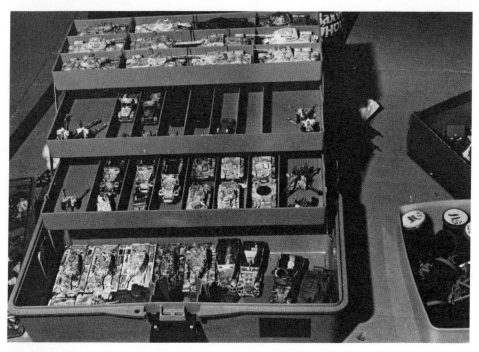

Part of an experienced war gamer's army in a tool box. — *Photograph by Sharli Powell*

Leader is to war gamers what Dungeons and Dragons is to the fantasy folks. The game deals with the Eastern Front in World War II but from the point of view of the squad leader—the single officer, NCO, and infantryman. The focus is on war as it seems at the bottom of the chain of command. In short, the game operates from the perspective of the ordinary man caught up in the throes of grand battles he can never hope to fathom. The history buff who enjoys *Red Badge of Courage* or *A Walk in the Sun* (in either book or film form) will immediately appreciate the attraction of Squad Leader. Since its appearance in 1977, the game has added a score of scenarios—all of which are both realistic and playable.

West Wall (1944) • Simulations Publications

This QuadriGame set is one of the most popular of all board game combinations. It features four battles on the Western Front during World War II: Arnhem, Hurtgen Forest, Bastogne, and Remagen. Somehow these simulations capture the confused, brutal, bloody aspects of modern war. Arnhem is especially realistic—and tragic. Well designed and filled with action, these are excellent games for the advanced novice. A good combination would be a day spent trying to break through Germany's "West Wall," followed by a screening of *Battleground*, the fairly realistic 1949 film which gives the "Willie and Joe" perspective on the Battle of the Bulge.

Agri-gamble, an educational simulation for visitors at Iowa Living History Farms. The game, like real farming, is indeed a gamble. —*Photograph by Mimi Dunlap*

Afterword: Serious Play

DURING three very foggy days in the summer of 1984, I visited the Fortress of Louisbourg on Nova Scotia's Cape Breton Island. To really get to know this massive living history museum, three days is a minimum visit. Members of the staff showed me their mountains of archaeological artifacts, historic records, and research reports covering all aspects of culture in the French community during the first half of the eighteenth century. I also spent many hours wandering through the historic fortress, observing the variety of interpretive programs which simulate the life of Louisbourg's inhabitants in 1744. The visit was both exhilarating and exhausting.

Toward the end of my stay, I had dinner with William O'Shea, Louisbourg's acting director. We talked about the scope of the living history movement and my field work for this sourcebook. Bill asked, "Do you think that living history has a real future? Or is it a fad? I think your new book needs to suggest an answer to that question." I hope that by now my answer is clear: the living history movement is a significant one that is here to stay.

The number and variety of living history activities are striking. A total of about ten thousand outdoor museums and historic sites, events, publications, organizations, suppliers, games, and films use historical simulation. Filing cabinets along my office wall are brimming with material for entries, many of which, sadly, I had to omit.

In short, the world of living history is not only kaleidoscopic but also continually growing. I have presented a stop-action portrait of this world in 1985. A decade from now, only a wide-angle lens will be able to capture the living history scene. I have no doubt that the movement will have doubled— surprising no one involved in it—and will cover aspects of life in North America's past that are currently neglected, such as the histories of minority groups. Insiders today take living history's popularity so much for granted that they are amazed to find articles in the popular press suggesting that an interest in history is on the wane. As far as living history is concerned, this assessment couldn't be farther from the truth. Living history is alive, well, and growing at a pace that often seems breakneck.

The movement manifests an increasing dedication to quality—a widespread desire to simulate life in the past more truthfully. Over and over as I talk with interpreters, reenactors, and history buffs, I hear the words "authenticity," "historical ac-

A makeshift militia at Williamsburg. —*Colonial Williamsburg Foundation*

The General Store at Iowa Living History Farms in 1880 and in 1980. The quality of the research is evident to both historian and layman. —*Photograph from 1980 by Mimi Dunlap*

curacy," "greater realism," and "honesty" used to describe their activities. Within the living history movement, there is growing pressure to improve quality. Museums pride themselves on being historically accurate. Events are limited to "authentics." New sketchbooks are given tough reviews in reenactors' magazines. I recently saw a good example of this pressure in action. One winter evening I went over to Asgard, a model and gaming store near my home, to watch my son Coll "push micro" with some friends. The battle they refought was a post-D-Day encounter in France between American and German armor and infantry units. There were about ten war gamers scattered around a large table in the shop's basement, each responsible for moving several tanks, cannon, infantry units, and so forth in and out of battle. The table looked like a model railroad setup, filled with miniature French buildings, farms, fields, and woods. When the battle had been raging for more than an hour, a German player asked, "Can I move my 75mm PAK 4 up this hill?" Everyone laughed. An older, more experienced player replied, "Of course not. Haven't you read the German manual on artillery of that kind?" I was astounded, but the players weren't. They seemed to take it for granted that a prerequisite for playing miniature war games well was a knowledge of history, especially battlefield tactics.

To achieve greater historical accuracy, people active in the living history movement are increasingly borrowing the tools and techniques of academic historians. This trend will certainly continue as more and more nonacademic historians within the movement recognize their need for quality control and realize that the academic has much to offer in historical theory, methodology, and knowledge of relevant primary sources. At one time we could speak of a gulf between academic historians and professional and lay "living historians." To some extent this gap has been bridged. Living history museums have hired hundreds of academically trained historians, curators, folklorists, and education specialists. Internships and special educational programs have been developed specifically for undergraduate and graduate students. Articles by recognized historians lauding the interpretation at serious living history museums such as the Fortress of Louisbourg or Plimoth Plantation are no longer unusual. But most important, the number of teachers and researchers who take part in living history as a form of recreation has swelled. Professional historians have increasingly realized that historical simulation can be a refreshing avocation. The participation of professional and lay historians alike has improved the quality of living history activities.

Living history's most significant characteristic is its vitality, an energy which is the direct by-product of the movement's experimentation with historical simulation. The usefulness of simulation as a tool with which to research, interpret, and reenact life in the past is amply illustrated by the 361 entries in this sourcebook.

One of our generation's contributions to the field of history (and ultimately to society) is our experimentation with historical simulation. By breaking away from strictly written accounts of the past, we have developed a "living history" that is often successful because it is dramatic, playful, experimental, and memorable.

Historical simulation is dramatic. It unabashedly uses our society's traditional mediums of cultural expression: ritual, ceremony, pageant, theater (including film, radio, television), games, sport, festivals, and celebration. The power and popularity of these forms is obvious. I am certain that my own interest in Civil War reenacting germinated from my mother's continual and vocal devotion to the film *Gone with the Wind*. My own children's view of race relations was unquestionably influenced by the televised miniseries *Roots*. No doubt everyone in North America can point to a similar encounter with the past which came to them through the medium of theater, pageant, festival, or a related traditional dramatic form. I have met Scottish-

A dramatic moment in the past brought to life for visitors at Williamsburg. —
Colonial Williamsburg Foundation

Americans whose interest in history was kindled by a "Burns Night Supper" or a "Highland Games," and in the South, hundred of thousands of families troop off every summer to outdoor historical pageants. After spending a cool summer evening watching one local variant—*Shakertown Revisited*, in which the Shakers of South Union, Kentucky, are celebrated in song, dance, and story—I asked a native why historical pageants are so popular. He thought for a moment, then replied, "Part of it is an interest in old things, history. That's traditional around here. But like all people, we do enjoy a good show. *Shakertown's* not Broadway, but in the summer, it's the best show in town."

Much past criticism of living history focused on its theatricality. There was an underlying message: if history is entertaining, then something must be wrong. The truth must have been sacrificed somewhere; history must have been bowdlerized. You could almost sense the ancient puritan mindset behind this criticism—to grin is a sin. Some criticism of living history's account of life in the past (as too clean, neat, peaceful, male, white, and so forth), however, was and is right on target. Just as there are poor history books, there are poor living history museums, events, films, games, and so on. Still, there are no *dull* historical simulations, and as the living history movement matures and emphasizes programs and activities of higher quality, its role in purveying history to our society should become more significant.

For many people, historical simulations have an aura of playfulness about them. Reenactors refer to living history as a "hobby." Games are considered a leisure time activity, and museum interpreters often describe their work as "fun and games." It would be wrong, however, to conclude that historical simulations are trivial. On the contrary, they are examples of "serious play." Tom Deakin, editor of *Living History Magazine*, once said to me, "Living history is one of the few hobbies that is intellectually demanding, that requires a commitment to historical research and plain old-fashioned book learning." After an encampment or battle reenactment, "you are bone weary but mentally invigorated." Living history synthesizes the mental challenges of the workplace with the physically and emotionally satisfying benefits of recreation. No wonder it has been described by people as "*the* participatory sport of the future." Recently, a friend of mine who is a historian by profession and an "admitted closet buckskinner" wryly noted, "When the Yuppies get tired of all their running and exercising, you watch—they'll turn to living history." His point was, of course, that serious hard-working people will eventually be attracted to serious, intellectually strenuous play. And living history will be waiting in the form of a historical dramatization such as the television series *The Jewel in the Crown*, a demanding board game such as Civilization, or a place in the ranks of an authentic reenactment unit. In the mid-1970s a Dupont chemist and his wife, a computer programmer, volunteered to work weekends at the Colonial Pennsylvania Plantation. One day I asked them why they were attracted to the rigors of historical interpretation. They agreed on one answer: "It's relaxing—but you never feel you've squandered your mind."

Living history is also experimental. Simulation is by definition an imitation of something real and so leads itself to experimentation. Rather than fight real wars, H. G. Wells suggested in his 1913 classic *Little Wars*, people could use mock conflicts to simulate reality, as they now do in war gaming. Vicarious battles with miniature soldiers, Wells wrote, can provide the drama, excitement, and even mental exercise of warfare—without the tragic consequences. You can "experiment" with war without anyone's getting killed or maimed or suffering from shell shock. The loser's ego might suffer, but that's the price for a winner's glory—and both players can return to "fight" another day. Well's sensible book didn't end real wars, but it did start a popular, worldwide hobby for amateur military history buffs interested in testing their tactical skills. In the six decades since *Little Wars* was published, simulation has also become an acceptable research tool for professional experimental archaeologists. Scores of voyagers have sailed the high seas in the wake of Thor Heyerdahl; in Denmark and England significant research centers have been established to conduct "imitative experiments"; and experimental projects have been interpreted for the public in American living museums such as Plimoth Plantation, Sleepy Hollow, and Colonial Williamsburg.

Plimoth's experience perhaps best illustrates the experimental potential of historical simulation at museums. In the early 1970s, the museum made the courageous decision to remove its original Jacobean artifacts from the re-created village and to replace them with reproductions. In essence, Plimoth was transformed overnight from a museum of historic furniture to a living historical village. Freed from the curatorial restrictions involved in caring for valuable antiques, the interpretive staff could now devote its energy to presenting a realistic picture of Pilgrim life. The plantation rapidly established itself as an innovator in first-person interpretation and effective educational programming.

Finally, historical simulation is memorable. It involves a total sensory re-creation of life in the past. A realistic living

Realistic presentations of Pilgrim and Wampanoag folklife at Plimoth Plantation. —*Plimoth Plantation, Inc.*

Tim McGill documents a reenactment of Charles Lindbergh's arrival at Wichita's
Rawdon Field, August 18, 1927. —*Photograph by Sherry Eslick Buettgenbach*

history museum or event can create the illusion that you have really traveled back in time and entered another world. Throughout my own involvment with living history, I have been struck by how often interpreters and reenactors talk about their experiences in *almost* bringing the past to life. The best you can do, of course, is authentically to *simulate* history, but everyone seems to savor the moment when you actually feel as if you are part of a particular historical period or event. The memory of experiencing what it really must have been like is a reward that anyone seriously associated with living history prizes. I remember showing a well-known museum curator around Living History Farms in Des Moines, Iowa. He happened to be blind. He insisted on involving himself in the historical lifestyles we were simulating at the three period farms. He wanted to touch the split rails of our pioneer fences, listen to the bells of the dairy cattle, smell the earthy aroma of a newly plowed field, and taste the full-flavored stew cooked over open wood fires. At the end of a long day of immersing himself in our facsimile of life in the nineteenth-century Midwest, he paid living history its highest compliment. "Thank you for the visit. You have brought the past to light. I'll see it forever in my mind's eye."

Glossary

Adventure Gaming. A general term for all varieties of simulation game playing.

Animation. Canadians prefer the term "animation" to "living history," but for Americans, "animation" means living history interpretation that doesn't involve demonstration or visitor participation.

Authentic. Historically accurate. "Authentic" is a key word in the reenactor's vocabulary. It denotes a high standard of historical realism, especially in regard to period clothing, equipment, and demeanor. Many reenactments or living history events require authentic clothing and other artifacts.

Buckskinners. Muzzle loaders who re-create the culture of the longhunter, mountain man, native American, and other historic frontier groups. Also called a "skinner."

Cantonment. A formal, long-term encampment. The best example is the Brigade of the American Revolution's annual meeting at the New Windsor Cantonment in Vails Gate, New York, where Washington's army camped in 1782 and 1783 while awaiting peace.

Costumes. Farbs and stage actors wear costumes. Reenactors and interpreters wear "period clothing."

Dioramas. Scaled-down historical scenes re-created with figures and models.

Dress Code. Rules adopted by reenactors to ensure authentic dress.

Encampment. A military event focusing on camp life in historic times. Most battle reenactments also feature an encampment, but an encampment may be held without simulated warfare.

Event. A planned, scheduled living history activity such as a rendezvous, battle reenactment, agricultural fair, or other celebration.

Farb. A reenactor who is not authentic. Derisive synonyms include "cowboy" and "polyester soldier."

Farb Fest. A living history event that is not authentic and attracts reenactors who are not serious historians.

First-Person Interpretation. At some living history museums, interpreters pretend they are actually living in the past and adopt a historical point of view. At Plimoth Plantation, for example, interpreters speak in Elizabethan dialects and remain in character even when visitors aren't present.

Historical Games. Simulation games which re-create historical events.

Historical Simulation. Simulation of the past through any medium, including film, living history, museum, board game, and so forth.

Historically Accurate. Realistic simulation of historic artifacts and activities. Museum interpreters prefer to reserve the term "authentic" for original artifacts actually made and used in the past. "Historically accurate" is generally applied to reproductions or re-creations that achieve a high level of verisimilitude.

Historic Site. An historically significant property (battlefield, fort, village, farm, urban district, and so forth) preserved in its original location. Fort Snelling and Colonial Williamsburg are good examples of historic sites.

Hivernant or Hivarano. An experienced mountain man reenactor.

Interpretive Garbage, or Trash. Historically accurate living history museums often litter their buildings, workshops, and farmsteads so that they look less like well-kept, twentieth-century museums.

Live-In. Some living history museums allow staff members or selected groups to stay at the site for a weekend or more and follow a historically accurate living routine. One of the best-known programs of this type is the Washburn Norlands' adult live-in, in which a small group actually simulates life in 1870 Maine for three days.

Living Historical Farm. An actual historic farm or outdoor agricultural museum which simulates a farm and its activities during a particular period in the past.

Living History. Simulation of life in another time. Usually the time is in the past and there is a purpose for the simulation: research, interpretation, play, or perhaps all three.

Living History Museum. A historic site or outdoor museum which uses living history as its primary mode of interpretation.

Living Museum. A living history museum.

Longhunter. Also called *coureur de bois*, or *boschloper*. Reenactors who re-create the culture of the eighteenth- and nineteenth-century frontiersman.

Miniature Gaming. The hobby in which historical events are played out with small scale figures. Also called "pushing micro."

Modeling. The hobby of building scaled-down replicas of ships, vehicles, structures, and so forth.

Mountain Man. A reenactor who recreates the culture of the early nineteenth-century western hunter and fur trader.

Museum Quality. A term used to describe historically accurate reproductions of original artifacts.

Muzzle loaders. A general term for enthusiasts involved in shooting muzzle-loaded firearms.

Open Air Museum. The European term for "outdoor museum."

Outdoor Museum. A collection of historically significant structures relocated to a central location and interpreted as a unit. Old Sturbridge Village is a good example of an outdoor museum.

Participation. Living history interpretation involving the visitor in the simulation. The involvement may be as simple as a conversation between an interpreter and a visitor or as complex as a weekend live-in at a historic site.

Period Clothing. Historically accurate reproductions or facsimiles of the clothing worn in a specific historical period. Interpreters generally refer to their outfits as "period clothing," never as "costumes."

Pilgrim. A novice mountain man reenactor.

Primitive Camp. At larger muzzle-loading events, an authentic encampment set aside for buckskinners who agree to live without modern conveniences.

Pushing Mirco. Miniature gaming.

Re-creation. Modern simulation of a historic artifacts or activity.

Reenactment. A living history event that simulates a particular historic event, such as surrender at Yorktown or the Battle of New Market.

Reenactor. Someone who acts out life in the past for recreational purposes.

Rendezvous. A living history event which informally simulates the historic seasonal gatherings (called "rendezvous" at the time) that occurred during the eastern and western fur trade eras. Rendezvous are especially popular among buckskinners and voyageur units.

Restoration Village. A dated term for outdoor museum.

Role Playing. Living history interpreters and reenactors often pretend they are people living in the past and adopt a role as actors do. Sometimes this role is called an "impression" and is based on extensive historical research.

Simulation Games. A general term for games which imitate real-life activities (sports, war, and so forth).

Sketchbook. An illustrated short guide to the period clothing, accessories, and accoutrements worn or used in a specific historical period or by a particular historic group. The best sketchbooks base their suggestions on authentic artifacts and on primary sources.

Stationing. The assignment of an interpreter to a particular post or location—such as a shop or workplace where a historic activity is demonstrated.

Third-Person Interpretation. At some living history museums, interpreters dress and act as if they are living in the past but don't adopt historical roles. They speak to visitors as one twentieth-century person to another.

Toy Soldier. Scaled-down replicas of soldiers.

Voyageurs. Reenactors who re-create the culture of eighteenth- and nineteenth-century French fur traders.

Please zerox this form and return to the author.

Nomination Form

Dear Jay,

You left out a good one! Here's my nomination for inclusion in your next edition of THE LIVING HISTORY SOURCEBOOK.

- ☐ Museum
- ☐ Event
- ☐ Book
- ☐ Article

- ☐ Magazine
- ☐ Organization
- ☐ Supplier

- ☐ Sketchbook
- ☐ Film
- ☐ Simulation Game

Name of entry:_____

Contact person:_____

Address:_____

Phone:_____

Reason for nomination:_____

_____

_____

Submitted by:_____

Address:_____

Return this form to: Dr. Jay Anderson
c/o AASLH Press
172 Second Avenue North, Suite 102
Nashville, TN 37201

Index